In this book Roger Spegele argues that in the past international
theorists have failed to recognise that there is not one conception of
international relations, subdivided into different theories and approaches, but at least three wholly different conceptions of the subject.
Though scholars are increasingly prepared to accept this, there is still
no consensus about what to call these conceptions, how to describe
them, and why they should be studied. This book attempts to fill this
gap. The author first examines two conceptions of IR – positivist-
empiricism and emancipatory international relations – which challenge political realism. He then defends a revised version of realism,
called 'evaluative political realism', from challenges arising from its
rivals, with the aim of defining a conception of political realism which
is coherent, viable and attractive.

D1525786

CAMBRIDGE STUDIES IN INTERNATIONAL RELATIONS: 47

Political realism in international theory

Editorial Board

Steve Smith (*Managing editor*)
Christopher Brown   Robert W. Cox   Anne Deighton
Rosemary Foote   Joseph Grieco   Fred Halliday
Margot Light   Andrew Linklater   Richard Little
R. B. J. Walker

International Political Economy
Roger Tooze   Craig N. Murphy

Cambridge Studies in International Relations is a joint initiative of Cambridge University Press and the British International Studies Association (BISA). The series will include a wide range of material, from undergraduate textbooks and surveys to research-based monographs and collaborative volumes. The aim of the series is to publish the best new scholarship in International Studies from Europe, North America and the rest of the world.

CAMBRIDGE STUDIES IN INTERNATIONAL RELATIONS

Series list continues after index

Political realism in international theory

Roger D. Spegele
Monash University

CAMBRIDGE
UNIVERSITY PRESS

Published by the Press Syndicate of the University of Cambridge
The Pitt Building, Trumpington Street, Cambridge CB2 1RP
40 West 20th Street, New York, NY 10011–4211, USA
10 Stamford Road, Oakleigh, Melbourne 3166, Australia

First published 1996

Printed in Great Britain at the University Press, Cambridge

A catalogue record for this book is available from the British Library

Library of Congress cataloguing in publication data
Spegele, Roger D.
Political realism in international theory / by Roger D. Spegele.
    p.   cm. – (Cambridge studies in international relations: 47)
Includes bibliographical references and index.
ISBN 0 521 55403 9 (hardcover). – ISBN 0 521 55635 X (pbk.)
1. International relations – Philosophy.   2. Realism.
I. Title.   II. Series.
JX1394.S744   1996
327.1′01 – dc20   95–40148   CIP

ISBN 0 521 55403 9 hardback
ISBN 0 521 55635 x paperback

CE

For my mother and father

Contents

Preface

It would not be misleading to describe the contemporary situation within international studies as a philosophical problem of the sort described by Ludwig Wittgenstein in the *Philosophical Investigations*: 'A philosophical problem has the form: "I don't know my way about".' The signs of international relationists not knowing their way about are just about everywhere: *from* the fragmentation attending the vast array of models, paradigms, approaches, conceptual schemes, research programmes, discourses (or whatever), strewn across the pitted surface of the academic study of international relations and wearily promoted by their creators *to* fevered calls for yet another debate conspicuously devoid of any indication of what the debate, *au fond*, is all about or even *who* is debating with *whom* about *what*. This study, by contrast, moves in a different direction: it deploys substantive arguments against identifiable rivals in defence of a genuine position – a somewhat different version of political realism which I call 'evaluative political realism'. As we shall see below, evaluative political realism stands in sharp contrast to neorealism, on the one hand, and in somewhat muted contrast to commonsense realism, on the other. Evaluative political realism sees itself embedded in a tradition of realist thought which accepts, for now and any foreseeable future we are likely to care about, a world which contains cultural and national communities with radically different values organised into nation-states. Given the diversity of ideas and ways of life resulting from the articulation of these values, any political conception of world politics should, according to the evaluative political realist, be *tolerant, democratic* and *pluralistic*. Although this study is not intended as a full-scale justification of this conception, it does attempt to develop the bases for a viable conception of political realism that moves toward such a justification; and it does so not only by meeting at least *some* of the major challenges of opposing positions but also by advancing a revised version of the realist position. So this study not only criticises rival opposing anti-realist conceptions but, more particularly, argues in favour of four theses which, it is claimed, constitute the core features of a realism which puts out the anti-realist fire but without recoiling into a neorealist frying pan.

To avert some possible misunderstandings, it might be useful to indicate how this study differs from other theoretically oriented works in the field. First, this study is *not* a survey of theories of international relations; there are already several useful works in the field that perform this task. It is worth remarking that such studies often have a decidedly 'conservative' import because they tend to reproduce the categories and concepts with which we are already familiar and, therefore, leave our understanding of international theory very much as we found it. This seems reason enough to try to move beyond the *genre*. Secondly, this book does not purport to offer a 'theory' of international politics, if by theory one means a linguistic structure whose purpose is to discover 'how things are in the world'. Since the very idea of theory in this sense is at issue between rival conceptions of international relations, assuming its correctness would be obvious question-begging. Thirdly, this work is *not* a 'philosophy' of international relations, if by philosophy one means a permanent, universal framework of thought that dictates the totality of possible descriptions of the world once and for all. In post-empiricist international relations we can no longer avail ourselves, if we ever could, of a God's-eye view of the world whose role is to weed out those assumptions and presuppositions which cannot be justified by showing that they either fail to be analytic truths or that they do not match up with the inert data of the world. Philosophical reasoning in international relations has many objectives but, for the evaluative political realist, the main one is to explain why, from *within* one's fundamental assumptions and presuppositions, someone might be tempted to accept an opposing viewpoint but still, all things considered, resist the temptation. Rather than try to persuade hostile opponents or to 'prove' that her version of political realism is true *tout court*, the evaluative political realist accepts diversity and even indeterminacy of viewpoint and proposes to clarify her own fallible beliefs in the light of the challenge arising from opposing considerations. To be sure, this raises the spectre of relativism which, as I shall argue below, can be largely circumvented. There is, in any case, no implication here that in giving up a foundationalist conception of philosophical reason, one can also get along without general conceptions of reason, truth, objectivity and knowledge. Post-modernist deconstruction has value in forcing us to think harder about international relations but goes wrong when it urges us, in a way strangely reminiscent of philosophical projects it opposes, to decon-struct everything we ever believed before about philosophical reasoning and argument.

But, then, what is this study if it is not these three things?

My self-conceived task here involves re-examining, with a view to revising, certain key assumptions embedded in the realist tradition. These assumptions are contained in four theses and concern state (and state-system), human nature, history and ethics. Although one may expect radical disagreements about what one can, and should, say about these topics, it is hard to believe that a conception of international relations sufficiently rich to count as one can avoid articulating (or at least having) thoughts on such matters. Since I focus on these topics rather than 'on the world' (whatever that might come to), my study may be viewed as a 'second-order inquiry'. To be sure, the idea of a second-order inquiry has to be understood in a quite restricted sense. A second-order inquiry normally implies that one is examining the examiners of the world rather than the world itself and there is a natural sense in which this study attempts to carry out just such a project. Often, however, the term 'second-order inquiry' resonates with an assumption that the results of such an inquiry could serve as logical imperatives in order to coerce first-order studies into a certain mould. On this view, the goal of second-order studies is to determine what must be done in first-order studies. That is certainly not what this study is all about. First of all, such an assumption implies that a sharp distinction can be usefully entered between second-order and first-order studies. Secondly, it implies that foundationalist epistemological projects are valid enterprises. For a variety of reasons which we need not rehearse here, neither of these assumptions appears warranted. For the evaluative political realist, there is a dialogic rather than a hierarch-ical relation between second and first-order studies. Second-order studies cannot logically dictate to first-order studies since they cannot describe, even in the highest-order logical language, all the possible objects there are in the world. However, second-order studies do permit those concerned about the conflicting implications of first-order studies to ask profoundly important questions about their assumptions, presuppositions and arguments. From *within* one conception of the subject – the revised form of political realism called evaluative political realism – my aim is to excavate the assumptions, presuppositions and arguments to be found in the principal alternative conceptions of international relations, to show why a certain kind of political realist either need not accept them (since they are uncompelling) or to state how this somewhat different form of realism might be reformulated to incorporate their 'acceptable face' into its own conception of the subject. If this means that political realism has to be reshaped in certain fundamental ways, so be it. Political realism is not now – nor was it ever intended to be – a set of timeless metaphysical truths that stretch beyond human needs and interests.

It is worth remarking that in carving out a revised understanding of political realism I assume the truth of a pragmatic/realist philosophy of science and a certain realist conception of ethics. The pragmatic/ realist philosophy of science in question needs to be sharply distinguished from any philosophy of scientific realism that accepts the correspondence theory of truth, materialism and associated doctrines; it rests, rather, on a realist view of reference to the effect that objects can be identified independently of any particular description of them. And the certain philosophy of ethical realism alluded to holds, in contrast with more foundationally ambitious versions of ethical realism, that some moral judgements *can be* true independently of people's choices and beliefs even though they may not be, in any interesting sense, part of the natural world. But although these two philosophies are said to ground evaluative political realism, I do not attempt to justify them directly. Rather, I defend them obliquely and only insofar as they play a role in shaping the constitutive beliefs of evaluative political realism, which I attempt to defend, more or less vigorously, against possible detractors.

This study, then, may be understood as a search for a viable and plausible (as opposed to 'conclusive' or 'proved') conception of political realism. Though I may or may not have succeeded in this task, I would like this study to be judged, as Henry James recommended as a propaedeutic for effective criticism, on the basis of what I have actually attempted to do and not on what I have *not* tried to do and therefore necessarily failed to accomplish!

It is true that my project is controversial, but I do not know how international theory can avoid controversy once it gives up (as it must) the foundational goal of justifying claims to truth and rightness by

showing them to be the conclusions of a rationally motivated consensus. There is no escape from a *political* conception of international
relations, and certainly not in orthodox social science or traditional
philosophy. The arguments which I advance below are not intended to
be knockdown and conclusive. Since they are arguments at the second-
order level, they will invoke a number of different metaphysical claims
which I could not even begin to list completely, let alone justify
through argument. We do metaphysics as soon as we open our mouths
to speak, go into a laboratory, or think about who to vote for. Since the
second-order arguments of evaluative political realism and rival conceptions of international relations invoke, often inadvertently, different
metaphysical claims the presuppositions of which remain partially
concealed, the arguments for rival conceptions will be inherently
inconclusive; and so, too, will be the basis for accepting evaluative
political realism.

For the evaluative political realist, there are certain characteristics
which any viable conception of international relations must have, *viz.*,
it must be *critical, coherent* and *tradition-informed*. It has to be critical,
not in the sense of pretending to disclose the fundamental interests of
mankind as such but, rather, in refusing to take for granted the
'unthought' – the shared conceptions and background practices human
beings have about their character, interests and capacities. It must also
be coherent, not in the sense of satisfying the ferocious standards of a
fully integrated and determined theoretical system but, more modestly,
by bringing themes, theses, ideas, rhetoric, talk, etc. into some intelligible relationship with one another. And it needs to be related to
tradition, not in the sense of simply reproducing past beliefs, principles
and norms, but in developing ideas that suggest some threads of
continuity with the conceptual and theoretical structures of the core
tradition in which its practices are located. To be sure, the search for a
conception of international relations that can satisfy these standards
will not be easy since it has to take place within the context of an
epistemological and metaphysical crisis that has been brought about
by the demise of positivism and the emergence of the time of great
debate.

Since the establishment of International Relations as an academic
subject at Aberystwyth, Wales in 1919, reflective international relationists have tried to specify the nature of the subject and how to
study it. They have, that is, invited us to answer the *what-question* and
the *how-question*. The what-question consists of philosophical thoughts

concerning the nature of international relations and requires a response to the anodyne question: 'what is international relations?' The how-question stimulates methodological thinking about the status of certain logical techniques of analysis and asks us to give a determinative answer to the question: 'How ought international relations be investigated?' From the 1930s to the 1950s the internal disciplinary debate in the Anglo-American community centred principally on the what-question with 'realists' arrayed against 'idealists'. Whereas for the realists the essence of international relations was power and security, the idealists argued that peace and justice ought to be the central concerns. In the mid-1960s this debate was replaced by a methodological controversy ostensibly designed to answer the how-question with the disputants organising themselves into 'traditionalists' and 'scientists'. Traditionalists argued that we should use historical methods to understand international relations, while scientists contended that we had to follow natural scientists in using the methods of scientific theorising, model-building and data analysis. This latter debate has continued down to our time with many twistings and turnings to protect the fundamental commitments of the disputants.

Important as answers to these two questions are, the third debate in international relations (in which we are still engaged) effectively urges us to incorporate what- and how-questions into the *why-question*. 'Why would intelligent adults spend their time and energy mastering the concepts and categories of international relations anyhow?' Crudely put, 'what's in it for you, me or anyone else?' The why-question invites us to be self-consciously reflective about the point of international relations. Three general responses, bound up with three alternative conceptions of the subject, vie for attention and support. A possible answer emanating from positivist-empiricism (see chapter 1 for a characterization of this term) would be that as a developing science, naturalistically understood, international relations holds out the prospect of eventually being able to make more or less accurate predictions of international events (within a certain limited scope) and of controlling the unwanted effects of such events or, more ambitiously, eliminating them altogether. On the other hand, someone committed to emancipatory international relations would hold that the point of studying the subject lies in helping us to understand how human emancipation can be actualised (or at least strongly advanced) in some historically relevant future. Evaluative political realism provides yet a third response to the why-question, one which involves affirming political values which defend pluralism and the modern democratic state-system. Discussions of these answers are best left to the body of the text.

The key point for us here however is just this, that when we try to give a serious answer to the why-question, we are moved to philosophical reflection. For the evaluative political realist, philosophical reflection is needed so that the tradition of political realism can re-evaluate and reform itself in the light of the new currents of ideas that have emerged to challenge it. This implies that political realism must be open to other conceptions, for it is only out of that openness that more reflective understandings of international relations can be forged, that different answers to the why-question can be conceived and defended. And this, in turn, will mean that international relations in general, and political realism in particular, will have to become more accessible to a fuller range of philosophical issues than has generally been thought necessary or desirable in the past. Philosophy is, in any case, an essential ingredient of any form of knowledge since it involves, as Hegel understood, a critical examination of the act of knowledge itself. Philosophy is not, on this view, some frilly extra whose dazzle provides panache to an otherwise lacklustre discipline: it is essential. As Hegel also observed:

> Philosophy may be thus called a kind of luxury insofar as luxury signifies those enjoyments and pursuits which do not belong to external necessity as such. Philosophy in this respect seems more capable of being dispensed with than anything else; but that depends on what is called indispensable. From the point of view of mind philosophy may even be said to be 'that which is most essential'.

Although for Hegel the philosophical standpoint of *mind* was 'most essential', for the evaluative political realist the philosophical standpoint involves not only *mind* but, crucially, *value* as well. Whereas the third debate in international relations has thus far focused mainly on mind in the form of theory, what the discipline requires today are reflections on how conceptions of science, reason and knowledge shape, and are shaped by, our understanding of value and practice. Focusing on theory and practice will wonderfully concentrate 'discourse' in international relations and help us to provide new answers to the naive why-question. It might even form the basis for a fourth debate. If it did, then the debating game would really be worth the philosophical candle – at least for the evaluative political realist.

Acknowledgements

In completing this book I received much help from people and institutions. I would like to thank the University of Chicago for a graduate programme which encouraged intellectual risk-taking and Monash University, my current institutional affiliation, for continuing an Australian version of the same programme. I gratefully acknowledge their identity and difference.

I owe a debt of gratitude to my friend and colleague Alastair Davidson whose understanding and help over the years has made this book possible. I am especially indebted to Richard Little not only for discussing many of the issues in the manuscript but for his gentle encouragement and unfailing support at a crucial stage in the writing of the manuscript. I would also like to thank Ralph Pettman, Morton Kaplan, Alastair Davidson (once again) and the anonymous referee at the University of Cambridge Press for their insightful comments about one or another version of the text. Much as I would like to hold them responsible for any errors of thought or expression which remain, honesty and fear compel me to say that the usual caveats apply in full measure. A special word of thanks goes to Daniela Basile, a very gifted Honours' student, for her consistently helpful, patient and encouraging attempts to weed out infelicities of thought and style. She is not responsible for any residual authorial recalcitrance.

Material in two chapters has appeared previously in journal articles. Part of chapter 4 appeared in 'Three Forms of Political Realism', *Political Studies* 35 (1987): 189-210 and part of chapter 8 has been published in 'Political Realism and the Remembrance of Relativism', *Review of International Studies* 21 (1995). I am grateful to the editors and journals of these publications for allowing me to incorporate in the book a substantial part of the material they published.

Finally, I would like to thank Anne West for her generosity of spirit and good nature in preparing the manuscript for publication.

Part 1

1   Theory and practice in international relations

I have endeavoured rather to show exactly what is the meaning of the question and what difficulties must be faced in answering it, than to prove that any particular answers are true.

G. E. Moore, *Principia Ethica*

Introduction

The principal preoccupation of this chapter lies in establishing a tripartite classification of international relations which will be deployed in subsequent chapters. In contrast to other such schemes in international relations, the classification presented below brings methodological and practical-moral concerns into the same schema from the outset. The establishment and development of such a schema not only permits increased critical purchase on rival conceptions of international relations, it also allows criticism of certain versions of political realism. It will therefore move us towards Part 2 of this study where I will defend four theses of a new version of political realism. This is not to say that this classification scheme is 'foolproof' or without its own set of difficulties; nonetheless it succeeds, I believe, in focusing our attention on the sorts of issues which need to be reflected upon. And that is all that one should expect from a classification scheme. In this connection, I hasten to point out that this chapter is followed by two subsequent chapters to make up Part 1 which, in general, has two principal goals: first, to loosen the grip on the proponents of rival conceptions of international relations by casting them in a somewhat different light and indicating the difficulties to which they give rise and second, to prepare the ground for devising a substantially revised version of political realism which is coherent, viable and attractive.

3

But we now must ask: 'what is the justification for such a study?' For one must grant that in the past philosophical discourse about international relations has tended to be dull and unilluminating. But with the recent subsidence of empiricism as the only legitimate theory of knowledge for international relations, philosophical discourse has suddenly become one of the exciting games in town. However belated the effort, serious attention is increasingly being directed to scrutinising the principal discourses which define and delimit the field.[1] On a number of topics for which empiricist epistemological and ontological assumptions had previously appeared to provide satisfactory solutions, there is now greater uncertainty, growing controversy and considerable confusion. For some, this is very bad news indeed since it undercuts the picture of a discipline progressively coming into 'maturity' as a 'science' which accumulates knowledge; but for certain philosophically minded international theorists it presents yet another opportunity to show that the discipline cannot be properly comprehended without coming to grips with the discourses and practices that give it life. Robust disagreements, on this view, are not signs of scientific impotence but a simple acknowledgement of the indisputable fact that rival schools of thought are producing rival answers to fundamental questions that do not have straightforward, or even necessarily recognisable, answers. Indeed, they may say, more radically, that there are no answers.

International theorists impressed with the rivalry in the discipline may now be searching for new ways to articulate the assumptions and presuppositions which are shaping and redrawing our conceptions of international relations. From the point of view taken up here, this period of rivalry and contention is to be valued not only because it helps to awaken international relationists from their dogmatic epistemological and metaphysical slumbers but also because, as a consequence of newly discerned tensions, theorists might be motivated to seek out new ways of conceiving international relations as a subject, possibly in terms which have not yet been precisely formulated or even genuinely comprehended. In fact, this search seems to have already born partial fruit since there is now greater recognition that there is no single compelling answer to the anodyne question: 'what is international relations?'.[2] On the contrary, several international theorists claim that there are at least three dominant discourses in recent international relations, even though they agree considerably less concerning their character or what they should be called. Alker and Biersteker call them 'approaches' and have labelled them 'behavioural', 'radical/Marxist' and 'traditional';[3] K. J. Holsti calls them 'theories' and denotes them: 'globalist', 'neo-Marxist' and 'classical';[4] and Michael Banks refers to them as 'pluralist', 'realist' and 'structuralist' paradigms.[5] On the other hand, I call them 'conceptions' and designate them as 'positivist-empiricism', 'emancipatory international relations' and 'political realism'. Each of these three conceptions – however labelled – makes different claims as to the nature of international politics; each holds that a case in its favour can be made out; each contends that its values are worthy of support from those who do not share them; and each insists that alternative conceptions go wrong in certain fundamental ways. Moreover, despite heroic efforts of synthesisers to reconcile, resolve or deconstruct these three conceptions of international relations, recent international theory has been compelled to recognise their intellectual stamina, their general coherence and their sheer recalcitrance to assimilationist manoeuvres which try to efface the genuine philosophical differences which animate them and make them worthy of our focused attention and concern. The extent and depth of disagreement among proponents of these three conceptions is hardly disputable. Nevertheless, in a discipline whose lingua franca appears to consist mainly of disagreeing about so much, there is an impressive degree of consensus on the 'threeness' of international theory. Seizing the threeness-moment has decisively shaped the frameworks devised for this study.

Three conceptions of international relations: general considerations

In this section I provide a schematic classification of the three main conceptions of international relations which dominate, in one form or another, theoretical discussion in Anglo-American international relations. I do not claim that these are the *only* conceptions of international relations available in current international relations; rather, the claim is that these conceptions have – though not in the form presented here – provided the main signposts for reflective discussion in Anglo-American international relations. Although the main lines of the discussion revolve around theory and practice, these terms are not the exclusive basis for evaluation of the conceptions; they should be understood, more modestly, as entering wedges whose purpose is to

5

engender reflective thought concerning the commitments, assumptions and presuppositions of these rival views of international relations. By seeing how the discourse one favours relates to others both from within and outside one's favoured conception, it becomes possible to reformulate one's own view and to move it in directions previously thought unacceptable, unpalatable or unattractive. On this view, we are not, as framework-dependent notions of the discipline might suppose, incarcerated within our conceptions: we are sometimes able to stand back from them, to criticise them and to reformulate them in light of internal and external reasons. In accepting this possibility, we shall be better placed to see what is shared by all three conceptions and what is specific to each, which differences are resolvable and which are 'non-negotiable' commitments.

Positivist-empiricism

Positivist-empiricism is an understanding of international relations which attempts to derive a coherent conception of the subject by drawing upon, and partially reconciling, the competing philosophical traditions of positivism (in its rationalistic form) and empiricism. The term 'positivist-empiricism' is intended to replace such misleading and anachronistic terms as 'behaviouralism', 'post-behaviouralism', 'the scientific approach', etc. with an historically more revealing label. The principal source of positivist-empiricism is to be found in the writings of Descartes, especially in *The Discourse on Method*, *Principles of Philosophy* and *Meditations* where he advanced strong claims for deduction and intuition as methodical innovations for overcoming sceptical doubt. The positivist-empiricist conception of the world was significantly advanced in a variety of different ways by Bacon, Hume, Locke, and, in certain respects which would need to be carefully qualified, by Kant, all of whom accepted an inextricable link between human progress and rationality. It achieved a certain notoriety in the studies of Auguste Comte who suggested in *The Positive Polity* that only adherence to scientific method would bring about human integration and harmony. A summary of its principal beliefs will help to show how positivist-empiricism links up not only with the positivist tradition but with rationalist tendencies as well. These beliefs include (for example): the identification of knowledge at its best with natural science and mathematics; the unity of the sciences thesis; theory-world dualism; the reduction of semantics to *a priori* analytic and *a posteriori*

6

synthetic statements; the reduction of philosophy to the 'logic of science'; metaphysical monism, i.e. the view that there is one real world; methodological monism, the idea that science ideally provides one best method for describing all facets of the one world in which we live; non-cognitivist ethics, i.e. the view that ethics has nothing to do with knowledge; and an emphasis on the social value of science and its practical effects. Positivist-empiricism, so understood, shares with rationalism a large number of views about knowledge, science, language, ethics and metaphysics.

With these salient characteristics in the background, positivist-empiricism has tried to construct an understanding of international relations based upon two leading commitments: *instrumentalism*, the notion that the main goal of theoretical reason is the production of systematic explanation, potential prediction and effective control to 'promote human progress';[6] and *moral non-cognitivism*, the idea that ethical *knowledge* does not exist, that morality is not 'in' the world but, at the very most, spread onto the world by us. Instrumentalism and moral non-cognitivism go hand-in-glove to form a putative *foundation* for international relations. In an instrumentalist understanding of science, means to ends can be evaluated by all who have the requisite competence; instrumental science is incompetent, however, to evaluate ends themselves. Moral non-cognitivism attempts to sustain this claim and promotes rationalistic moral philosophies and theories whose most notable feature is that they 'slot in' with the instrumentalist requirement that precludes 'strong evaluations' of human goods which give direction to choice and action.[7] These two commitments are not at all innocent of metaphysical implications. For, instrumentalism effectively presupposes a dualistic metaphysics which opens up a gap between theory, reason, language, mind, etc. on the one side and the world, hard data, reality, and body on the other, while moral non-cognitivism involves a partially overlapping form of dualism in its enthusiastic acceptance of a dichotomous distinction between facts and values. Dualism creates a distinction between two kinds of things – mind-dependent things (theories and values) and mind-independent things (reality and facts) – and thus creates the inevitable problem of bridging the gap between the two. By characterising positivist-empiricism in terms of the two principal elements of instrumentalism and non-cognitivism, we shall be better placed to grasp why certain research programmes from within it have attempted to bridge the gap between theory and

7

the world by effectively 'theoretising' the contents of the world itself, while others, such as research programmes influenced by Kant, have accepted the gap but have tried to defuse its sceptical implications by showing that international relations is necessarily bound up with universal normative principles that we can only grasp through reason itself. In chapter 2 we shall see how positivist-empiricists in international relations attempt to grapple with the theoretical issues which emerge from their varied commitments. However, it is important to see that there are other conceptions of international relations and that they pose incisive challenges to the theoretical and practical legitimacy of positivist-empiricism.

Emancipatory international relations

One consequence of the subsidence of positivism as the dominant methodology of the social sciences has been the strong emergence of theories of international relations whose principal goal is the transformation of international relations, both in theory and in practice. Unlike positivist-empiricism's static naturalistic assumptions, theories falling under the general rubric of Emancipatory International Relations propose ways of conceiving the theory of international relations which purport to assist us to change its practice, and the world with which it is inextricably bound up, for the better.

Emancipatory international relations is not all of one piece. Though there is a potentially infinite set of emancipatory theories, for our present purpose, it is helpful to distinguish four sorts: classical Marxism, international critical theory, poststructural theory and feminist international theory. These perspectives fall under the same emancipatory rubric in the sense that they adopt some liberationist modality as an explanation for why we should focus our attention and interest on international relations. These views accept the central thought not only that there is something drastically wrong with the way human life is lived on planet Earth, but also that people live in certain ways because they have an erroneous understanding of what their individual and collective existence ought to consist of. Positivist-empiricism aims to keep theory apart from practice on the grounds that practice is always partisan and theory should be value-neutral. By contrast, emancipatory international relations holds that theory in international relations is a form of practice and a vehicle for promoting social and political change. Emancipatory international relations requires that *theory* be connected up with *practice* in a certain way, namely, that if the theory is correct and people 'put it into practice', their lives will go better individually and collectively. The validity of changing people's practices is related to the fact that they satisfy the requirements of genuine freedom. With this as backdrop, let us mark out some of the main emancipatory alternatives relevant to international relations, keeping in mind that the distinctions put in play here are intentionally blurred and the categories themselves always revisable.

According to classical Marxism, the fundamental categories and concepts which Marx devised to explain the nature and consequences of capitalism can – indeed *must* – be applied to the context of international relations. Despite massive setbacks for states which have explicitly identified themselves as 'Marxist', Marxist theory remains a vital resource for any emancipatory understanding of international relations. The rout of Marxism in Central Europe notwithstanding, it is hard to take exception to Fred Halliday's insistence on 'the relevance of Marxist theory as such to the discussion of the central concepts of international relations ... Marx and Engels established a theoretical system ... that is of great importance for international relations as a whole.'[8]

Supporters of the classical Marxist approach tend to presuppose the truth of Marx's understanding of historical materialism in their efforts to analyse the significance of the acquisition of territories and the creation of empires, in seeing war as a function of class conflict, and in preparing the world for the inevitable collapse of liberal international capitalism and its replacement by scientific socialism. Proponents of this view treat Marx's thought as a radical 'break' with 'bourgeois' thought; it cuts a fault line between previous thought which is profound in depth and progressive in time. Classical Marxists tend to emphasise the extent to which the world capitalist system is in crisis as a result of intensive capital accumulation, capital's increasing internationalisation and growing class conflict. They generally accept the idea that the Third World has been underdeveloped by capitalism and that structural dependencies widen the gap between poor states and rich ones. Although classical Marxists tend to perceive a world in severe economic crisis, there is far less consensus among them concerning whether there are genuine prospects for revolutionary change towards world socialism. Notwithstanding recent depredations in the ranks of classical Marxists, this

9

theoretical position still represents a powerful strain of emancipatory thought in international relations but it would take me too far afield to consider it in this work.

International critical theory has many incisive and determined advocates. Despite striking differences in theme and method, international critical theorists evidently share a desire not only to develop a deeper understanding of international human emancipation but also to provide the materials in terms of which human beings will change their self-understandings and therefore act in ways that are self-consciously freer and more satisfying. Only when human self-understandings result in the destruction of historical structures that prevent social and political emancipation will international relations, on this view, become a form of rational freedom. International critical theory takes its bearings from an Enlightenment view which posits an inner connection between rational action and moral autonomy and which forms, as Habermas puts it, 'the horizon of a new historical consciousness which has kept modernity in constant motion until the present'.[9] The founders of the Enlightenment saw themselves as engaging in intellectual labours which would emancipate humankind from prejudice, superstition, convention and tradition. In following the founders, recent international critical theory manifests a passionate insistence on the self-sufficiency of human reason and a belief that reason can determine the ground of political theory and practice in international relations. The various theoretical alternatives falling under this category – notwithstanding their great differences in other respects – share some version of the liberationist goal, i.e. the goal which says that international relations can (and in some versions *will necessarily*) free itself from structures which prevent individuals and human communities from actualising flourishing ways of life. In chapter 3, I shall consider international critical theory in more detail and give two recent examples of its deployment.

By contrast, poststructuralist international theory hopes to articulate an alternative to both classical Marxism and international critical theory *without* losing all grip on the liberationist modality which draws it into the emancipatory net. It attempts to develop such a theory out of a disparate set of materials, such as, for example: deconstruction; belief in an imminent world crisis of thought; and certain Nietzschean ideas of self and morality.[10] Whether these materials can be combined to produce a coherent and attractive understanding of international relations which also remains faithful to emancipatory international relations is beyond the scope of this work. A certain scepticism, none-theless, seems in order.[11]

Feminist international theory is another emancipatory modality in international relations. To be sure, not all feminist theories of international relations are emancipatory, but there has been, as one would expect, a strong tendency towards liberationist modes of thinking in recent feminist international relations. Notwithstanding great differences in feminist perspectives, there is general agreement that the aim of feminist theories of international relations is radical improvement in the lives of women. Nonetheless, a distinction needs to be marked between feminist theories which call for radical improvement in the condition of women and feminist theories which attempt to bring theory and practice into unison. In terms of the way in which emancipatory international relations has been characterised above, only the later sort of theory would count as emancipatory. To see how this shapes our understanding of the state of play within feminist international theory, let us divide up the main theoretical approaches in terms of the following three categories: feminist empiricism, feminist standpoint theory (FST) and feminist postmodern theory (FPT).[12] Given this schema, one finds that although all three perspectives embody commitments to overcoming patriarchal power, only FST and FPT can be said to count as emancipatory. That is, feminist empiricism, as a *genre* of positivist-empiricism, holds out the possibility that a non-gendered observer can study the reality of world politics objectively and impartially. When such a position is taken up, one will understand that women in Western culture have been denied many possibilities and opportunities because men have exercised power over them. But there is no claim in feminist empiricism that once this is understood, if it is, that anything will be done about it. Theory can be value-neutral, non-partisan, non-gendered and only accidentally related to practical change.

The same cannot be said for either FST or FPT: each in its own way is emancipatory. FST reflects the view that women occupy a social location that affords them privileged access to understanding social phenomena. The central idea behind FST was developed by Nancy Hartsock who drew an analogy between the Marxist claim of a privileged epistemic standpoint and feminism.[13] Just as Marx held that the proletariat knew more than the bourgeoisie about society because of the proletariat's special experiences with it, so Hartsock claimed that women are epistemically superior to men because their experiences with the world are uniquely different and cognitively superior. Hartsock attempts to sustain this view by claiming Marxism as a true moral framework which, given certain revisions from a feminist materialist psychology, provides a basis for an emancipatory feminist view of the world. Hartsock shows the extent to which she follows the canonical Marxian understanding of theory and practice when she writes: 'Feminist theorists must demand that feminist theorising be grounded in women's material activity and must be a part of the political struggle necessary to develop areas of social life modelled on this activity.'[14] Since, for Hartsock, feminist theorising *must* be part of a practical political struggle, her account, and those which follow from it, is clearly emancipatory.

To recapitulate so far: the aim of FST is to emancipate the subject, to empower her and help her to escape the social roles that exploit and oppress her. The theory emancipates a subject by removing her reasons for accepting or conforming to these roles. To succeed, the subject *needs* to be convinced that her reasons are not good reasons but ideological reasons, and she will not be convinced of this unless she accepts the view of her world offered by the theory. In other words, acceptance by the subject is relevant because the aim or end of the theory is to get the subject to do something – namely resist – and her acceptance of the theory is the means to secure her resistance. This is what accounts for the tendency in FST to proselytise, to propagandise and to oversimplify: for the theory to be true women have to be made to act on it. But there is an alternative to FST: FPT. To be sure, although FPT does not explicitly present itself as an emancipatory view, it is not difficult to see the extent to which it expresses a modality of gender liberation.

FPT adopts an epistemology which reveals the futility of any attempt to define an essential female nature or to replace masculinist epistemology with feminist epistemology. It denies that any totalising framework, including Marx's, will result in emancipation – at least not an emancipation one would want to write home about. For FPT, we (men included) must reject all subject/object dichotomies including the dichotomy, redolent in FST, which says that men and women are fundamentally different and women are superior. FPT aims to emancipate women not by seeking a unitary absolute and transcendent truth but by subverting, displacing, disrupting and transgressing all dichotomies, normalisings, unities and totalities. According to Christine Sylvester, one of its most incisive proponents in international relations, postmodern feminism 'looks for differences in voices and standpoints and marks the connections that may exist across the differences. It looks for new forms and mobilities of subjectivity that can replace single-subject categories ...'[15] In 'Riding the Hyphens of Feminism, Peace and Place in Four-(or more) Part Cacophony', Sylvester describes three story lines within the feminist peace literature with a view to deconstructing the dichotomy between war (male)/peace (female).[16] Sylvester suggests that we must ride the hyphens of all the story lines, that is, we must effectively excise the *emancipatory content* of all canonical positions but without using the assembled material to construct a unitary Self. She holds that feminists would do well to equivocate with regard to all canonical positions including feminist postmodernism. Sylvester makes two additional points. First, she suggests that peace standpoint feminism, in clinging to peace as women's property, unwittingly valorises war by retreating to wars' socially inferiorised other. By clinging to the peace standpoint, war looms as a self-preoccupation. Second, Sylvester holds that FST is afraid of the indeterminacy of postmodern politics, a politics which produces no programme, has no project nor goals except to deconstruct the dichotomies which have led to gendered politics. The old categories of race, class, culture and colonial experience are pieces of tired architecture which fail to come to grips with the postmodern condition.

In her more recent work *Feminist Theory and International Relations in a Postmodern Era*, Sylvester becomes more explicit in her commitment to postmodern feminism (in contradistinction to feminist postmodernism) which, on her view, 'exposes the smokescreens, and the histories of the screens and the smoke, in brilliant, eye-opening ways'.[17] The path to emancipation lies neither in assimilation nor in the overthrow of male dominance and its replacement by female (or feminist) dominance. Emancipation comes about through looking at 'other identity allegiances within ourselves and our context of knowledge with an empathetic-critical gaze'.[18] It comes from 'listening to and engaging canon-excluding and canon-including subjectivities'.[19] Rejecting doctrinaire feminist postmodernism, Sylvester develops and deploys the concept of *homesteading* to articulate what women require in the face of their homeless condition. According to Sylvester, homesteading leads to emancipation 'through a radically empathetic conversational politics that helps us to learn the strengths and limitations of our inherited identity categories and to decide our identities, theories, politics and daily concerns rather than continue to deride them out of hand because they come from established authority sources'.[20] For Sylvester, 'homesteading is always a politics of disturbance that unsettles and ploughs up inherited turfs without planting the same old seeds in the field ...'[21] It emancipates, we are told, through 'an unravelling-reworking process' such as the one that took place at Greenham Common. Emancipation is a matter, on this view, of shaking up foundations and always maintaining ambiguity and 'a Janus-faced politics of disturbance'.[22] Emancipation here *is* an anarchism. Notwithstanding its great interest, feminist international theory will not be considered further in this study.

Even from these cursory descriptions, it should be clear that the gulf separating poststructuralist theory, critical international theory, classical Marxism and feminist international theory is enormous. For the first two 'schools', Marx's theses are, if true at all, only contingently true, viz., true insofar as they sustain genuine, non-transcendental steps towards human emancipation. For classical Marxism and Hartsock's version of FST, on the other hand, Marx's theses are true *tout court* and the knowledge gathered in terms of them is objective. By the same token, it is also worth pointing out that much of the criticism of emancipatory international relations is actually directed at the pretensions of hyperbolic forms of degenerate classical Marxism; but even devastating criticism of this 'school' would leave largely untouched the core ideas of those other strands, including Hartsock's revisionary historical materialism, which have earned independent title to the emancipatory legacy. This consideration is of some importance since it will help us to avoid 'cheap and easy' dismissals of emancipatory thought and practice.

Political realism

Political realism typically claims to be 'the natural view' of international relations, one which arises from ordinary, pre-philosophical and intuitive reflections on 'the way things are' in world politics. In terms of its own self-understanding, political realism requires neither philosophical foundation nor rational justification; it simply articulates the commonsense truths of everyday political life. Nevertheless, its claim to being the commonsense view is vitiated somewhat by the manifest internal division within this conception between what I shall call *Concessional Realism* (or neorealism) and *Commonsense Realism*. By concessional realism I mean the idea which concedes the validity of the principal methodological claims of positivist-empiricism broadly considered and, in particular, the claim that theories of international relations are structurally homomorphic to natural scientific theories. Theories of international relations are not, on this view, mediated by language, mind and value; they do not require the use of 'subject-related terms', 'contexts' or 'practices'. Concessional realists still consider themselves realists because they conceptualise international relations (in the material sense) as consisting of sovereign states in adversary relations with one another; but they increasingly tend to accept the following methodological idea: that rationalism – in the form of rational choice theory and the theory of games – will transform older forms of realism into acceptable scientific structures and ward off anti-realist challenges.

Although the writings of Robert Gilpin,[23] Stephen Krasner[24] and Joseph Grieco[25] represent significant contributions to concessional realism, we shall concentrate here on the work of Kenneth Waltz.[26] According to Waltz, theory is an activity of representing or picturing. In one of his articles he distinguishes 'theory' as 'artifice' from 'facts ... that permit explanation and prediction'.[27] He cites Ludwig Boltzman's article 'Theories as representations' as support for his view that 'theory is a depiction'.[28] In his earlier work, *Theory of International Politics*, Waltz had called theory 'not an edifice of truth nor a representation of reality but a picture, mentally formed, of a bounded realm or domain of activity'.[29] But what is 'a bounded realm or domain of activity'? Evidently, it is the isolated individual Cartesian theorist who decides what is in the realm and how it is bounded. But in terms of what criteria? 'Usefulness' is Waltz's answer.[30] To the question 'usefulness for what purpose?' Waltz responds that 'usefulness is judged by the explanatory and predictive powers of the theory that may be fashioned'.[31] Circularity seems to threaten here. This prompts us to push the question further back and to ask why it is useful to explain and predict. Waltz's answer reveals his commitment to instrumentalism: 'The urge to explain is not born of idle curiosity alone. It is produced also by the desire to control, or at least a desire to know if control is possible.'[32] Control, a central feature of positivist-empiricism, turns out to be a major feature of Waltz' philosophy of science as well.

In his more recent work, Waltz has emphasised that his understanding of theory is not committed to the correspondence theory of truth, i.e. the increasingly discredited idea that truth is determined by matching up language with reality. Waltz writes: 'Theories ... are not useful merely because they may help one to understand, explain, and sometimes predict the trend of events. Equally important, they help one to understand how a given system works ... To achieve "closeness of fit" would negate theory. A theory cannot fit the facts or *correspond* with the events it seeks to explain.'[33] Although Waltz is evidently prepared to give up the idea that a true theory is one which corresponds with facts, this leaves unclear just what cognitive status theories are supposed to have and how Waltz can avoid scepticism about their alleged 'usefulness'. For if we have a dualistic theory-world view and we do not have a correspondence theory of truth available to match theory up with reality, the sceptic would seem to be justified in saying that there is no basis for believing that there is any relationship between the picture and what the picture is supposed to represent. In *Theories of International Politics*, Waltz has told us that theories are 'neither true nor false'.[34] He has indicated that he agrees with the statement 'made by many that theories can never be proven true'.[35] Waltz goes on: 'Theories do construct *a* reality, but no one can ever say that it is *the* reality.'[36] Two things appear to lie behind the obscurities of these statements.

First, there is the idea that theories, on Waltz' construal, can never have the slightest epistemic access to the world or reality. The truth of our theories stretches beyond the limits of our cognitive powers. Truth, on this view, is radically non-epistemic. No matter how much evidence there may be for a theory, it can never be 'proven' and it can never be 'true'. Since the described reality may be wholly different from reality as it is, Waltz is effectively committing himself to a metaphysical position, i.e. metaphysical realism, which reinforces scepticism. Second, Waltz' conception of theory as an activity of representing is an understanding of mind which stretches back to Aristotle: Hilary Putnam calls it 'a Cryptographer's model of mind'.[37] The leading notion here is that concepts are 'representations in the mind', that the way in which we account for sameness in some concept such as, say, 'international-political system' is that different uses of that term are associated with the same mental representation. However, Putnam has persuasively argued that the traditional mentalistic account of meaning that lies behind Waltz' view fails and this for two reasons. It fails, first of all, because 'what is in people's brains or minds, their mental representations or mental descriptions or mental pictures, does not in general determine the reference of a word that they know how to use'.[38] And it fails also, according to Putnam, because it does not give due weight to the contribution of the environment to reference. The things that we refer to themselves contribute to speakers' reference. That is, reference does not necessarily change because of difference of mental representation, but rather because the substances, things or objects to which they refer are different. In the light of these failures, it is quite unclear how Waltz' notion of 'theory' can be sustained.

A sharply opposing view falling under the rubric of political realism is commonsense realism. It regards realism as a conception of international relations intimately bound up with the concepts and categories of the tradition of political philosophy, especially as these are discernible in the writings of Thucydides, St Augustine, Machiavelli, Hobbes, Spinoza, Rousseau, Hegel and de Tocqueville. Such thinkers form a tradition of political realism in the sense that they see themselves as participants engaged in an enduring discourse about the nature of political action and ethical activity as these apply, or would apply, to international relations. It is a conversation which is tradition-dependent and authority-oriented; and it has often taken as one of its main themes the ineliminability of the tragic in politics, as a place where human beings, especially statesmen and stateswomen, are evidently self-compelled to make choices which they regret having made. In general, commonsense realists think it essential to build an understanding of international relations on the 'truths' of political and ethical life derived from traditional political thought. Failure to do so will lead, in their view, only to a truncated and greatly impoverished understanding of international relations which is false – false to 'the tradition' and false to the reality of 'how things are'. In chapters 4 through 9 of this study I shall argue in favour of a form of political realism – evaluative political realism – which builds upon and extends commonsense realism but which hives off some of the baggage that has made it vulnerable to criticism from rival alternative conceptions. Evaluative political realism proposes to achieve this by incorporating some new elements from a pragmatist/realist philosophy of science and a certain realist understanding of ethics. Emphasis will be placed on showing that although it bears a 'family resemblance' to other versions of realism, evaluative political realism does articulate a distinctively different conception of international relations.

Evaluative political realism has four features that are worth noting in advance of our more comprehensive discussion below. The first holds that international relationists should determine the content of their discipline by advancing reflective answers to the 'philosophical' and 'quasi-philosophical' problems which the subject matter evokes. As we shall see, there are a good many such problems, including: the ontological status of state and state-system; the epistemological problems that relate to claims about human nature; the degree to which we can legitimately describe history as truth-telling; and the basis for making cognitive ethical claims. In reflecting on these problems, evaluative political realism urges us to abandon all absolute, global and unified accounts of 'science' and determine *from within* the discipline whether the deliverances of international relations constitute knowledge, ideologies of domination, texts, bad poetry, rhetorics or whatever. To be sure, this is not to imply that international relations should attempt to inoculate itself from discourses outside its traditions and develop an account of itself in terms which are wholly or mainly divorced from its own past. That would be harmful even if it were conceptually possible. Human beings are embedded creatures and, as such, are never able to completely detach themselves from their culture, language and traditions. This does mean, however, that international relationists should abandon the practice of adopting fully blown philosophical accounts of what science, knowledge or reason consists of, whether expressed in a post-positivistic commitment to models of explanation and prediction or articulated in a scientific realism advancing programmes for international relations based on a naturalistic or physicalistic relationship between language and the world. An internal pragmatist/realist philosophy of science is all the philosophy of science international relations needs.

The second feature of evaluative political realism worth emphasising here lies in its commitment to explanation by reasons or, as I would prefer to say, 'ordinary-life explanations'. An ordinary-life explanation involves the claim that to explain human behaviour, in general and with appropriate *ceteris paribus* clauses attached, we need to appeal to someone's reasons for acting within a certain historical and environmental context. In other words, we correctly account for the behaviour of statesmen and women on the basis of attributing to them belief-states, desire-states and intentional-states. From within the capacious category of ordinary-life explanation, we may say that past statesmen have chosen policies for their nation-states on the basis of reasons concerning the desirability of certain ends or purposes; we have access to those reasons by imaginatively putting ourselves in their place and judging whether those reasons were 'good' or 'bad' reasons. Ordinary-life explanations, thus understood, have deep resonance in the explanatory accounts traditionally offered by political realists and stand in sharp contrast to the rational choice explanatory modes which neorealists typically rely upon.

The third notable feature of evaluative political realism lies in its firm commitment to history, not just in the sense of a commitment to history as methodology (historiography), but to history as a way of understanding and interpreting ordinary life. Since ordinary life is principally characterised by 'historicity' and human beings are the 'bearers' of history, they generally have access to the implicit ordinary-life explanations that underlie their 'traditional' and 'customary' ways of interpreting themselves. History is the public speech which creates heritages and the cohesive narratives of different cultures, communities and nation-states. Insofar as we are all participants in the shaping of our heritage and the cohesive narratives of which they are a part, history is meaningful and this makes historiography possible. But although history is meaningful, there is, on this view, no predetermined *telos* that will make the whole course of events naturally and fully intelligible: there is an ineluctable gap between historiography as a *practice* and historiography as a vicarious *theory* that projects a pre-given *telos* for the whole.

A fourth feature of evaluative political realism worth mentioning in this summary lies in its commitment to a quasi-realist ethics for international relations. A quasi-realist ethics is one which says that it is both human beings and the world – in a sense that requires spelling out – that determine the success of our ethical practices and not, as in an alternative Kantian view, reason and the will. The problem for evaluative political realists is how to bring an internal pragmatist/ realist philosophy of science into coherent relation with a quasi-realist ethics so that they can claim ethical knowledge of the world. One route to sustaining this claim – explored below – lies in rejecting an absolute conception of the world and the rationalism which is supposed to ground it and replacing it with a participant's conception of the human world – the world of human action – which makes a place for both pluralism and ethical objectivity. Evaluative political realism may thus be viewed as the attempt to make a place for a partially cognitive ethics within a non-absolute, but realistically conceived, pluralist world. More of this later.

Conclusions

It should now be clear that the differences animating these three conceptions of international relations are neither theoretically nor practically vacuous: understanding what they are and what they imply for the way we conceive international relations *is* what international theory is all about in our time. Even at this very elementary descriptive level, the sheer complexity of these three conceptions is remarkable: each involves different epistemological assumptions, theories of language and meaning, philosophies of science, moral philosophies and different metaphysical positions. And as if this were not enough, each of these three conceptions has its own history – rooted in different Western political and philosophical traditions – which has not yet even begun to be told.[39] In the face of these profound differences, it seems reasonable to begin a discussion and analysis of them by taking a philosophical shortcut: I shall characterise these three conceptions initially in terms of the central concepts of *theory* and *practice*.

There are at least three reasons for focusing on theory and practice. First of all, it will enable us to maintain constant contact with the deep differences which animate these alternative understandings of the subject and thus help us to see what is valuable in each conception. Secondly, the concepts of theory and practice have an ancient philosophical lineage and so discussion of them will help us to place our particular conception within an informative historical context. There is a critical need to avoid a truncated view of international relations which locates thought about the subject exclusively in the present. And, thirdly, the concepts of theory and practice are very much bound up with two partly overlapping discourses which are central to any genuine understanding of international relations, viz., those that concern science and those that relate to ethics. Science, understood as reliable beliefs about the world and ethics, conceived as the search for human goods, are central features of any human science and therefore of any conception of international relations.

This opening towards considering theory, practice and their relation stands in marked contrast to attitudes developed in the 1960s and 1970s. During the heyday of logical empiricism, it was generally thought that 'theory' had a strictly axiomatic or formal definition which could be applied to all knowledge-acquiring disciplines regardless of their great differences. By the same token, it was thought that 'practice' (and in particular ethics) was outside the scope of what constituted genuine knowledge. With the demise of logical empiricism, the strong resurgence of emancipatory theory with its special under-standing of the relation of theory and practice, and the rise of poststructuralism, the stage has been set for redeploying these two concepts for expository purposes, keeping in mind, of course, that the central purpose of this study lies more in *locating* and *revising* political realism than in providing a comprehensive account of the three conceptions themselves.

2 Positivist-empiricism and international relations

The force of illusion reaches its zenith here ...
Nietzsche

Introduction

Chapter 1 indicated in a general way what positivist-empiricism consists of. The purpose of this chapter is to tease out some of positivist-empiricism's core assumptions and presuppositions, and in particular its assumptions about theory and practice, keeping in mind that this is to be done not from some putative position of neutral observation but from within the perspective of a certain revisionary form of political realism. Of particular concern from this point of view is how positivist-empiricism intends to cope with the challenge of scepticism to which, it is claimed, commitment to assumptions and presuppositions deeply embedded in its understanding of *theory* give rise. Attention will also be given to the positivist-empiricist's conception of *practice* and the understanding of the self with which it is bound up. Such an understanding is erroneous: it captures neither our common intuitions nor our moral perceptions.

Theory and practice

Positivist-empiricism: general considerations

Let me illustrate how the three conceptions relate theory to practice by offering Figure 2.1. Positivist-empiricism, emancipatory international theory and political realism are here depicted as articulating different understandings of theory, practice and their relation. To avoid later

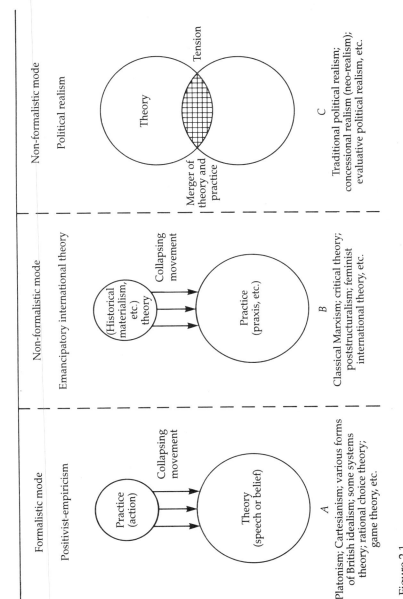

Formalistic mode

Positivist-empiricism

Practice (action) → Collapsing movement → Theory (speech or belief)

A

Platonism; Cartesianism; various forms of British idealism; some systems theory; rational choice theory; game theory, etc.

Non-formalistic mode

Emancipatory international theory

(Historical materialism, etc.) theory → Collapsing movement → Practice (praxis, etc.)

B

Classical Marxism; critical theory; poststructuralism; feminist international theory, etc.

Non-formalistic mode

Political realism

Theory ⟨Tension / Merger of theory and practice⟩

C

Traditional political realism; concessional realism (neo-realism); evaluative political realism, etc.

Figure 2.1

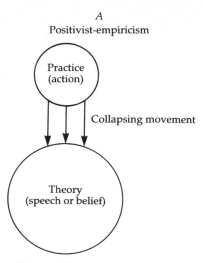

A
Positivist-empiricism

Figure 2.2

misunderstanding, it needs to be pointed out that the distinctions depicted in Figure 2.1 are not meant to be neat delineations: the boundaries are intended to be fuzzy and their identifying features are supposed to interweave and overlap. Their value lies in showing that certain partially concealed connections between past philosophical thought and some on-going current research programmes in international relations may be uncovered and made perspicuous. Let us consider Figure 2.2.

According to positivist-empiricism, formal definitions of both theory and practice are the indispensable starting point for describing these two concepts. A theory in a logical sense might then be defined as a set of statements which does not contain the contradictories of all its theses, or in some similar way. The main reason for the formalistic emphasis is epistemological, *viz.*, that without formal definitions and clear meanings, one would not be able to determine whether certain observations confirm or disconfirm theoretical statements. And if this cannot be accomplished, then the very idea of providing reliable, i.e. scientific, knowledge about international relations would be put at considerable risk. So the formality serves the vital purpose of providing grounds for determining what we can know and whether such knowledge is reliable. Positivist-empiricism aims to base knowledge, not on sense-perception or facts, but on theoretical reason's capacity to

24

correct potentially deceptive sense-perception. Theoretical reason is always prior to sense-perception.[1] Although any such starting point may be regarded as contrary to commonsense, positivist-empiricism refuses to be cowed; it holds that knowledge claims derived from our common prereflective understandings of the world are uncertain, unreliable and replaceable with something demonstrably better, i.e. scientific knowledge. On this view, assertions about international relations are ideally expressible in a theoretical, formalistic language; international relationists should make use of this language to select facts, explain events and to predict, where possible, future conditions in world politics. For positivist-empiricism, scientific activity in international relations brings theory to bear on facts in ways that permit explanation and prediction and accepts only those theories which bear a formal logical relationship, deductive or inductive, to whatever constitutes the database.

To achieve reliable knowledge, practice too, like theory, should be defined in formalistic terms and made ready for scientific reconceptualisation. For positivist-empiricism, politics, law, religion and morals are best conceived of in neutral and external ways so that the intrusion of the subjective which describes how things appear and feel to a particular person may be minimised or, possibly, eliminated altogether. No 'subject-related' properties are admissible to any scientifically conceived conception of practice.[2] To eliminate such properties and to develop a universal morality which goes hand-in-glove with a universal science, we need to be committed, it is held, to a single framework. Consider, for example, Ernst Hass' epistemological project. He writes: 'Knowledge about any phenomena cannot be accumulated unless the practitioners share a single frame of reference ...'[3] Since only a single frame of reference allows 'knowledge to accumulate' and since, as we also learn, the single focal point requires commitment to absolute objectivity, reality has to be stripped of its secondary characteristics, of how things feel and appear to human beings, of what Charles Taylor calls 'the desirability characterisations' of things.[4] On Haas' view, if we commit ourselves to 'the rational-analytical way of thinking' we will be able to resolve our practical problems by using 'Western reason' which 'offers us both the possibility of attaining consensual understandings of problems requiring solutions' and 'an incremental step toward achieving a universal morality yet to be conceived'.[5] A universalistic understanding of theory engenders a universalistic moral project.

We might call the general attitude which conceives practice in terms of the categories of theory, 'the theoretisation of practice', that is, the disposition to conceive practice – morality, religion, history and politics – in terms which, in depreciating the value of a reflective practical attitude, make the absolute objectivity of science stand over against reflective practice. When viewed from the absolute perspective of a single frame of reference, scientific theorising of practice has two alleged advantages: negatively, it allows one to avoid the deleterious effects of bias, prejudice and tradition and, secondly, it provides an opportunity, according to its proponents, of grasping the world in a precise and objective way. By theoretising practice, positivist-empiricists believe they are justified in replacing an ontology of 'desirability characterisations' with a scientific ontology of identical units which potentially permit explanatory control and the possibility of predicting future configurations of events in the world. Insofar as practical concepts fail to satisfy minimal scientific standards of objectivity and precision, they will tend to create uncertainty, sow confusion and prevent genuine progress. Hence, either they must be reduced to facts or data of some kind, or consigned to the realm of the non-cognitive. Only by validating practical reason *theoretically* can we hope, on this view, to lay an epistemological foundation for practice. In sum, positivist-empiricism is rooted in prior epistemological commitments about what constitutes reliable knowledge and, in particular, in the idea that any practice must be substantiated by the same sort of apodictic methods which obtain in the natural sciences. But such standards may be impossible to meet, and hence, they may cement the very scepticism which poses so many difficulties for positivist-empiricism in both theory and practice. In the theoretical realm the principal difficulty lies in overcoming methodological scepticism. In the realm of practice the epistemological demands placed on morality and ethics contribute to a spectacular narrowing of the scope of practical reason and to its general impoverishment in the field of international relations. But what is the source of this conception of international relations?

Descartes and 'The Age of the World Picture'[6]

The principal provenance of the positivist-empiricist understanding of theory and practice lies in the philosophy of Descartes. For Descartes, all rational inquiry derives from a self-conscious commitment to a single methodology as articulated in a programme of 'unified science'.

Descartes' conception of reason in its relation to practice was instrumental in character. He effectively redefined practical ends themselves in terms of theoretical categories and regarded theoretical reason as the sole instrument of their achievement. He called for the replacement of the '[s]peculative philosophy ... taught in the schools' by a 'practical' one which would render us 'the masters and possessors of nature'[7] and 'enable us to enjoy without any trouble the fruits of the earth and all the good things that are to be found there'.[8] If we use reason and theory to achieve practical goals, Descartes tells us in the Author's Letter to the *Principles of Philosophy*, we shall be able to transform our pre-philosophical moral practices into the 'most perfect moral science which, presupposing a complete knowledge of the other sciences, is the last degree of wisdom'.[9] Although Descartes admitted that it was 'improbable' that 'the whole body of the Sciences should be reformed', nonetheless, concerning his own pre-scientific opinions which were not sciences, Descartes implied we should follow his lead and 'sweep them completely away, so that they might later on be replaced, either by others which were better, or the same' once they had been made to 'conform to the uniformity of a rational scheme'.[10] In other words, we need to follow a certain uniform method, originated by Descartes, called *the method of doubt* which delivers us from our prejudices and provides confidence that our claims to knowledge are based on a solid foundation rather than on the shifting sands of contentious opinion. Descartes suggests that the application of the method of doubt will lead us to discover the foundations of knowledge in mathematics, metaphysics and physics which will lead, in turn, to greater knowledge in the 'branches' of physics (medicine, mechanics and morals).[11]

Although considerable attention has been given to the application of Descartes' method to philosophy and science, its extension to practice has been relatively neglected. In one of his late works, *Passions of the Soul*, Descartes redefined and reconceptualised the Aristotelian virtues, reducing them to the single passion of *générosité*, the self-recognition of natural self-mastery. Whereas Aristotle enumerated a range of moral and intellectual virtues which required reinforcing through constant doing, Descartes reduces all these to the sole good of *générosité*, which does not require reinforcing because it is congenital and natural.[12] The theoretisation of practice, on the present construal, refers to the Cartesian tendency to make all sciences and arts 'conform to the uniformity of a rational scheme' irrespective of the reductionist consequences for practical life. There is a paradox here worth pondering:

Descartes had hoped that his method would enable human beings to fulfil their practical aims but his excessive concentration on method led him to devise a conception of theory of such a formal purity and totalistic character that it radically reduced the scope of practice itself. Within the Cartesian framework, practical activities were reconceptualised in thoroughly abstract terms and made remote from the real, complex and frequently opaque doings of ordinary human beings in their everyday lives. Since the method of doubt reinforces theory's dominance over practice, we can anticipate the prospective collapse of practical activity into the leading premises of an architectonic theoretical system (as depicted in Figure 2.2). The resulting depreciation of history, law and morals – a notable feature of recent positivist-empiricism – might then be understood as part of an historically identified effort from within this tradition to transform practical questions into theoretical ones in the instrumental interest of a unified science in which the vagaries of practice are squeezed into a radically theoretised framework to achieve certain predefined methodological goals.

In the Cartesian framework, the instrumentalist's understanding of theory's relation to practice collapses into scientific imperialism: theory is supposed to absorb or replace practice with a version which conforms to its own theoretical self-conception. For Descartes and Bacon, knowledge is progressive, to be used for mankind's general benefit; it is nothing if not an aggressive activity self-determined to eliminate the confusions of everyday experience. And since its value is greatly reduced if not generally used, there is an internal dynamic tendency to promote the social uses of science and to expand its 'benefits' to a greater number of domains. For the descendants of Descartes and Bacon within recent positivist-empiricism, scientific theory is to be guided by reason conceived as method and is supposed to yield, in one of the current jargons, *useable knowledge* for the benefit of human beings, i.e. to prevent self-destructive wars, global famine, destruction of the world's environment and so on *ad indefinitum*. But, from a different perspective, useable knowledge may be yet another instrumentalist vehicle for replacing a traditional notion of practice as ethical knowledge with a hypertrophic, imperialistic conception of theory whose upshot in international relations would be to replace the fractious pluralism of interstate conflict with a comprehensive rational ordering inimical to pluralism, democracy and difference.

Positivist-empiricism in international relations

However, at this point one might ask: 'This is all very well, but to what extent are recent theories of international relations committed to an instrumentalist understanding of the subject?' To be sure, there is no intimation of direct lines of influence from Descartes to positivist-empiricists in recent international relations. It would be better to say that 'a tradition' has been identified whose 'fuzzy' boundaries neither permit nor require precise demarcation. Still, positivist-empiricism *is* a tradition and one which tends to dominate the writing, research and rhetoric of Anglo-American international relations. A few citations from the writings of some well-known international relationists (positivist-empiricists in my terms) will help to suggest the extent of its influence:

  (i) Oran Young: ... the development of viable theories *is the best procedure available for those who wish to make accurate predictions, whether in the physical sciences or the social sciences.*[13]

 (ii) Kenneth Waltz: Theoretical notions *find their justification in the success of theories that imply them.*[14]

(iii) Karl Deutsch: Knowledge is ... a process in which subjective and objective limits meet ... Maps, as well as time diagrams, can do more than summarise existing knowledge. They *can suggest ways of looking for knowledge, and help to predict regularities that may or may not be confirmed by later experience or measurement.* We can do these things through the operation of prediction.[15]

 (iv) Ernst Haas: *Knowledge is the sum of technical information and of theories about the information which commands sufficient consensus at a given time among interested actors to serve as a guide to public policy designed to achieve some social goal.* Knowledge incorporates scientific notions relating to the social goal.[16]

  (v) Nazli Choucri: Theory generally performs several functions in the course of empirical investigation: It provides a coding scheme for storing and retrieving information, and *it serves as a search instrument that guides the investigator toward relevant questions and appropriate data.* Theory preserves and facilitates inspection of data; theory also preserves and focuses upon what the theorist sees as relevant. Through its built-in capabilities for dissociating and recombining information (in terms of

29

first- and higher-order symbols), theory provides a means of accommodating new information and new combinations of ideas and concepts.[17]

(vi) R.J. Rummel: For me science or quantitative research are not the aims, but tools to be pragmatically applied to doing something about war ... [18]

(vii) McGowan and Shapiro: Many social scientists feel today that social science is a *tool* in the struggle for a better world – for example, a world with a more equitable distribution of wealth and less violence.[19]

(viii) Richard Rosecrance: ... if y increases, one can expect x to change in a predicted direction ... [20]

(ix) Robert Keohane: ... the rationalistic theory ... implies hypotheses that could be submitted to systematic, even quantitative, examination. For instance, this theory predicts that the incidence of specific international institutions should be related to the ratio of benefits anticipated from exchange to the transaction costs of establishing the institutions necessary to facilitate the negotiation, monitoring, and enforcement costs of agreements specifying the terms of exchange ... The rationalistic theory could also help us to develop a theory of compliance or noncompliance with commitments. For international regimes to be effective, their injunctions must be obeyed ... [21]

It would seem that formalistic and abstract modes of conceptualising theory are pervasive in recent positivist-empiricism. How practice is conceived in such terms is incisively summed up in an introductory text in a brisk formulation: 'Why do we want to understand international relations? An obvious answer is that we want *to increase our ability to control events*. Thus assumptions about the understanding and controllability of international relations are very much related, imperfect understanding almost always results in poor policies.'[22] For this author, and many others in the positivist-empiricist tradition, there is a profoundly intimate triadic relation between theory, control and successful practice.

Now, although there are differences in emphases between these disparate positivist-empiricist perspectives, for our purposes here it is important to see what they share: first, the notion that human subjectivity lays the world open to potentially infinite, transparent representation directed towards the acquisition of knowledge; secondly, the idea that theory, reason or science is essentially an instrument for understanding and practical goal-achievement. And, thirdly, the view that practice (ethics or morality) has nothing to do with scientific knowledge and should therefore either be developed scientifically or excluded altogether from the discipline's ken. On the positivist-empiricist's instrumentalist understanding of theory, the commonsense world as we experience it has no descriptive import; our theories of the world are simply devices for deriving observational consequences when certain variables are manipulated in certain ways: theories are tools for generating controlled explanations or predictions.

Language, too, for the positivist-empiricist is treated as instrumental since it is regarded as a tool which determines whether 'reality' can be made intelligible or not. From the positivist-empiricist point of view, the ability to use language is grounded in some prior grasp of the non-semantic contexts in which we find ourselves. It is only because we have first understood the nature of reality that we can then come to comprehend the meaning of the words we use. Language is seen as a tool for communicating and ordering this prior grasp of reality. Since the theorist – in her Cartesian mode – thinks of herself as having a practical, prior grasp of reality, her task then becomes the mastery of language itself as a propaedeutic to theoretical mastery.[23] The clear assumption behind the Cartesian idea of language is that human beings first 'grasp' the world's reality, 'decide' upon their goals and then, taking up some external Archimedean position, 'use' language as the instrument towards reaching these sub-vocally articulated goals or purposes. Although the idea that we can grasp the meaning of reality independently of language itself is of doubtful coherence, it continues to play a large role in the positivist-empiricist's understanding of international relations.

Despite wide differences in style and content, the spirit of positivist-empiricism (and the instrumentalism bound up with it) lives on, albeit in considerably attenuated form, in such theoretical formulations and research programmes as game theory, rational choice theory, systems theory (in many of its formulations), functionalism, neofunctionalism, integration theory, regime theory and so on. What these otherwise very different theories from within positivist-empiricism share, though not necessarily explicitly, is the idea of science, knowledge, reason or theory as sets of rules for calculating how to obtain theoretically conceived goals for the advancement of human 'subjective' ends or purposes. Subject, on this view, is dichotomously divided from object.

31

The resulting understanding of self grounds neoliberal conceptions of human agents as rational self-determiners of their ends. Such a conception of self is 'thin', a pure subject of agency stripped of its complex attributes and pre-poured into the objectified, concrete category of rational chooser. Since states, too, can be understood, given certain problematic philosophical extensions, as individual actors as well, the principles which apply to individuals are conceived to be transferable to the explanation of state behaviour. That individuals and states are then conceived to be self-compelled, as a matter of rationality, to act in terms of their self-interest lies at the heart of neoliberal institutionalism, an understanding of international relations which has played a large role in recent positivist-empiricism. Neoliberal institutionalism has been elegantly formulated and eloquently defended by Robert Keohane.[24]

Another self, another liberalism?

Neoliberal institutionalism articulates a view of the self as a self-contained, self-determining subject which is unencumbered and thin.[25] We shall call this conception of the self: 'the self-as-actor'. In neoliberal institutionalism, the self-as-actor is an agent contingently related to its preferences. It does not matter, for this purpose, whether individuals are viewed as utility maximisers, 'satisfiers' or preference satisfiers as long as they are the sole choosers of their ends and sufficiently detached from their constituting selves to be able to take up an impartial and impersonal perspective on value choices. On an alternative 'thick' view, the self is conceived to be partly constituted by its ends so that one cannot wholly distinguish between self and ends.[26] The self, on this view, is inherently made up of ends that it does not choose; it discovers them by virtue of its being at least partially embedded in some shared social context such as, for example, being a member of the French nation-state. On the thick view, the choices the self makes do not enable the agent to define her identity. By contrast, Keohane is supposing a notion of the subject 'individuated in advance and given prior to its ends'.[27] On this model, the self-as-actor has only the bare capacity for choice itself. The paradigmatic relation of self to ends is supposed to be one of rational, detached choice and not of discovery or self-discovery. From the alternative thick point of view, the thin, self-as-actor understanding is self-defeating for international relations because it cannot account for the persistent division of competing communities in the world.[28] Only a conception of the self which leaves scope for self-focusing human beings who have the capacity to act as co-participants in the joint venture of realising shared cultural goals within a unified community of some sort can account for the evident fact that people want to live in separate communities, notwithstanding the drawbacks of doing so in terms of rational choice theory. Human beings find themselves, through no fault of their own, living in certain historical contexts which lay out a range of possibilities that they can express in being agents in the world. But they also are driven towards community-infused ends which direct the agent's future actions. Human beings are historical creatures such that it is possible for them to formulate meaningful goals for the future in the light of what the community to which they belong reveals as consistent with its heritage and tradition. History is accidental to the extent that historical events might have turned out differently, but history is also binding on human beings because it defines who they are and who they can be.

The neoliberal institutionalist's conception of self-as-actor derives largely from positivist-empiricist assumptions and presuppositions. It finds a resonance in Descartes' conception of *générosité* and has surged into prominence with the rise of certain market-oriented versions of liberalism. It is a form of liberalism which draws more from neoutilitarian accounts of liberalism than from strong forms of civic liberalism.[29] It is a liberalism which proposes to be methodologically tough-minded, quantitative, and computational. It is a version of liberalism where only 'weak evaluation' of alternative actions is possible; strong evaluations, which give direction to choice and action, are regarded as epistemologically suspect.[30]

To be fair, Keohane recognises some of the defects to which the self-as-actor view leads and attempts to cut a path outward to a conception of self and international relations which would permit a far greater role to morality than considerations bearing on rational choice and efficiency would normally permit. In particular, he attempts to develop the notion of diffuse reciprocity which, contrary to rational choice theory, would incorporate notions of obligations, trust and benevolence.[31] But Keohane fails to acknowledge that the 'thicker' notions of morality which he wishes to import into positivist-empiricism require a thicker understanding of the self, one which recognises the capacity of human beings to determine the intrinsic worth of their moral desires. The self-as-actor view to which positivist-empiricism is wedded, however, can neither yield the moral evaluations which Keohane's newer view requires nor can it simply be abandoned without also replacing the epistemological assumptions upon which positivist-empiricism is based. And this it cannot do because positivist-empiricism defines itself in terms of prior epistemological commitments about what constitutes reliable knowledge and, in particular, in terms of the implicit goal that any conception of practice must be substantiated by the same sort of formalistic methods which (allegedly) obtain in the naturalistic sciences. Evidently, the only alternative for the positivist-empiricist who wants to stay within the parameters of traditional epistemological commitments is to eschew thick conceptions of the self and the accompanying talk of intrinsic worth and to opt for a thin conception of the self-as-actor and its talk of preferences, utilities and mutual benefits.

Keohane's conception of the self-as-actor however, even when expanded to allow for diffuse reciprocity, is incompatible with central features of moral experience and human identities. The fact is that we can and do discover, through critical self-reflection, that there are certain valued ends to which individuals (or communities) are attached and that these are not chosen but discovered to be essential to what individuals (or communities) are. The power of discovery enables us to constitute our identities in the light of our self-knowledge, a power which we lack on any notion of the self-as-actor. Although the self-as-actor engages in reflection, it always looks outward to how others can stand over against it rather than inward to moral experience itself. Reflection amounts to a kind of prudential reasoning that could in principle be carried out with equal or greater success by an outside expert who knows relatively little about the agent but a good deal about the alternatives involved and the sort of interests and decisions they typically satisfy. The selves who are making the choices are intersubstitutable. The self-as-actor – that is a self with no pre-attachments to community, nation, ethnic group or country – is simply too thin a creature to bear the burden of sacrifices of the sort required for building identity relations between self and community. What is needed, rather, is a self partially constituted by its ends so that human beings cannot wholly distinguish between self and ends. The resulting self would not be *an actor* but, to use a felicitous term of Charles Taylor's, a self-interpreting animal.[32]

In the last analysis, neoliberal institutionalism embodies a rationalistic conception of the self – the self-as-actor – that is inconsistent with our moral perceptions and our self-understandings. So what? One might think the concept of the self-as-actor to be without much significance for international relations. Cursory reflection suggests otherwise. The concept of 'the actor' has been doing a lot of philosophical work in recent positivist-empiricism in international relations and deserves close attention. This judgement, interestingly enough, seems to be supported by one of the early exponents of the actor-concept, Arnold Wolfers. Wolfers said that the 'identity' of the ' "actors" – those who can properly be said to perform on the international stage – is a matter of dispute which raises not unimportant problems for the analyst, for the practitioner of foreign policy, and for the public'.[33]

As Wolfers warns us here, one consequence of using the term 'actor' is that 'one may lose sight of the human beings for whom and by whom the game is supposed to be played'.[34] Replacing, as Keohane does, human beings with the self-as-actor, then, would be, in effect, to choose (in a distinction due to Martin Hollis) *Plastic Man* rather than *Autonomous Man*. The former 'is a programmed feedback system, whose inputs and inner workings can be given many interpretations' while the latter 'has some species of substantial self within'.[35] But Keohane is certainly not alone in reading Plastic Man into his concept of actor. The forms Plastic Man as actor has assumed in positivist-empiricism have been as varied as they have been unreal. This ghostly figure has appeared as congeries of expectations and dispositions,[36] as structures of social action,[37] as decisional processes,[38] as communication channels,[39] as 'the processes of networks and organisations',[40] as a calculating 'problem-solving machine',[41] and as hypotheses about human behaviour which fail to treat behaviour as expressions of mind.[42] But whatever the self-as-actor's Banquo-like shape, it will not manifest itself as a persisting, thinking and feeling *animal*. Evidently, with the self-as-actor concept we are light years away from the notion of human beings as a 'natural kind'. Below we shall argue that we need a concept of self or human nature distinctively different from the self-as-actor, a concept which resuscitates the animality of human beings, i.e. of their being members of a natural kind.[43]

Another consequence of the neoliberal idea of the self-as-actor lies in its tendency to give support to models of social control and social engineering. As such, it goes along with the suffocation of the self as experienced in modern states with their dreary bureaucracies and their techniques of social manipulation. To see how this might shape international relations, consider the implications of George Modelski's rejection of 'older' concepts of world politics and their replacement by a 'geocentric' conception of the subject. In taking up an Archimedean point of view on political science in terms of which 'politics itself will undergo radical conversion',[44] there will be, quite obviously, certain consequences for the self, though Modelski is not explicit about these. It turns out, however, that Modelski's vision of a geocentric world politics does at least entail the analytical dissolution of the personal 'I' into 'processes of networks and organisations', where individuals are to be regarded as 'contributors to the output of public goods'.[45] This 'theoretical' dissolution of individuals into systems, to which international relationists are urged to give enthusiastic endorsement, not only contracts the subject matter of morality and ethics in international relations, it also reduces the scope for possible criticism of those political activities which obstruct the achievement of the very end – the elimination of world inequalities – which provides the *raison d'être* of a geocentric understanding of world systems. In conceiving human beings fundamentally in terms of their contribution to the output of public goods, one would appear to be licensing a social-engineering approach to human satisfaction in which the global managers of world politics choose the systemic economic, social and political moulds for the globe's entire population. Understood in this way, it appears that the self would lack two features which have generally been thought to be constitutive of it: separability and character. Lacking these, it is not at all clear whether any such understanding of the self can be made coherent. It would certainly not be able to sustain a conception of practice for international relations in which the scope for ethical reflection and action would be capacious.

We have seen that the concepts of theory and practice from within positivist-empiricism have a certain shape. It is a shape dominated by a hypertrophic, colonising understanding of theory modelled on the natural sciences. Such a conception of theory engenders a sceptical attitude to its own deliverances. By the same token, positivist-empiricism allows little or no space for an independently conceived understanding of practice. For practice, in the form of ethical reflection, is supposed to adhere to the same apodictic standards as the natural sciences. But this, too, is a recipe for scepticism since there is little prospect of our moral reflections satisfying standards implicitly derived from the physical sciences. So scepticism arises from both the theory and practical components of positivist-empiricism. We thus reach the central difficulty which positivist-empiricist's attachment to a Cartesian perspective on the world invokes: scepticism.

Scepticism in positivist-empiricist international relations

The sources of scepticism

In the light of the paucity of literature on scepticism in international relations, readers might be forgiven for thinking that the idea has little to do with the subject, that scepticism is a special 'philosophical' problem concerning belief in 'the external world' to be addressed by philosophers rather than political theorists. Such a view is untenable. Cursory reflection on the current state of international relations suggests that scepticism is becoming increasingly established in the discipline and represents a formidable challenge to positivist-empiricism's epistemological authority. The rise of poststructural international relations,[46] of radical historicism and feminism,[47] the growing popularity of 'deconstructionist' conceptions of international relations and a growing pessimism concerning whether the goals of a scientific international relations are achievable may all be viewed as new forms of Pyrrhonic scepticism.[48] These changes internal to the discipline pose a formidable challenge to the positivist-empiricist: how to defend the deliverances of one's research programmes from sceptical dismissal. 'Why should I believe *that*?' is the persistent question of the new Pyrrhonic sceptics to the continued outpouring of *findings* accumulated by empirical research. Focusing on the dualism which is built into the positivist-empiricist project, the Pyrrhonic sceptic holds that positivist-empiricism conceptualises the external world of physical events (facts, research, evidence) in objective terms, while the mental world of theory (models, mathematical axioms, analytical conceptual schemes and so on) is conceived of in a distinctly subjective way. So the two languages which articulate these worlds are categorically different. But then how, the Pyrrhonic sceptic asks, are they supposed to be related to one another? For the Pyrrhonic sceptic, the naturalistic theories of international relations to which positivist-empiricists aspire are doomed to fail since all that we require, and all that we can have, are the appearances that randomly present themselves to human consciousness. Furthermore, there is a Pyrrhonic counterpart to conceptual scepticism in the practical realm: moral scepticism. Pyrrhonic sceptics contend that there may be no *rational* answer to the question of whether 'ethnic cleansing' – or any other action in international relations – is right or wrong. The putative basis for claims to moral knowledge is absent because human beings are neither able to observe any properties of rightness or wrongness in the world nor to twist free of the historical circumstances and contexts which create the incommensurable moral codes by which collectivities of people live. But such circumstances present positivist-empiricism with a difficulty.

If positivist-empiricism grants the Pyrrhonic sceptic these claims, it would evidently be compelled to accept its main consequence, i.e. that positivist-empiricism, incapable of establishing a foundation, constitutes just another picture which, contrary to its explicit claims, is incapable of providing 'genuine' knowledge of international relations. Under such circumstances, scepticism concerning its claims would be justified. Moreover, attributing a sceptical problematic to positivist-empiricism is not simply a consequence of accepting trendy new views about international relations. These new views simply exploit a condition which has long been an internal feature of positivist-empiricism in international relations. For example, Charles McClelland, an early exponent of systems theory, expressed a dualistic view of the world sufficient to justify the attribution of scepticism when he wrote: ' "out there" is the world in flows of a stream of occurrences involving mankind: "in here" *in our minds* is the desire to understand what the occurrences signify.'[49] The problem, as McClelland posed it, clearly derives from the Cartesian analysis of thoughts into mental acts which are available for introspection, on the one side, and an extra-mental world, 'out there' which exists apart from any mental ideas and acts. And the problem which the sceptic latches on to is how anyone would know whether the mind was accurately representing what 'the occurrences' signified; for, from some commonsense perspective, the question could always arise of whether the signs of the mind actually signified what was really there in the reality outside it and on what basis we could know this.

The Cartesian model of the mind not only bolstered sceptical views of mind-world relations but also created the basis for depreciating commonsense appeals to mental states as potential explanations of human behaviour. Consider, in this connection, Bruce Russett and Harvey Starr's defence – in a well-known popular textbook of international relations – of a behavioural theory of mind.[50] The authors write: 'A good theory is one that can be supported or rejected through explicit analysis and systematic use of data. A theory that cannot be tested – and for which there is no conceivable way that it might be tested – cannot get us very far.'[51] So far this is just the standard, and increasingly abandoned, verificationist account of theory confirmation in international relations. But now consider the authors' sequel:

> Think, for example, of the proposition 'People always act to advance their own self-interest, no matter how much they delude themselves or others into thinking they are acting in someone else's interest'. Since the proponent of such an argument can always suggest new reasons to support the argument (the person in question is deluding himself about his motives), and that statement cannot be checked with evidence (*we cannot get inside the person's mind to look*), the self-interest proposition cannot be disproved. It is not a scientific statement, because any evidence can somehow be interpreted to 'fit'. It is also a useless statement, because it doesn't tell us what the person's specific behaviour will in fact be.[52]

Apart from the propensity to *non-sequitur* and question-begging argument (e.g. has anyone ever held that 'people always act to advance their self-interest' no matter what they may do to show otherwise?), these statements posit a robust link between a sceptical understanding of mind and a programme for eliminating explanations which depend on people's mental states. Since 'we cannot get inside the person's mind to check', any statement about people's motives is untestable and, therefore, according to Russett and Starr, without scientific import. Any such statement would be 'useless'. To avoid making scientifically useless statements, we must, on this view, avoid making statements that go beyond possible evidence; and since, presumably, all statements about 'what's going on in the mind' fall into the proscribed category – the mind being inaccessible to observation – we must eliminate altogether putative explanations which attribute mental states to human beings. This proscription would apply not only to motives but to forming intentions, making plans, goal-setting, choosing and so on – all of which presumably play a more or less capacious role in our ordinary common-sense realist understanding of the world. Without that understanding it is hard to see how one could explain people's actions in international relations or, indeed, in ordinary, everyday life. But the key point here is that any radically self-denying ordinance concerning the use of mental terms would not even have got off the ground in the first place without the Cartesian model of mind as presupposition and, in particular, without the central idea which Russett and Starr implicitly invoke, that perception of the inner states of others is a matter of inference from behavioural data. If behavioural data cannot give us a sound basis for reliable inference, we have no grounds, on this view, for providing attributions of mental states to others.

However persuasive this argument may seem to its proponents, it is a dismal failure. The main reason is that it violates Wittgenstein's strictures against 'private languages'.[53] A private language is one in which words refer to a speaker's inner experiences and since these experiences can be apprehended only by the person whose experiences they are, it follows that someone else is incapable of understanding the language which gives them expression. The private linguist is claiming to be able to understand and utilise the words of his private language because he confers meaning on them. This is just the capacity which Russett and Starr are attributing to the person who says that 'people ... act to advance their self-interest'. But, the Wittgensteinian says, the attribution is impossible since the so-called private linguist would not be able to distinguish incorrect from correct uses of sign 'X' to refer to the signified in question. The key point at issue is whether there are any criteria available to the private linguist to determine whether he is using the same sign 'X' correctly each time he uses it? The problem for him may be expressed this way: before he can use his memory of the sign 'X' to refer to the same signified as on a previous occasion, he must be able to show that his memory is correctly describable as a memory of sign 'X'; but the difficulty here is that the only standard available for distinguishing between correct and incorrect uses of 'X' is the memory of the sample itself. Before the private linguist can intelligibly use his memory of 'X' as a standard of correctness, he must first employ it as a standard of correctness in order to check upon its suitability for that role. According to this diagnosis, the private linguist is pushed into circular argument from which there is no escape. Here, too, positivist-empiricists appear to be trapped into sceptical modes of thinking by unarticulated commitments to a Cartesian philosophical system. However, positivist-empiricists have developed a number of strategies designed to resolve or obviate sceptical conclusions and thus make good on their claim to provide a 'scientific' foundation for international relations.

Anti-sceptical strategies

Let us consider two such strategies.

The Inductivist Strategy.[54]

One way to try to overcome scepticism is to take the traditional route of empiricist philosophy and to claim that there are certain kinds of self-authenticating entities which would enable international relationists to accumulate genuine knowledge about their subject.

One proponent of this strategy in international relations is J. David Singer according to whom all genuine knowledge is grounded in 'data'; traditionalists, on the other hand (according to Singer), seek to collect 'mere facts ... which do not constitute data, nor can they in and of themselves be said to constitute knowledge in any but the most modest and fragmentary sense of the word'.[55] Although in this early article Singer did not give an analysis of 'fact', he implied that concerning facts there could be no intersubjective agreement. The basic unit, 'a fact', is interpretive, and interpretations necessarily differ since the situations in which facts are said to exist differ. Data, by contrast, are certain kinds of non-verbal experiences with objects, each episode of which presupposes no other knowledge; data are reports which consist of the direct sensing of mental particulars. No interpretation is necessary on the observer's part to identify the impression of an object as one to be counted as being of a certain kind. As long as there is an element of discernment concerning what is to count as 'the same' impression, there will be unarbitrable differences of judgement among observers. The problem for Singer and similarly minded empiricists is to specify how the direct sensing of a mental particular could itself be a kind of knowing and yet not, at the same time, be the knowing of facts. And if it is the knowing of facts, then such direct sensing involves the exercise of concepts which introduce the possibility of error and of legitimate sceptical challenge.

To be sure, Singer and associates have been aware of the problem of scepticism and have attempted to 'resolve' it. Consider another work by Singer and Jones entitled, appropriately enough, *Beyond Conjecture in International Politics*. For readers of Descartes' *Meditations*, the self-motivation to go beyond 'conjecture' is reminiscent of Descartes' parallel aim of overcoming what he calls prejudice. The title of the book, we are told, 'is no accident'.[56] Although they grant that no

41

science can move ahead without conjecture, their own contribution, we are informed, is not to advance conjecture but to accumulate 'knowledge'. When conjecture is identified with knowledge, 'knowledge is not easily differentiated from folklore or astrology'.[57] But how, in the authors' view, do theorists move beyond conjecture to knowledge? The answer they give is: 'evidence'.[58] But what is it about evidence that gives it this privileged status, that allows bearers of it to move beyond conjecture and towards knowledge? Although they say that there are certain 'criteria for inclusion' which will tell us how evidence can move us beyond 'conjecture' to knowledge itself, we are lamely informed that these are only suggestive and not determinative. Singer and Jones give us no basis for believing that evidence will determine knowledge and therefore provide no grounds for thinking that 'we' can go beyond conjecture to knowledge itself. Thus, for example, there does not seem to be any way of establishing connections between evidence and hypothetical claims about the causes of war. Singer and Jones might want to argue that an hypothesis is evidentially adequate when it has no false observable implications, that is, when it is compatible with observable events in general. But whether or not an observable implication is compatible with observable events must be inferred from whether it accords with actual observations and these might go wrong in a variety of ways. So we arrive at a position that not only fails to overcome scepticism but collapses into its clutches. If we assume that empirical evidence is the only route out of conjecture and towards knowledge in the form of accepting hypotheses, then no inductive conclusion can be justified. Scepticism cannot be defeated simply by appealing to evidence.

Let us consider a more recent example of inductivist justification, namely, John Vasquez's attempt to 'devastate' realism in *The Power of Power Politics: A Critique*.[59] Vasquez attempts to accomplish this feat by reconceptualising political realism as a series of single hypotheses which he then claims to disconfirm as empirically inadequate. Apart from the question of whether empirical evidence alone can justify any inductive conclusion, we have the additional problem of whether the inductivist strategy is coherent, of whether, that is, it even makes sense to attempt to assess the value of any richly-textured theory or conception of international politics such as political realism by determining the empirical adequacy of single hypotheses imputed to it by others. A serious drawback of Vasquez' strategy is that it ignores the impact of two of the most important contributions to the philosophical semantics of our time: the contribution, due to Austin, Wittgenstein and other English philosophers, that there are many different sorts of meaning and that the task of analysis is to try to discover how they work and not to measure everything by the canons of formalist standards and to pronounce all others defective; and the contribution, due to Quine, that it is useless to try to verify our sentences one-by-one against the world. The meaning of sentences is interdependent; it is only the whole theory that has observational consequences. So nothing other than the whole theory can be falsified by experience. Vasquez' attempt to circumvent scepticism and to provide a thoroughgoing refutation of political realism on a proposition-by-proposition basis flounders on these two rocks of recent philosophy of language.

Given the lack of plausibility in such inductivist strategies, we move on to consider a second anti-sceptical strategy.

Intuition: can it overcome scepticism?

As is well known, Descartes relied centrally on the method of intuition to overcome scepticism. In *Regulae 3* Descartes identified intuition as follows: 'By intuition I understand, not the fluctuating testimony of the senses, not the misleading judgement that proceeds from the blundering construction of the imagination, but the conception which an unclouded and attentive mind gives us so readily and distinctly that we are wholly freed from doubt about that which we understand.'[60] Descartes summed this up with characteristic precision: 'No science is acquired except by mental intuition or deduction.'[61]

Several centuries later, Donald Puchala has made strong claims on behalf of intuition, linking these with an attempt to rescue 'something' from claims, vigorously advanced in the 1960s and 1970s, promoting international relations as a naturalistically conceived science. Forthrightly admitting that the behavioural revolution has been an unmitigated failure, Puchala ascribes this not to the effectiveness of its critics but to its having 'hit an epistemological iceberg'.[62] He admits that he is no longer 'looking to build an empirical theory of international relations by listing and heaping propositions or by otherwise working methodically from the facts to the whole'.[63] Rejecting the inductive approach, Puchala writes: 'Scientific theories are simply not born by inducing wholes from parts.'[64]

But what are scientific theories? Puchala uses the now favoured ocular metaphor and calls them 'pictures'.[65] He writes:

43

> Those generally recognised as leading international relations theorists today have earned their stature through accomplishments in wholistic image-building ... What they have been doing in their writing is *painting* for us bold-stroked, broad-brushed pictures of social reality and telling us that the real world is like their pictures. It may be empirically unobservable, except in a partial and piecemeal way, and its wholeness may be different than the sum of its parts, but they, the theorists, know what it looks like.[66]

Puchala concludes that 'relying on human intuition is a fully legitimate avenue to knowledge'.[67] The interesting part of this 'defence' from within positivist-empiricism is that the author admits *ambulando* that 'intuition is the basic stuff from which metaphysics are made'; so, international relations rests on a metaphysics, on this view. The purpose of intuition as a metaphysics, we learn, is to 'properly deal with the nature of unobservable reality'.[68] Apart from the undefended commitment to metaphysical realism embedded in this passage, Puchala's appeal to intuition to overcome scepticism is unconvincing. The main problem is that when intuitions conflict, as they so often do, intuition itself is impotent to resolve the conflict. Moreover, if someone – in thrall to Cartesian dualism – is genuinely perplexed, say, about how 'theories' hook onto 'reality', surely it is unhelpful to receive the response: 'it's all a matter of intuition'. So if one has no better basis than intuition for resolving differences when intuitions conflict, one has no basis for overcoming or avoiding scepticism.

Will a new empiricist philosophy of science help?

The failure to overcome scepticism and its corrosive effects have led some positivist-empiricists to defend their position by adopting a form of empiricism whose roots are to be found in the work of Thomas Kuhn and Imre Lakatos. For example, Keohane aspires to 'employ the conception of a "scientific research programme"' as 'explicated ... by the philosopher of science Imre Lakatos'.[69] The purpose of his doing so, we are told, is that it 'provide[s] criteria for the evaluation of theoretical work in international politics'.[70] On Keohane's reading, 'Lakatos developed the concept of a 'scientific research programme' as *a tool* for the comparative evaluation of scientific theories ... '[71] He goes on to explicate Lakatos' view as follows:

> Theories are embedded in research programmes. These programmes contain inviolable assumptions (the 'hard core') and initial conditions,

defining their scope. For Lakatos, they also include two other very important elements: auxiliary, or observational hypotheses, and a 'positive heuristic', which tell the scientist what sorts of additional hypotheses to entertain and how to go about conducting research. In short, a research programme is a set of methodological rules telling us what paths of research to avoid and what paths to follow.[72]

This unidimensional picture of Lakatos' philosophy of science is a travesty of Lakatos' views. Keohane fails to give any weight to the incontrovertible fact that Lakatos constructed an *historical* philosophy of science, that a research programme is an *historical* reconstruction and not simply 'a concept for evaluating' theoretical work. As an historian of science, Lakatos was careful to avoid any suggestion of a reductionist rationality. In Lakatos' methodology, 'there can be no instant – let alone mechanical rationality. *Neither the logician's proof of inconsistency nor the experimental scientist's verdict of anomaly can defeat a research programme in one blow*. One can be "wise" after the event.'[73]

The essence of Lakatos' rational reconstructions lies in the capacity to predict novel facts. As Lakatos admitted 'all research programmes I admire have one characteristic in common. They all predict novel facts, facts which have had been either undreamt of, or have indeed been contradicted by previous or rival programmes.'[74] Can this be applied to a social science of international relations? Are there any theories in international relations which enable us to predict novel facts? Is international relations capable of predicting anything in any way comparable to what can be done in most natural sciences? Many international relationists have been at pains to show that a science of international relations is possible without being able to predict. Although this view cannot be dismissed out of hand, it is also true that one cannot consistently deny that international relations need not predict novel facts and still claim that one's theoretical constructions are supported by Lakatos' philosophy of science. Removing the capacity to predict novel facts would not be a minor change in Lakatos' methodology. Without being able to predict known facts over competitors in a novel way, there would be no criteria for determining progressive problem shifts. And without this, there is no basis for saying which research programmes are rational. The very heart of the schema, in its application to international relations, would be torn away.

But Keohane is not alone in the recent effort on the part of positivist-empiricists to obtain the imprimatur of the philosophy of science to legitimate their own research programmes or conceptions of international relations. John Vasquez and Stephen Krasner have attempted similar manoeuvres.

In *The Power of Power Politics*, Vasquez claims to be inspired by Kuhn's philosophy of science and influenced by Lakatos and other new empiricist philosophers.[75] Although Vasquez makes frequent allusion to Kuhn and Lakatos, an examination of his account shows that he maintains more or less strict adherence to positivist-empiricist methodology: claims to have incorporated Kuhn's philosophy of science are quite misplaced. In particular, the Kuhn to whom Vasquez claims to be committed bears little resemblance to the commonly understood anti-positivist Kuhn; he resembles, rather, a Kuhn transfigured by the assumptions and presuppositions of the sort of empiricist and positivist philosophies of science Kuhn rejected. 'Theory construction', according to Vasquez and in contrast to Kuhn, is not haphazard but systematic and theories are subject to clear and decisive tests.[76] Many of Vasquez' remaining commitments have their source in the canon of positivist-empiricism: meanings are either stipulated or operationalised;[77] evaluation 'differs from description';[78] paradigms are 'stipulatively defined';[79] 'a paradigm must produce knowledge';[80] 'knowledge itself is a semantic concept';[81] and knowledge involves primarily 'empirical corroboration of hypotheses'.[82] Given such commitments, a certain scepticism about Vasquez's degree of commitment to Kuhn's philosophy of science seems to be in order. The paradox is that Kuhn's philosophy of science itself may be seen as a determined effort to overcome positivist-empiricism's legacy of methodological scepticism.

One of the main difficulties for Vasquez seems to lie in accepting the positivist-empiricist's idea that knowledge consists of bits and pieces of self-authenticating knowledge which one obtains by direct encounter with objects and which are non-inferentially known to obtain. But there is no kind of knowledge which presupposes any other bit of knowledge; knowledge building is always holistic. If this is correct, the correspondence theory of truth has to be abandoned as incoherent: Stephen Krasner seems to agree. He approves of Lakatos' lack of concern 'with correspondence theories of truth which view science as looking for the real world. He sees no firm distinction between theory and observation'.[83] In the same article, however, Krasner refers to the significance of 'Kuhn's paradigms' and 'Lakatos' research programmes' as a way of developing 'intersubjective agreement on the meaning of variables. The most fundamental differences among research programmes are about what variables to use, that is about what the "real" world is, more than they are about specific causal relationships.'[84] Here, Krasner seems to be bringing in by the backdoor the central idea in a correspondence theory of truth which he threw out by the front: matching *thought* and *the real world*. That is, Krasner seems to presuppose the positivist-empiricist's traditional reliance on metaphysical realism and its insistence on 'theoretising' a mind-independent reality which our chosen variables are designed to capture. It is worth pointing out, however, that the claim that theories are about the 'real' world, however construed, is directly opposed to both the letter and spirit of Lakatos' and Kuhn's philosophies of science. For example, Kuhn writes: 'There is, I think, no theory-independent way to reconstruct phrases like "really there"; the notion of a match between the ontology of a theory and its "real" counterpart in nature now seems to me illusive in principle.'[85]

But whatever Kuhn's view, the idea of a statement's corresponding to the 'real' world is indefensible. As Hilary Putnam has shown, we know, as a model-theoretical fact, that even if we could somehow fix the intended truth-values of our sentences, this would not determine a unique correspondence between words and items in the universe of discourse.[86] The idea that lies behind the claim which Putnam refutes is that there is just one theory of the world and one world of which it is true and this is a idea which neither sits well with the adoption of Kuhn's philosophy of science nor is it, in any obvious way, true. In general, the problem of scepticism could perhaps be dissolved by accepting the new empiricist philosophy of science; however, such acceptance is unlikely to be effective so long as that philosophy is distorted by prior philosophical and methodological commitments derived from positivist-empiricism.

For political realism – at least the revised form of it I am calling evaluative political realism – positivist-empiricist philosophy of science is just one more effort by traditional Western metaphysics to control the way in which we think of the world and ourselves. In this respect, evaluative political realism agrees with Richard Rorty's harsh assessment that this kind of philosophy of science is just another failed project designed to make human beings responsible to 'non-human power'.[87] That non-human power is expressed (in my view but perhaps not Rorty's) by the 'scientising' of the human sciences which characterises positivist-empiricism as it searches to avoid scepticism without letting go of the naturalistic framework which engenders it. In rejecting the scientising (and the ideas bound up with it), evaluative political realism encourages us to escape from a stultifying rationalism and its self-defeating consequences.

Conclusion

We have characterised positivist-empiricism as dominated by a certain relationship between theory or language and 'reality'. Located in the Age of the World Picture, Cartesian philosophy and method, the positivist-empiricist view of the relationship between language or theory on the one hand and reality on the other has given rise to themes dominated by empiricist epistemology: the dichotomy between the language of theory and the language of observation, the correspondence theory of truth, the distinction between facts and values and so forth. According to positivist-empiricism, the relationship between language or theory and the reality which theory and language are about is metaphysically realistic. Objects, facts, and events – the objects of our observations – are all on the same metaphysical level – the level of the objective, physical world – while language and theories are on another distinct level. The objects, facts or events are 'out there' waiting to be experienced by an observer and discovered by the scientist, and theory formation is the process of constructing the right theory in order to 'hook on' to those objective facts. Observation and experimentation are the important processes of providing evidence for theories by focusing our attention upon the crucial facts or events. Objective facts thus serve as the beginning and end point of theory formation. The consequence of this way of viewing the relationship between theory and reality is a chasm between facts, objects and events 'in reality' on the one side and language or theory, which supposedly describe those facts, objects and events on the other. Attempts to bridge this gap between theory and fact to avoid scepticism have not only occupied much of positivist-empiricism since the seventeenth century but have also been one of the main projects of recent positivist-empiricist international relations.

Scepticism is a notable feature of recent international relations. Michael Donelan (in my terms a positivist-empiricist) clearly expresses this feature when he writes: 'Consider physical and human nature. The essences of these, things in themselves, the Good, Ends, and Laws of Nature are not accessible to us and cannot be discovered by reasoning.'[88] Yale Ferguson and Richard Mansbach, also writing from within positivist-empiricism, are compelled to admit that in the study of politics 'concepts ... lack objective referents ... '[89] Sceptical doubts may be seen, in this case, as tacit admission of the uncertainty which the references of our words and concepts possess and, given the tight connection between reference and truth, on the truth-value of our sentences. This kind of scepticism does not deny the independent existence of the world. What it denies is the possibility of gaining any genuine knowledge about these objects considered as referents of our familiar and scientific concepts. Scepticism, in this sense, is not simply an intellectual parlour game nor is it just a 'philosophical' doctrine. It is, as Pyrrhonic sceptics have always claimed, a serious challenge to the positivist-empiricist model of theory and practice.

Notwithstanding the seriousness of the challenge, the way to avoid scepticism, as we shall argue below in chapter 4, is not to 'buy into' the dualistic metaphysics which creates it in the first place. We can refuse to accept the dichotomistic relation between theory (or language) and reality; we can reject the very idea that there is a universal way of structuring human experience; and we can deny that there is a universal 'scientific' methodology. If we take this route, we shall be, in effect, replacing the monistic metaphysics to which the positivist-empiricist is wedded with a metaphysically pluralistic metaphysics. For what lies behind the positivist-empiricist conception of the world is a deep commitment to a monistic metaphysics to the effect that there is one world and only one conception of it that can be true. This assumption accounts for the persistent scientism in international relations theory, those repeated (and failed) attempts to adopt a vocabulary derived from the natural sciences or mathematics in the form of field theory, cybernetics, reductionist systems theory, rational choice theory and so on. It is this scientism which is the breeding ground of scepticism. The monistic assumption, however, does not stand unchallenged. According to the pluralist perspective adopted by evaluative political realism, human beings inhabit not one world but many. There is, on this view, no uniquely 'correct' version of the world, only different correct interpretations: scepticism here can get no grip.

The monistic conception of the world has shaped the positivist-empiricist's conception of practice as well. The positivist-empiricist attempts to develop a conception of practice consistent with the theoretical materials inherited from the Cartesian rationalistic tradition and this has typically meant, in recent international theory, reliance on utilitarianism, welfarism, game theory models and rational choice theory. Positivist-empiricists search for theories of morality and practice which satisfy the same methodological standards available in the natural sciences and mathematics. In our time, this disposition has led to the search for a single computational principle of rationality and to the belief that morality must satisfy that principle. The view seems to be that once that principle has been correctly determined, then any interference with it would be irrational, inefficient and unjust. The failure to find such principle has reinforced sceptical responses and has led positivist-empiricists to accept understandings of the self which inflate the individual's capacity for self-determination. In so doing, positivist-empiricists drastically underestimate the value of living in communities and therefore fail to grasp why human beings live, and evidently want to continue to live, in nation-states. For evaluative political realists such failures suffice to motivate the search for alternative conceptions of international relations. To foreshadow arguments in part 2, one such alternative is evaluative political realism, which in deep contrast with the monistic assumptions of positivist-empiricism, supports a pluralist understanding of politics. The basis for this view has been beautifully captured by Isaiah Berlin:

> The notion that there must exist final objective answers to normative questions, truths that can be demonstrated or directly intuited, that it is in principle possible to discover a harmonious pattern in which all values are reconciled ... that we can uncover some single central principle that shapes this vision, a principle which once found, will govern our lives – this ancient and almost universal belief, on which so much traditional thought and action and philosophical doctrine rests seems to me invalid, and at times to have led (and still seems to lead) to absurdities in theory and barbarous consequences in practice.[90]

Throughout this study we will be acquiring grounds for accepting Berlin's assessment and thus for rejecting positivist-empiricism and its monistic view of theory and the world.

3 Emancipatory international relations: a first cut

There is no such thing as a world without loss.

Sir Isaiah Berlin

Introduction

Stage-setting

Emancipatory international relations is a capacious category intended to include a large range of theories whose sources lie in German idealism, the Enlightenment and Marxism. In Chapter 1 we sorted emancipatory international relations into classical Marxism, critical international theory, poststructural theory and feminist international theory on the understanding that such categories be treated as examples only: the range of possibilities for emancipatory theory appears endless. The point of this chapter lies not in trying to capture these widely disparate and seemingly indefinite possibilities but rather to describe certain tensions within a certain version of emancipatory international relations, tensions which undermine the plausibility of its claim to unify theory and practice. These tensions stretch back to the sources of the conception; the subsequent failure to resolve them suggests why certain difficulties continue to plague more recent theoretical offerings falling under the rubric of emancipatory international relations. The goal, then, is not to follow the White Queen of *Alice in Wonderland* fame by doing six impossible things before breakfast, such as refuting or even adequately describing the theoretical alternatives opened up by this conception but, more modestly, to throw the project of emancipatory international relations into enough doubt so that students of international theory will be motivated to consider political realism – at least in its evaluative political realist version – as an alternative conception. And this purpose can, and should be, accomplished not by claiming that an emancipatory conception of international relations is unintelligible. On the contrary, it is not only intelligible, it is also extremely attractive and appealing. All the more reason, according to the evaluative political realist, for subjecting it to a searching critical scrutiny which does not presuppose its falsity.

I will begin by describing emancipatory international relation's distinctive understanding of the relation between theory and practice. Secondly, I will identify certain features of international critical theory and, without implying that my description is comprehensive or even very precise, raise certain difficulties for this popular version of emancipatory international relations by critically examining certain ideas of Andrew Linklater and Robert Cox. In the final section I will intimate, by developing certain ideas of Jean-François Lyotard, that all efforts to make international critical theory coherent may fail. Although such criticisms will still leave open the prospect of establishing the validity of international critical theory and other versions of emancipatory international relations, such projects too might come to seem problematic if certain considerations adduced in Part 2 of this study turn out to be veridical.

Emancipatory theory and practice

According to Figure 3.1, emancipatory international relations conceives theory to be less significant than practice; hence, the circle designating theory is smaller than the circle designating practice.

A second feature of emancipatory international relations which Figure 3.1 attempts to capture is its self-annihilating property: there is an inherent tendency, on this view, for theory to collapse into practice. Emancipatory international relations is intended to emancipate members of oppressed groups, e.g. workers, women, artists, etc., by making them aware of the structures and forces hindering their self-realisation. Internal to this conception lies the assumption that if privileged subjects are prepared to accept certain theoretical reasons as explanations of the frustrating situation they find themselves in, they will deploy those theoretical reasons to eliminate it. Increased self-understanding comports with an increased desire to replace

B
Emancipatory international theory

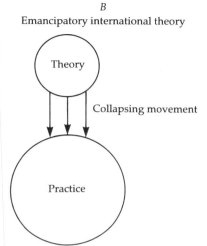

Figure 3.1

oppressive structures and conditions with those which enhance human autonomy. If the conditions are eliminated and practice wheeled into line with these theoretical reasons, there will be nothing left for theory to do. Theoretical reasoning works itself out of a job, so to speak, when it fulfils its function of replacing current oppressive practices with non-oppressive ones. Subjects accept a role that is oppressive and harmful to their interests, on this view, because they mistakenly believe that it is fair, harmless, or 'natural'. For example, the lead female character in the movie *Sex, Lies and Videotape* thinks it natural that she should stay at home, clean the house and serve as a sexual object for her husband, even though her life is intellectually vacuous and she is sexually unfulfilled. An emancipatory theory shows that her belief is ideological and thereby does her, and other women in similar situations, harm; revealing the damage does not immediately eliminate the conditions which brought it about but it does offer her reasons to oppose it. If she succeeds in eliminating those conditions by acting in concert with others, then the emancipatory theory which described the ideological bases that made those conditions possible would become obsolete. In international relations the emancipatory theory might, e.g. address as privileged subjects the oppressed peoples of the Third World in a self-conscious effort to show that their impoverishment is not a natural condition but the result of an ideology, say, of neoclassical economic theory and its views about efficiency, markets, comparative advantage and free trade. If theoretical reasoning is able to demonstrate the ideological nature of neoclassical economic theory, Third World people will not thereby have eliminated their poverty; but they will have gathered up reasons for opposing the ideology and, perhaps, for joining with others to overturn it and the conditions derived from its use. The theoretical reasoning in question, however, must not only describe how the world really is but must also show how the theoretical reasons are to be put into practice in order to replace oppressive political structures. If the goals of the theory are reached, the theory's usefulness will have come to an end: theory will have collapsed into practice.

Emancipatory international relations, then, may be understood in terms of how its variants propose to make theory obsolete or, what amounts to the same thing, how theoretical reasoning will eliminate the conditions which prevent the liberating goal, end or state of affairs from coming into being. To be sure, different theories identify different members of the community as subjects to be liberated. For classical Marxism, it's the proletariat. For critical theory, it's all those who are oppressed by irrational social formations. For poststructuralist theory, it's dissenting, marginalised voices. For feminist international theory, it's women. But no matter which members of the community require liberation, each theory is obliged to show how it leads, not just to enhanced understanding or knowledge of the constraining conditions, but also to the acceptance of theoretical truths in such a way that sufficient motivation is gathered up to end the stultifying practice(s). The test of a theory's truth, on this view, lies precisely in actions being taken which change the offending practices and bring about the required emancipation. Emancipatory international relations hopes to tie theory to practice in an inextricable knot. The test of a theory is a matter of what is to be done with it. And the correct or best theory is one that leads to the most successful practice.

This is all that needs to be said at this point concerning the general features of emancipatory international relations. I now wish to explore one version of this theory, in particular, the version identified in Chapter 1 as international critical theory.

Constructing a progressivist understanding of international relations

A brief characterisation

International critical theory may be understood as the self-conscious effort to develop a progessivist, Marxian understanding of international relations as conceived and developed by the Frankfurt School of Social Research and, in particular, by Jürgen Habermas. Two of the most noted representatives of international critical theory in international relations are Andrew Linklater and Robert Cox.

Andrew Linklater's emancipatory project for international relations is discernible in his lucid books *Men and Citizens in the Theory of International Relations* and *Beyond Realism and Marxism*.[1] Linklater puts us on notice that he is attempting to develop a theory of international relations which is emancipatory in the sense that reason's increasing self-consciousness provides us with grounds for believing in the coming into being of emancipated humanity. As Linklater remarks: 'Reason has a history; it develops a determinate and progressive content from its expressions in various forms of social life.'[2] But this is not the end of the story. For Linklater, any theory of international relations must not only be in accord with Reason's imperatives, but be 'critical' as well. Being critical for Linklater seems to mean that a theory is inextricably bound up with certain imperatives from the marxian legacy. For although any critical theory of international relations has to go 'beyond ... Marxism,'[3] it must also be open 'to the influence of Marxism'.[4]

Robert Cox, too, associates critical theory with Marxism. According to Cox, critical theory's 'foremost source' is 'historical materialism' and, as one might expect given the source, critical theory has a considerable agenda. First, 'it deals with changing reality' and hence 'it must continually adjust its concepts to a changing object it seeks to understand and explain'.[5] Secondly, critical theory has to ensure that problem-solving theory is sublated. As Cox writes: 'Critical theory contains problem-solving theories within itself, but contains them in the form of identifiable ideologies, thus pointing to their conservative consequences, not to their usefulness as guides to actions.'[6] Yet a third task for critical theory is transcendental/utopian. According to Cox, critical theory, though just as practical in its aims as problem-solving theory, 'approaches practice from a perspective which *transcends* that of the existing order, which problem-solving takes as its starting point'.[7] But then this implies that critical theory, too, could have some difficulties in achieving its goals. Cox admits as much. He writes: 'Critical theory ... contains an element of *utopianism* in the sense that it can represent a coherent picture of an alternative order, but its utopianism is constrained by its comprehension of historical processes.'[8] Cox argues that 'theory can serve two distinct purposes'.[9] First, it can 'be a guide to help solve the problems posed within the terms of the particular perspective which was the point of departure'.[10] Cox calls this 'problem-solving theory', by which term he evidently means all non-emancipatory theories whether they call themselves 'utilitarian', 'realist', 'systems analysis', 'pragmatist' or whatever. By contrast, there is critical theory which calls 'institutions and social and power relations' into question 'by concerning itself with their origins and how and whether they might be in the process of changing'.[11] For Cox, critical theory enables us to grasp those changing forces of material production which will hopefully, though not necessarily, move us towards the practice of world order. It is these historical, dynamic and universal interests which distinguish critical theory from what Cox refers to as 'problem-solving theory'. Cox finds no difficulty in dismissing this latter type of theory with undisguised contempt as 'non-historical or ahistorical', a *genre* of theory which serves 'national, sectional ... class' and 'conservative' interests.[12] Although these two characterisations are helpful in providing some rough outline of what international critical theory consists of, the picture needs to be filled out and made more concrete. In addition to the foregoing, international critical theory may be understood to consist of such beliefs and attitudes as:

The class-based character of the capitalist state

International critical theorists take the view that the state, under capitalism, is the expression of a ruling class such that the vast majority of the world's people suffer structural domination. The main thrust of international critical theory is to maintain 'a classical Marxian concern to analyse the state as a class-based apparatus' while searching for mechanisms for transforming that apparatus from a condition of social inequality to social equality.[13] For example, G.A. Cohen's *Karl Marx's Theory of History* provides a powerful defence of the view that the state under capitalism is class based and that under socialism a class-based state could be replaced by a system of collective ownership of the means of production.[14] Although some international critical theorists may still accept this traditional view, more recently they have been worried by the loss of workers' rights under state socialism and prefer the establishment of worker cooperatives, self-managed enterprises, or some alternative which escapes both ruling classes and state power.

Anti-nationhood

International critical theorists tend to be 'haters' of nationhood which they equate with state-created 'nationalism', i.e. a form of nationalism which has legitimised power and oppression and continues to play a major role in generating militarism, colonialism and imperialism. On this view, nationalism is so closely associated with state power that virtually no conceptual resources remain for an independent conception of nation within the boundaries laid out by international critical theory.[15]

Economic forces as the dominant historical agent

International critical theorists hold that underlying economic forces – classically referred to as 'productive forces' – either determine or, less conclusively, shape in decisively important ways the social, political, and legal structures of international relations. Some international critical theorists continue to insist on productive determinism. However, many international critical theorists now seem to be satisfied to wave vaguely and innocuously towards quasi-determinism since the heart of their theoretical offerings lie in reason's increasingly self-conscious awareness of itself.

New social movements as agents of historical transformation

Recent international critical theorists admit that the classical Marxist vision of a proletarian uprising has to be set aside and replaced by the idea that new social movements could well serve as possible instruments of social transformation in international relations. For example, while recognising that critical social movements are often regarded as 'marginal and powerless', R.B.J. Walker sees room for optimism in the thought that some of these movements 'have generated energies that empower people to get things done...'[16] Among international critical theorists, the identification of new social movements as potentially revolutionary subjects is pervasive.

Human global emancipation via a theory of history

Although international critical theorists are prepared to accept the idea that certain features of classical Marxism's aspirations for human emancipation are utopian, they nonetheless adhere to *some* version of historical materialism, a version which contains within it the claim that a just and harmonious international community is not a utopian, unrealisable or impractical goal. Human emancipation, on this view, is within reach of real societies in futures we could actually care about. But herein lies a major issue.

Does international critical theory offer an understanding of human emancipation which is reasonable, non-utopian and practical? We can, of course, grant that international critical theory has very broad support within emancipatory international relations. Aspects of international critical theory have been articulated by people holding a wide variety of political positions. The concept of human emancipation, for example, has been a feature of various versions of neo-Kantianism;[17] it has star billing, notwithstanding certain reservations, in various forms of post-Marxist thinking relevant to international relations;[18] it plays a renewed role in debates about security;[19] it finds resonance in some feminist writings on international relations;[20] and it continues to illuminate debates concerning the very possibility of an emancipatory international relations.[21] But the fact that international critical theory has wide support does not mean that it is coherent. For this one would need to show, rather, that the goal of human emancipation is reasonable, non-utopian and practical. But what does human emancipation consist of and how is it to be achieved? For an answer to the first part of this question, international critical theory has crucially depended on its Marxian legacy.

Marxism is surely the greatest emancipatory project in the history of Western and non-Western thought. In 'On the Jewish Question', Marx made a telling distinction between political and human emancipation. According to Marx: 'political emancipation is the reduction of man, on the one hand, to a member of civil society, to an *egoistic, independent* individual, and, on the other hand, to a *citizen*, to a juridical person'.[22] On the other hand, human emancipation was a question of bringing into unity elements which had previously been separated by social forces. Human emancipation requires the development of critical self-consciousness. Marx writes: 'Only when man has recognised and organised his *forces propres* as *social* forces, and consequently no longer separates social power from himself in the shape of political power, only then will human emancipation have been accomplished.'[23] Theory and practice will lead to human emancipation on this view only when consciousness and reality are brought into unison and this means that our conception of consciousness, conceived as 'theory', will be historical. According to Marx, there has to be some way for theory to *become praxis* and there is: 'theory becomes a material force when it grips the masses'.[24] The requirement to unify theory and practice meant that a new theory of history, fusing not only consciousness and culture but also productive forces and economic structures, was needed.[25] That theory was historical materialism. But what is historical materialism? The problem with asking this question in its bald form is that there seem to be as many answers to it as there are Marxian social theorists. Given this, let us see how two international critical theorists, Linklater and Cox, deploy (or fail to deploy) historical materialism in order to persuade us of the plausibility of the project to emancipate humanity.

Why focus on Linklater and Cox? First, they both accept some version of historical materialism, and the emancipatory project contained within it, however attenuated their relationship to these concepts may turn out to be. Secondly, insofar as many international relationists continue to look for alternatives to the dominant paradigms of liberal internationalism and neorealism, Linklater's and Cox's theoretical projects (or portions thereof) have merit. And, thirdly, these projects have just the sort of interesting differences required to bring out two sides of the international critical theorist's coin in international relations: Hegelian Marxism and Marxian materialism. For whereas Cox is committed to a strong productionist version of materialism as a way of moving to global struggle, Linklater relies on the movement of self-conscious reason to make emancipation a reasonable goal. So in examining these two alternatives, we will effectively be critically examining two different ways of maintaining a grip on Marx's emancipatory project for international relations. It is important to keep in mind that my objective here is not to review the corpus of Linklater's or Cox's work but, rather, to critically assess their respective claims to ground a critical, emancipatory theory of international relations. As such, my analyses of their work will be developed along a narrow axis.

59

Linklater and Cox

Linklater

In the third part of *Men and Citizens*, Linklater deploys a set of arguments intended to 'suggest how the study of international relations might accommodate the study of human freedom'.[26] Using 'Marx's principles of historical periodization', Linklater first identifies the logic of three stages of international relations – *tribal community, political society*, and *emancipated humanity*. Secondly, he tries to show, if only in a speculative way, how these stages are dialectically and progressively related to one another. Since the movement of history through these stages is necessary rather than contingent, Linklater has to show how emancipated humanity – the last stage – is already prefigured in the dynamics and logic of development of the two prior stages. For, it is only on this basis that Linklater can hold his theory to be rational in the required sense, namely, that the end of political society and its replacement by global humanity are objective conditions which have already been formed in previous social structures or categories. The category of emancipated humanity takes the two other categories and posits itself as that which gives them their determinateness and so, on this view, gives a non-arbitrary rationale for the belief that the world's rational construction will culminate in the liberation of humanity. But just how does Linklater think he can explain this?

Although he is not specific about this, it would appear that Linklater depends on implicit appeal to historical materialism. Each of the three stages, we are told, is necessary for the development of the previous ones as the dialectical movement of history draws individuals, embedded in its rational swirl, towards greater moral autonomy. The *telos* of this movement is 'ethical universalism' which, Linklater contends, dissolves 'both the state's right to determine when it will use force and the government of international relations by principles based upon the consent of its constituent sovereign parts'.[27]

How does Linklater attempt to justify a commitment to such a conception of international relations? To understand the problem Linklater faces, we need to examine Linklater's conception of philosophical history. According to Linklater, philosophical history refers to a view of reason which is developmental.[28] On this view, 'rational, critical thinking' governs the world.[29] So despite half-hearted, occasional waves in the direction of materialism, Linklater follows Hegel in claiming that the world is driven by 'consciously chosen rational principles'.[30] Linklater goes on to insist that reason involves principles 'which are specific to human subjects'.[31] However, the human subject does not have consciousness of its final end as such, but only of certain other ends by which the final end can be said to be mediated. And herein lies a difficulty, for, unless Linklater can show how the mediating ends are internally related to the self-formulation of the final end of humanisation, he will lack the resources to defend himself against the charge that his belief in the actualisation of the final end is arbitrary, i.e. a state of affairs which Linklater would like to come about rather than one which must, or even has any likelihood, of occurring. Linklater seems to have taken a certain worldview as a preferred end-state of a developmental-logical process and then read the stages of the development back into the process. The issue here is whether Linklater can make sense of the idea that the final end is internally related to the process in terms of which he claims it develops. If this cannot be done, the idea that there is a final end on behalf of which certain things must occur in history, e.g. the humanisation of international relations, will be vacuous.

In *Beyond Realism and Marxism* Linklater calls upon a Habermasian theory of communicative competence to substantiate his developmental views.[32] Will such an appeal help? According to Habermas, the development of a species-wide rationality that is inherent in language is not simply a convention of a specifically Western tradition: cognitive adequacy with language takes place over time, a hypothesis supported by rational reconstructions of the logic of that development. The question is whether the kinds of distinctions we make, the worldview we inhabit and so on, can be shown to reflect a higher level of cognitive adequacy than other 'undifferentiated' world-views. That is, how does Linklater think he will be able to justify equating the categorical distinctions we find necessary in Western culture with 'rationality' and 'humanity' once we admit, as we appear compelled to do, the existence of cultures that have done without them? How can we prove our communicative competence to reflect a higher stage in a species-wide developmental process if all the speculative research that we undertake in order to show that it is higher already assumes what is to be proven? How do we escape the vicious circle in which we accept as a principle of research precisely that which is at issue: namely, the greater cognitive adequacy of speculative research? Without non-question-begging answers to these questions, it is quite unclear how appeal to Habermasian distinctions will help justify Linklater's project.

Nonetheless, although the foregoing arguments may tarnish Linklater's project, they are probably too abstract to undermine its overall attractiveness. For even if it can be shown that the concepts Linklater deploys for moving from tribal society to emancipated humanity are suspect and that his story about how the transition is to take place is not coherent, it would still be open to Linklater to claim that this does not prove that his vision of a humanised world is unrealisable. Perhaps a new and different story, using other concepts, can be told. In the face of such a possible claim, we need to consider whether certain non-institutional facts can be cited which would make Linklater's theory so implausible as to render it incoherent. To facilitate such an analysis I will list the activities which Linklater thinks are required to realise the condition of humanity and comment on their feasibility in the light of the theoretical knowledge and commonsense practical experience we have acquired, not only of the world in which we now live, but of possible worlds sufficiently like our own world that they would not automatically count as mere fictions or fantasies.

State replaced by global legal and political system

Linklater gives the state the truly monumental task of moving the world from political society to emancipated humanity but, nonetheless, envisages its replacement 'with a global legal and political system which affords protection to all human subjects as moral equals'.[33] Effectively, the state itself will diminish greatly and be replaced by a global legal and political system (GLPS). The organised use or threat of force greatly diminishes because the conflicts of interest that require coercively backed adjudication will have been eliminated. Since people will no longer view other people's needs and desires as levers to be manipulated for their own benefit, cooperative rather than conflictual interpersonal relations will come into existence. However attractive Linklater's goal may be, there are obvious difficulties with realising it. One of these is that even if a global, legal political system is instituted, there seems nothing except reason's self-conscious freedom to prevent GLPS from changing the rules of the game in the future. Unless we claim, inconsistently, that reason's self-conscious freedom will become internalised and eternal, the possibility of rule changes cannot be excluded on some *a priori* basis. What GLPS gives it can take away.

There is no way to guarantee that the rules of the game will never change unexpectedly. Since an individual member of the community can never be certain that whatever changes take place will necessarily be in her interest, there is always *potential conflict* between GLPS and the individual which will engender suspicion and fear about whatever institution replaces the state. If this is so, then even in the absence of the state, there will be some conflict between whoever happens to be maintaining and controlling GLPS and any individual member of the global community.

The demise of self-interest and the rise of selflessness

In reaching the level of humanised international relations, Linklater holds out the prospect that human self-awareness will constrain the forms of life in which men and women will be willing to enter. In place of 'self-interested beings or maximisers', individuals must become 'progressive beings with fundamental obligations to all other members of their species'.[34] The contrast which Linklater relies upon here between self-interested beings and progressive beings does not leave any scope for a middle ground. Perhaps there is none. But, then, that seems to imply the possibility of a world of global selflessness. The people in such a world would have no concern for their own interest, except insofar as it was required to further the interests of everyone else. Although we cannot rule out *a priori* the possibility of such selfless people – there have already been a certain number of such people in human history – the generalisation of this idea certainly strains our credulity. For one thing, there may be a strong biological basis for thinking that most human beings could not achieve anything like the selflessness that Linklater's project seems to require. For another thing, it should be noted that the achievement of selflessness would have to be globally simultaneous. For suppose a situation in which even a very large global majority became selfless while a small minority remained selfish (remember – there is no middle ground). Then the latter would have little difficulty in manipulating the altruistic attitude of the majority to suit its self-interested goals. But the prospect of a simultaneous global shift to selflessness seems pure fantasy.

Universal rules

According to Linklater, universal rules provide the basis for believing in a loyalty that not only extends 'beyond the parameters of the

63

sovereign state' but which also creates the possibility of 'an advanced form of moral consciousness, an intimation of a higher kind of international political life'.[35] The idea that 'universal rules' will be able to provide a basis for loyalty which extends beyond the state constitutes a throwback to Kant's moral formalism; it stands in marked contrast with Hegel's important notion of *Sittlichkeit*, a 'thick' ethics for real communities designed to protect existing moral institutions and foster their moral development. Without socialisation into the existing forms of life that embody moral values, ethics and morality would be thin, formal and uninteresting. Commitment to ethical life involves identifying with its demands so thoroughly that we resist taking seriously the possibility of giving them up. A life without them would no longer be recognisable as our own. It thus turns out that Hegel's analysis of *Sittlichkeit*, though hardly the last word on ethics, provides persuasive reasons why we should not adhere to Linklater's abstract Kantian notion of 'ethical universalism'. Without an understanding of the relationships involved in the various forms of life in a particular culture, it is hard to see how Linklater could maintain any grip on emancipation. If there is no domain of shared convictions, what is it that one is being liberated from?[36]

Monistic conception of the good society

According to Linklater, '*the* adequate theory of international relations is one which is committed to *the* emancipation of *the* human species'.[37] This and other statements to the same effect show that Linklater is committed to the idea of a single true theory of international relations. On this view, there is neither a plural set of possibly true theories of the world nor different valid practices within it. There is only *one* correct practice and there is only *one* correct theory of international relations. These are metaphysical assumptions which, at the very least, will be hard to defend in the face of increasing acceptance of diversity in both thought and practice.

Equal distribution of material resources

Although Linklater recognises the need to analyse 'the nature of economic life', he makes no analysis. He seems to be content with a substitute to the effect that 'we must measure in international relations by the extent to which particularistic economic activity has given way to a universalistic perspective sympathetic to the goal of world distributive justice'.[38] His theory thereby implies commitment to a distributive paradigm of justice which leaves little room for such non-material aspects of justice as integrity, power or opportunity.[39] Still, let us assume that Linklater is on the right track when he says that freedom involves 'ensur[ing] individual rights of access to a basic level of economic and social resources'.[40] Though a bit more cautious, this is quite similar to Marx's view that in the humanly emancipated society there would be considerably more freedom than in capitalist societies because the extraordinary abundance generated in the former would enable everyone's basic material needs to be satisfied. Both these views presuppose that human scarcity can be eliminated. But to accept this idea, we would have to ignore certain non-institutional facts about the world in which we live and will, so far as our best theoretical and practical experience tell us, continue to live in the future. In such a world there will be a relative scarcity of technological knowledge, an episodic scarcity of good human judgement and a profound scarcity of time.[41] Given such permanent features of the human condition and their obvious consequences, the idea that everyone's basic material needs will be satisfied seems very hard to accept.

Further, there would be certain untoward political consequences if one tried to achieve it. Consider what Linklater has to say about 'global control of social relations'. Since freedom is understood as global control of social relations in order to maximise species-powers, neither the organisation of material resources nor the management of claims between persons can be monopolised by, or take place within, separate sovereign states. International relations as relations between particularistic forms of organisation give way to a universal society in which members equalise their access to material resources subject to their common ownership and collective control.[42]

To see the bearing of this claim, we need to consider it in the light of Linklater's acceptance of the idea that capitalist institutions, including the state, restrict liberty. On this view, state sovereignty is a way of distributing *freedom* and *unfreedom* – freedom to the wealthy capitalist states and unfreedom to the poor non-capitalist states. But how will this situation change in a global emancipated society? As just indicated, Linklater contends that freedom should be 'understood as global control'. But if freedom is so understood, then why should one believe oneself to be more free under a condition of emancipated humanity than under the condition of political society where capitalism dominates? Why shouldn't one call a situation of global control, a condition of *collective unfreedom*? To press the point, even if we are forced to concede, as I think we must, that workers are *forced* to labour under capitalism, why should we think this won't occur under a condition of global control? After the 'revolutionary triumph of the international proletariat', workers will not, by hypothesis, be able to acquire property. Workers will have no alternative to working for the world-wide state, community or society and this surely means they will be *forced* to labour. But then what kind of freedom is it in which one is forced to work? Humanised workers, like their counterparts in capitalist political society, will find themselves in situations in which their productive forces are subject to the control of others in a way which suggests that the lot of the worker will not be very different from what it is in capitalist political societies. If this is not to take place, Linklater owes us an argument to explain why not.

In the last analysis Linklater's project of attempting to find a reasonable ground for a non-utopian critical theory – in the form of a humanised international relations – fails and this for two reasons. First, the structure of Linklater's argument depends on tacit appeal to an *a priori* rationalism which his argument officially excludes. Secondly, Linklater fails to show how his theory avoids a frictionless utopianism. In particular, Linklater seems to have given little thought to the idea of theory's guiding the coming into being of reality's self-consciousness via a revolutionary agent. Since there is no proletariat *or any other special revolutionary agent* in Linklater's abstract theory, we are left wondering how reason is to become fully conscious of its own freedom. For Marx, reality only becomes comprehensible with the emergence of the proletariat; for, only this class's knowledge would understand the decisive importance of the class situation. The proletariat is at one and the same time the subject and object of its own knowledge. Linklater, like most other revisionary Marxians, eschews proletarian epistemological and practical privilege. However, he implausibly suggests that *states* take on the role which Marx and Engels assigned to the proletariat! Apart from its unpersuasiveness, this move is reification at its very worst. After all, states are artefacts and as such cannot, so far as we know, be conscious of anything. At the very least, Linklater owes us an argument here. The claim that states are privileged subjects is extraordinarily far-fetched and Linklater provides no basis for our thinking otherwise. We turn to consider Cox's alternative form of international critical theory.

Cox

In turning from Linklater to Robert Cox, we are moving away from a Hegelianised Marxism to a more traditional Marxian view grounded in the materialist forces of production. In *Production, Power and World Order* Cox spells out his revisionary historical materialism. He is lucid about the point of doing so, namely, 'to consider the power relations in societies and world politics from the angle of the power relations in production'.[43] The whole of Cox's schema is anchored in 'patterns of production relations called modes of social relations of production ... the dynamics of these modes, their interrelationships, and how they are affected by the nature and activity of states and international forces'.[44] The main problem with this foundationalist manoeuvre is not that production is unimportant but that it becomes, in Cox's framework, the unquestioned metaphysical referent point for grasping the totality of social reality.

Cox's historical materialism, unlike Linklater's, takes account of the fact that there are *perceiving* subjects in the world, that subjects are not solely collected up into classes as objectively *real* entities, as Marx had thought, but produce created realities ineliminable from any objective understanding of the world. To sustain this view Cox resuscitates the metaphysics of Leibnizian monads. Monads, as Leibniz understood them, are spatial-temporal points – crucially linked to the metaphysics of substances – from which information about the past and projections into the future can be made. But how does resurrection of Leibnizian monads help Cox? Monads have three properties which make them attractive to productionist Marxists: substantiality, individuality and self-transformativity.[45] Cox implicitly uses these properties to accomplish three things: first, to maintain the real material underpinnings of the social relations of production without having to explicitly *defend* a materialistic metaphysics; secondly, to posit world orders which contain temporal-spatial points, i.e. 'individual' structures as states and state-systems; and thirdly, to have a basis for claiming continuous changes in world orders which are internally self-directed, even if we cannot *know* or be able to predict these changes. Notwithstanding the ingenuity of this foundational part of Cox's thesis, the deployment of monads will not help him to anchor social relations of production, productive forces, world structures or anything else.

For one thing, postulating monads is an empty gesture if one cannot also say – and Cox does not – how all-too-human creatures can get

67

access to them. We seem to be faced with two unpalatable choices here. On the one hand, we might claim that we grasp monads on the basis of intuition. The trouble with choosing this option is that one person's intuition is likely to be different from another's and there would be no basis, *ex hypothesis*, upon which conflicting intuitions could be adjudicated. Another possibility would appear to be more congenial to Cox's project, *viz.*, to posit a *structure* in the world which, as a set of essences, singles out some sort of implicit correspondence between the monads and social relations of production. In this way, we would have slipped 'materialism' into performing a foundational role but without having to spell out the problematic relation between language and mind-independent entities. Although positing monads may provide us with the sense of having anchored our 'constructions' in *The World's* ontology, we don't seem to get any increased understanding of how we can get to live in better world orders. To see this let me turn to the 'Conclusions' of Cox's book.

Here, Cox emphasises that 'critical awareness of potentiality for change' has to be distinguished from 'utopian planning' and claims that his approach makes a place for the transformation of existing orders.[46] For Cox, the way to understand change in international relations is to examine 'the conditions favouring the maintenance of existing social order...' and he holds that there are three such conditions, in particular, which have been found 'propitious for transformation'.[47] These 'include': (i.) 'a weakening of global hegemony tending toward a more permissive world order in which it would be difficult for a dominant power or group of dominant powers to enforce conformity to its norms'; (ii.) the 'existence of different forms of state' which have differential effects on 'the stability of world order'; and (iii.) 'the mobilisation of forces into new counterhegemonic historic blocs ...'. What these three conditions 'add up to' is 'a diffusion of power'.[48] And it is here that we arrive at the *content* of Cox's claim to be a *critical/emancipatory* theory of international relations rather than, say, positivist descriptive history. For Cox, emancipation is not contained in the idea of 'equal moral autonomy' understood as the free association of producers, as it evidently was for Marx, but in the more modest goal of a greater diffusion of power in the international system. But now, if this is the goal, how is it to be distinguished from the time-honoured realist programme one purpose of which is to obtain greater autonomy for individual states in the international political system? It would appear that Cox's reductionist, objectivist historical materialism, though less objectionable to scientific realism than Hegelian Marxism, has no place for a dynamic, necessitarian, antithetical route to emancipation. Emancipation would have to come about not as the teleological consequence of revolutionary world struggle, but as the result of 'rational' criticism of ideologies and contingent individual and group action. This is a pale reflection of Marx's view and leaves Cox without the resources for achieving anything remotely similar to the Marxian *genre* of human emancipation. Although Cox may regard this as a gain in plausibility, it certainly leaves us wondering if there is any basis for distinguishing Cox's theory from positivism. If there isn't, then Cox's theory, whatever else it may do, seriously threatens international critical theory's claim to being a distinctive social theory, i.e. one which brings together theory and practice.

Unlike classical Marxists, Cox evidently sees no alternative to breaking the inextricable tie between theory and practice. He makes this clear in his final discussion of *modes of production*. 'One way', Cox writes, 'to think of the mode of production' is in terms of 'the discovery of the inner essence of capital, giving rise to notions like the "logic" of capital or the "laws of motion" of capital'. Cox implies that Marx 'meant something like this', but whatever Marx's view, 'his approach has rather been *to infer structures from observable historical patterns of conduct*'.[49] It would seem, then, that Cox is prepared to abandon the teleological elements in Marx's philosophy so that his theory will pass scientific muster in terms of the principles of scientific realism. If this is so, then what is left of *historical* materialism and its claim to frame the dance of modes and structures from one stage of history to another as the rational and progressive movement towards human betterment? At least for Marx the idea that there could be emancipation from capitalist structures without invoking some teleological grounds for believing in a possible transformation to something better does not even seem to have been considered.

So the leading question here is why Cox would think it rational for us to believe that world order 'can be built only through a political movement capable of uniting sufficient of the segmented elements of existing societies into a counterhegemonic bloc'.[50] Since Cox is committed to a form of materialism which precludes those Hegelian elements of Marx's thought which would provide a rational basis for believing in the necessary movement to communism, why would people, groups, or movements be sufficiently motivated to make the sacrifices required to join a counterhegemonic bloc?[51] If no sacrifices are required, would the bloc have sufficient strength to be genuinely 'counterhegemonic'? Just what is Cox envisaging here, a coalition of all the world's 'wage labourers' against capitalism? A coalition of peasants and marginals against the military bureaucracies of the world? A coalition of new social movements? A coalition of all the wretched of the earth against the surveillance states? Is the counterhegemonic bloc going to be a revolutionary agent which takes political power and sets up new relations of power? Doesn't this presuppose that the over-whelming majority of people living in the counterhegemonic bloc are unhappy, frustrated and, more importantly, sufficiently confident that there is a viable, superior alternative to what currently exists? Does Cox provide us with any arguments that such an alternative will become available at the global level? Isn't the very idea of a counter-hegemonic bloc, given the present configuration of forces, just a big dose of mystification mixed with precisely the sort of political romanti-cism that Marx deplored?

Although he, quite rightly, notes that a society without 'the profit motive ... will not come about from wishing for it',[52] Cox, unlike Marx, doesn't seem interested in giving much weight to the practice which makes wishing for it beside the point. Instead, he adopts a form of rationalism in evidently supposing that reflection alone suffices to generate dialectical, antagonistic movement to world order. The in-tellectual 'task begins' we are told, 'with an *awareness* of the present social divisions generated in the production process'.[53] However, we are given no account of how this awareness moves through stages to a condition which is more than marginally better. On a more classical Marxist understanding – not defended here – dialectical theory is inherently radical insofar as it engages in self-criticism as a way of preparing revolutionary agents to bring about revolutionary change.[54] But theory, for Cox, is evidently only about making people 'aware' of what the world is like, of providing them with reasons and 'hoping' they will act upon them rather than, for example, transforming their self-understandings so that they *will* act to eradicate their suffering. But in stripping theory of its inherent radicalism in the evident interest of providing a more satisfactory 'scientific' conception of international politics, we lose all purchase on providing a basis for belief in the movement from a condition of alienation to a condition in which things are radically better; we sacrifice emancipation and thus call into question the critical/emancipatory goal which Cox offers as the *raison d'être* of his theory. But is not the whole point of critical/emancipatory theory for Cox to offer not only a theoretical assessment of a way of life which is inadequate because frustrating and unsatisfying to those who lead it, but to identify how society *will* (or at least *can*) change that way of life? If international critical theory cannot have that, if it must rest content with a world dominated by natural necessity only marginally different from 'bourgeois capitalism', why would potentially revolutionary elements be at all motivated to join a party, a movement or even to hand out leaflets? Or to put this somewhat differently: who would want to spend most of his/her life rotting away in one of Mussolini's prisons for marginal changes towards '[a] more participant society'?[55] Productionist Marxism seems far too sanguine about its power to change the world by intellectual means alone and far too willing to give up the very emancipatory goals which have distinguished Marxism from forms of left-wing positivism. In so doing it fails to provide international critical theory with sufficient grounds for believing that an emancipatory order is a reasonable, non-utopian and practical goal for international relations in our time. Given these difficulties with two versions of international critical theory, we have now gathered a sufficiently solid basis for considering whether these difficulties have a common source.

Emancipatory IR meets Lyotardian postmodernism

Lyotardian postmodernism and revisionary realism: an unholy alliance?

Why should revisionary realists turn to Lyotard to generate arguments – hardly determinate in any case – for rejecting an emancipatory view of international relations? For three reasons. First, Lyotard has raised issues which have also been considered by revisionary realists, such as, for example, whether attempts to bring Kant's emancipatory project from the realm of the suprasensible to the causal-determinative realm is utopian in an objectionable sense. If revisionary realists can show that positions developed outside their own favoured perspective are nonetheless compatible with it, they would then be better placed to sustain it against rival alternatives. Secondly, practising political realists may, in considering Lyotard's work, find grounds for rejecting strong versions of globalism as forms of moral dogmatism to be

71

resisted in the name of freedom and independence. And, thirdly, one may be able to find renewed arguments for forms of human political relations which recognise the ethical value of separate nation-states.

Without ignoring obvious differences between any form of political realism and Lyotard's hyperbolical anarchism, let us consider what Lyotard shares with one form of revisionary realism, namely, evaluative political realism. Both see emancipatory proposals as dangerously vague philosophical abstractions, as excessively rationalistic and utopian; both are pluralistic and regard pluralism as a way of expanding the scope of human freedom relative to totalistic theories; both hold that the universal perspective which international critical theory paradigmatically exhibits is excessively theory prone; and both advance projects to expand the scope and significance of *practice vis-à-vis theory*. For the purposes of this section, I shall assume that realist views on these matters do not require textual support, i.e. that we can confidently hold that realists – at least evaluative political realists – are anti-utopian, pluralistic and opposed to the unification of theory and practice (see Part 2 for an extended discussion). Lyotard's views on these matters are less well known and their relation to political realism, so far as I am aware, unexamined.

Lyotard's rejection of utopianism

For Lyotard, the rejection of utopianism, and the human emancipation bound up with it, is an obvious feature of the world in which we live; we should accept it as a self-evident description of 'how things are'. As Lyotard states it in *The Postmodern Condition*: 'We no longer have recourse to the grand narratives – we can resort neither to the dialectic of Spirit nor even to the emancipation of humanity as a validation for postmodern discourse.'[56] In rejecting the use of metanarratives to legitimate universal emancipation, Lyotard's position provides a partial basis for rejecting international critical theory and sustaining realist anti-utopianism. For Lyotard, metanarratives are narratives of emancipation. Such narratives often allude to conditions in which men, women and children are oppressed. The point of such narratives is to show that attempts to *legitimate* such conditions through the use of myth, religion and ideology should be exposed. Neither Lyotard nor political realists would object to using narratives for such purposes. But metanarratives don't stop there; they also point forwards to a future condition in which subjects are free. In metanarratives, Ideas (in the Kantian sense), e.g. concerning freedom, enlightenment, material abundance and so on, are held to have legitimating value because they are posited as bound up with a story which presupposes the reality of universal human needs and values. In assuming the validity of such posits, metanarratives confuse the realm of the suprasensible with the realm of phenomenal cognition. Lyotard rejects what he regards as an impermissible extension of the Kantian notion of Idea and the cognate notions with which they are associated.[57] Metanarratives, in any case, appear to be just the sort of narratives which international critical theorists and many emancipatory theorists in international relations presuppose.

Lyotard's 'hostility' towards metanarratives is related to his understanding of modernity, against which he advances several claims. Lyotard insists, first of all, that the development of consciousness, of technology, of science – the very things which modernity vigorously promoted – has paradoxically rendered human emancipation impossible. The philosophical basis for this thought lies in understanding one consequence of modernity's substitution of epistemology for ontology: after modernity neither society, nor labour, nor any privileged group of human subjects would have an essence in the sense required to make emancipation intelligible. In undermining the very idea of 'an essence' of infinite development, modernity, ontologically speaking, creates a condition in which there is literally *no-thing* from which 'humanity' can be emancipated: there are no structures *in the world* from which to be liberated. Moreover, there is, correlatively, no privileged subject to do the freeing. To say that there is something called 'humanity' which would be the (possible) object of an emancipatory Idea is, for Lyotard, just question-begging.[58] Modernity's promise of emancipation passes beyond the limits of what can be reasonably offered in this way; for, just as there is nothing from which to be emancipated, so there is no 'we' in whose name the emancipation can be realised. Of course, classical Marxists attempted to legitimise a 'universal historical subject' by universalising the workers' movement but, according to Lyotard, the fate of the workers' movement was a 'telling example' of why the Kantian idea of emancipation was bound to fail.[59] Quite clearly, Lyotard's views are consistent with the tradition of political realism and, if valid, would give additional support to the realist's equivocal attitude to emancipatory conceptions of international relations.

Lyotard's second claim against modernity – his rejection of the Enlightenment view of justice – creates more interesting possibilities.

According to Lyotard, modernity characteristically seeks a theory of justice which has certain properties: universality, comprehensiveness and necessity. To Lyotard this suggests that it thinks a theory of justice should be scientific in form. Lyotard and evaluative political realism reject this claim, though on different grounds. For Lyotard, questions of justice are always bound up with whether the institutions which are in place should continue to exist as they are. If this is the central political issue, then there is no escape from the question of whether a group of people affected by certain institutions should *prescribe* changes. But the act of prescribing is a far different speech act from the act of truth-telling and does not lend itself to scientific thinking. According to Lyotard, when such political philosophers as Plato and Marx held that there was a 'true being of society', that actual societies 'could be held to be just' if examined in the light of exemplary standards, they were effectively confusing description and prescription.[60] This, Lyotard claims, is a logical error. For Lyotard, discourse about justice is not a matter of observing the world in an attempt to find out its true workings, but a matter of listening. For 'there are language games in which the important thing is to listen, in which the rule deals with audition. Such a game is the game of the just. And in this game, one speaks only inasmuch as one listens, that is, one speaks as a listener, and not as an author.'[61] When justice is at issue, we need to begin with *hearing* what people in particular social and political contexts actually say about their practices on the understanding that no *voice* is privileged. The call to be just always precedes norms of rationality. On this reading, Lyotard's work supports political realism in rejecting utopianism as frictionless universalising, a genre of thinking which deprives itself of the resources to come to grips with local contexts and different understandings of justice.

Lyotard's pluralism

A second reason why revisionary realists might want to make contact with Lyotard's ideas is that they provide a somewhat different ground for supporting pluralism, a traditional feature of political realism.[62] The form of pluralism relevant to evaluative political realism involves recognising that the legitimate ends of nation-states are many and varied, and that there is no blueprint devised in philosophical reason (or anywhere else) which would provide those who gained access to it with knowledge of how people actually living in nation-states should live their communal lives. This is not to say, of course, that people or governments cannot make moral judgements about other nation-states. Claims that pluralism collapses into relativism are red herrings.[63] Lyotard's *genre* of pluralism, one hastens to add, is not directed towards defending realist pluralism; nonetheless, one consequence of his position is that it provides a useful basis for helping to reconstruct realist pluralism in somewhat different, i.e. linguistic, terms.

The main vehicle for this is Lyotard's Wittgensteinian understanding of language games as activities or 'moves' with or against players speaking one's own or another language. On this view, the world always contains a multiplicity of language games which cannot be transcribed into or evaluated in terms of any totalising metadiscourse. Thus, for example, attempts by Marxian totalisers to remove the differences between nation-states should be countered, on the Lyotardian view, by the practice of paralogism; that is, by attempts to defer consensus, to produce dissension and undermine totalistic efforts to impose commensurability among existing language games. From this practical and local perspective, the globalist would be diagnosed as someone who, *malgré tout*, is determined to uncover and impose the so-called common elements in different foreign policy language games which culturally diverse nation-states use in their ongoing struggle to satisfy their needs and interests against others using their own or a different language.

But Lyotard's pluralism goes beyond claims concerning the diversity of language games. In *The Differend* Lyotard conceives language as made up of *phrases* – 'the only givens'. Phrases are vehicles for grasping the world: 'a phrase presents what it is about, the case, *ta pragmata*, which is its referent'.[64] But phrases cannot belong to a single universe since this would entail the existence of a world 'prior to the phrases'. Phrases are linked together by genres or regimens of discourse which are always local; discourse sets down rules for the linking of phrases within a non-universal context. These regimens are intended to ensure that the discourse in which phrases are articulated 'proceeds towards its generically assigned end: to convince, to persuade, to inspire laughter or tears, etc'.[65] Given a heterogeneity of phrase regimens, Lyotard's pluralism may be expressed by doubting the very coherence of 'common subordination to a single end'.[66] To be sure, Lyotard recognises that alternatives to heterogeneity have been offered in the form of 'some metaphysical will' or in 'a phenomenology of intention', but these alternatives, Lyotard insists, fail to resolve Kant's problem (in the *Introduction to the Third Critique*) of how to bridge the gaps between dispersive discourses.[67] After canvassing a variety of preferred solutions to Kant's problem, Lyotard concludes that the order of the philosophical day is: 'Incommensurability, heterogeneity, the differend, the persistence of proper names, the absence of a supreme tribunal.'[68] Resistance to the integration of different language games is political activity recalcitrant to totalising international politics in the name of human emancipation or whatever.

To sum up this point: Lyotard's emphasis on the heteromorphous and wholly conventional style of language games implies a radically different, critical conception of ideology, one that abandons the search for foundations and totalising truth and instead embraces the logic of particularity and context-dependence. From this standpoint, a *grand récit*, a particular type of (potentially) hegemonic language game which functions as a mask of the conditions of its own engendering, would be the very epitome of ideology. The term 'ideology' would not apply, however, to *petit récit*, 'the quintessential form of imaginative invention, most particularly in science'.[69] In other words, 'ideology' may be the appropriate pejorative term for language games which endeavour to represent and secure themselves as general, global or universal. Understood thus, we can then make a fruitful distinction between non-ideological language games and ideological language games. The former may be understood as local, context-laden language games. By contrast, ideological language games are those which, in presupposing universal truth, demand their general adoption and, therefore, the exclusion and/or repression of every other *particular* language game. So conceived, the Lyotardian critique of ideology would break decisively with the political aim of international critical theory in its attempt to devalue the false universality of an opponent's language game by presenting its own as unassailable. If Lyotard is correct in his controversial views of language – and there does seem to be something right about them – then we have a version of pluralism which enhances political realism.

Lyotard on theory and practice

We have now reached the third and final way in which a revised realism may be able to find support in Lyotard's reflections. Lyotard strongly endorses replacing the theoretical apparatus of a scientific understanding of politics with a new conception of practice. As such,

he questions the role 'theory' would play once we give up, as
presumably we must, the idea that there is a universally or globally
just society.[70] Lyotard's general redrawing of the boundaries of theory
and practice is continuous with commonsense realism and its general
suspicion of 'abstract theory'. In Lyotard's view, attempts to discover
and justify a theory of the unity of theory and practice are 'futile'. No
theory of persons or society can generate the universal consent
required to bring theory into unison with practice without massive
coercion. And if massive coercion is used, then political practice
becomes a form of terrorism. Since theories of justice (and especially
world justice) are always riddled with indeterminacies, the idea that a
theory of justice can prove its truth – an idea shared by Plato and Marx
– cannot even arise. Any conception of the unison of theory and
practice cannot be sufficiently determinate to obtain the massive,
uncoerced consent required for it to become a global revolutionary
praxis, the acting on which proves the theory's truth. If this is so, the
gap between theory and practice becomes conceptually unbridgeable.
This means, for example, that justice 'cannot be thought from the
theoretical and the apophantic'.[71] Justice, on this view, is more a matter
of the making of practical judgements by judges 'worthy of the
name'.[72] Lyotard goes on to say that the making of just judgements are
statements about *doxa*, that is, of opinion or dialectics; what they
cannot be are statements of truth or theoretical statements articulated
in a science of justice.[73] If this view is correct, there are some rather
devastating consequences for international critical theory.

Without a theoretically persuasive account of how theory and
practice link up to yield a rationally grounded route to universal
justice, international critical theorists are caught in a dilemma. They
can either renew the claim that international critical theory articulates a
valid understanding of the unity of theory and practice, showing why
this is so notwithstanding the sort of criticisms brought against it by
Lyotard (among others), or they can give up the claim to possess a
theoretical conception of the unison of theory and practice. Being
impaled on either of these horns would be distinctly uncomfortable. In
choosing the first horn, international critical theorists would be obliged
to do what has never been accomplished before, namely, find a
conception of the unity of theory to practice which is coherent,
nonutopian and acceptable. But if they choose the second horn, they
would have to give up what Marx, and presumably international
critical theorists as well, considered the *raison d'être* of this conception

of people and society: to bring human emancipation.[74] If there is a third way, one would certainly appreciate learning of it.

Lyotard summed

Totality is the centrepiece of Lyotard's attack on modernity. He views totality as an anachronistic effort to reconcile theory and practice in the name of universal history, an effort which has led to campaigns of terror against real communities with named individuals in concrete temporal-spatial locations. For Lyotard, universal narratives (theories) are forever (partially) divorced from universal Ideas of practical freedom. Consequently, such Ideas as freedom, emancipation, equality and so on 'cannot be verified by empirical proofs but only by indirect signs, *analoga* which signal in experience that this ideal is present in people's minds...'[75] But this means, on Lyotard's reckoning, that any discussions of emancipation will be "dialectical' in the Kantian sense, that is, without conclusion'.[76] Since Ideas are not mirrors of the world they are meant to represent, 'there will always be a profound tension between what one ought to be and what one is'.[77] In the context of scrutinising critical/emancipatory international relations, one form of totality involves absolutising the Kantian Idea and then trying to find, *per impossible*, something to confirm it, whether this involves declaring reason's increasing self-awareness of freedom or reducing reality to modes of production.[78] But whether they take one form or the other such posits eliminate the profound tension between what ought to be and what is. They can also lead to terror. 'Terror acts on the suspicion that nothing is emancipated enough – and makes it into a politics. Every particular reality is a plot against the pure, universal will.'[79]

Totalitarianism borrows the Idea of freedom from modernity and attempts to legitimate it by the use of myths. The most important of these is the naming of a *we* and an end to human history. By announcing the singularity of a *we*, one would then be in a position to assert the possibility of a universal history of humanity and of humanity's possible emancipation. What prevents this claim from going through, however, is that no universal history can actually be written. Why not? For there to be universal history there would have to be 'addressees who were themselves "universal"'.[80] But this is impossible because the 'addressees' of narratives are always rooted in named, spatial-temporal particularities. Names, as links to reality, are learned in cultures and grasped through particular narratives. Such narratives are *sui generis* and 'absolutely opposed to the organisation of the grand narratives of legitimation which characterise modernity in the West'.[81] So, for Lyotard, reflection on the nature of universal narrative will show its practical impossibility. Once we grasp the link between the Idea of humanity's emancipation in history and modernity's attempt to legitimate this myth for political ends, we shall be less vulnerable, Lyotard suggests, to totalising formulas and the totalitarian political 'solutions' they engender.

Conclusion

I have argued that globalism – in its philosophically most interesting form of international critical theory – is bound up with an understanding of human emancipation which finds its numen in Marxian understanding of theory and practice. Many research programmes in international relations – even those which 'officially' reject any Marxian idea of human emancipation – nonetheless attempt to keep some grip on a critical/emancipatory understanding of international relations. I have argued that certain ideas of Jean-François Lyotard may be deployed to provide grounds for taking up an anti-emancipatory stance in international relations. In putting Lyotard's contribution into intimate contact with a revisionary realism, we get the following few points as yield.

First, the goal of international critical theory is essentially a demand to privilege the Western state-system over other possible sorts of state-system. The ideal of a universal humanity which effectively denies nation-state difference allows privileged groups within nation-states to ignore the ways in which their own group differs from indefinite others. Ignoring difference may encourage cultural imperialism by permitting norms which express only the point of view of certain privileged groups in their effort to appear neutral, impersonal and universal. International critical theory presumes that there is 'a place from nowhere' from which one can view individuals and nation-state collectivities, and that this unsituated 'place' will allow 'us' to judge entire nation-states *in terms that are nation-state neutral*. But, for Lyotardian postmodernists and revisionary realists, there is no such nation-state neutral point of view since the place from nowhere which would legitimate it does not exist. Human beings, societies and nation-states are always situated.

Secondly, the demand for international critical theory is an assimilationist demand at bottom. The insistence that states give up their 'sovereignty' effectively holds up to the world's people a demand that individuals and cultures everywhere 'fit', that their values, purposes and goals conform to those laid down by production-driven institutions in advanced Western societies. In terms of this conformist ideal, status quo institutions and norms are assumed as given and disadvantaged groups are expected to conform to them. By the same token, a transformationalist ideal as embodied in forms of international critical theory recognises the large role that the interests and perspectives of dominant groups will play in institutions. Achieving the goals of international critical theory, therefore, requires altering institutions and practices in accordance with allegedly neutral rules within an allegedly neutral and impartially conceived international system. From the transformational perspective of international critical theory, any conception of international politics that asserted the positivity of nation-state difference might be regarded as reactionary and anachronistic. But from a Lyotardian point of view, nation-state difference, recalcitrant to universal emancipation, might well be considered liberating and empowering for particular peoples. If the marginalised states of the Western Pacific, Latin America, Africa and elsewhere were to reclaim their national identity and insist on their cultural rights as nation-states, we might be less inclined to distort their distinctive experiences by focusing on them through lenses ground in the entrenched grand narratives of Western modernity.

Although emancipatory international relations has not been refuted here (*quelle idée!*), enough has been said perhaps to understand why someone might want to consider examining another conception of international relations. This is the task of Part 2.

Part 2

4 Evaluative political realism: a beginning

The beginning is more than half of the whole.
Machiavelli

Introduction

Having critically examined some other conceptions of international relations, I will now outline an alternative view, the one I've been calling 'evaluative political realism'.[1] In this chapter, I will first distinguish commonsense realism and concessional realism with the idea of indicating what evaluative political realism would like to appropriate from these views as it struggles to develop its own identity within the realist tradition. I will then go on to show that evaluative political realism is committed to a different conception of theory and practice than rival conceptions of international relations. Positivist-empiricism's conception of theory and practice is one in which theory stands over against the world and the world, being outside the space of concepts, is unable to deliver justifiable judgements. This leads to scepticism. Recoiling from these sceptical entanglements and their adverse implications for social and political life, emancipatory international relations, especially in its postmodernist versions, tends to depict theory as involving engagements which have no empirical constraints associated with them at all: theory connects up with practice to avoid scepticism but falls into the clutches of frictionless utopianism. Evaluative political realism constitutes a third way. As against emancipatory international relations it holds, as commonsense suggests, that reality is independent of our thinking; but since our experience of that reality is a rational constraint on our thinking, this need not drive us back to the sceptical dichotomies found in positivist-empiricism. Unlike these

83

rival conceptions, evaluative political realism pictures theory and practice as mediated by a conceptual content that allows us to identify (at least in the best of circumstances) 'how things are'. In subsequent chapters of Part 2 I will advance arguments intended to sustain four theses which, if true, will go a long way towards sustaining evaluative political realism against its principal rivals, positivist-empiricism and emancipatory international relations. At the end of the line of argument there will be, evaluative political realists claim, a conception of political realism which is neither 'an operator's manual' posing as a 'social theory' nor the 'name for a discourse of power'.[2] There will be, that is, a highly defendable conception of political realism.

The arguments mapped out below form, I claim, a coherent conception of a somewhat different version of political realism. I shall also hold that the arguments advanced on behalf of the four theses of evaluative political realism in the following chapters are true or approximately true, that is, not only do they hang together to form a reflectively coherent whole but they also say, if one is not misled, how things are in international relations. In identifying the arguments which, in my view, constitute a coherent and true conception of international politics, I shall be elucidating their content and saying why I am convinced of their truth. If, despite my efforts to justify them, others remain unconvinced, I might have to say, following Wittgenstein, that they 'stand fast' for me even though, as Wittgenstein also put it, 'that something stands fast for me is not grounded in my stupidity or credulity'.[3] Although I know that my arguments cannot be proven, their standing fast for me means that belief in them is warranted not only by virtue of attempts to show their truth but also because of the central role they play within a certain political practice, i.e. the ongoing practices of statesmen and stateswomen in international relations.

Commonsense and concessional realism

Just as there are varieties of religious experience, of the use of metaphor and of the nature of pragmatism, so too there are varieties of political realism; or so at least it will be argued here. The two forms of political realism discussed in this section – commonsense realism and concessional realism (or neorealism) – have different emphases; each claims that its version of realism is correct and seeks support from others; and, most importantly, each has a different understanding of the philosophy of science and the role it is supposed to play in political realism. Commonsense realism regards the philosophy of science as mainly irrelevant to the study of international politics and claims that a prereflective, prescientific perspective suffices to determine how things are in world politics: we do not need, and probably cannot have, a theoretical justification for international relations, on this view. The content of commonsense realism is well known: it holds that human beings are basically selfish; that states largely pursue their interests; and that power is the primary coin of diplomatic and military exchange. By contrast, concessional realism, though it agrees with these substantive premises, attempts to justify them differently in terms of certain foundational principles of scientific empiricism and/or utilitarianism. Concessional realism hopes to reconstruct realism methodologically by bringing our understanding of the subject into line with these principles, no matter how much strain this puts on our 'ordinary' understanding of international relations. Evaluative political realism – the view favoured here – rejects concessional realism and, notwithstanding certain affinities with commonsense realism, it insists, unlike that view, on the desirability and the possibility of a plain realist philosophy of science. By distinguishing these various versions of political realism, I hope to accomplish three things: first, to show that valid arguments against one version of realism don't automatically have force against other versions; secondly, to suggest that no adequate version of international relations can escape the philosophical and ethical issues with which international relations is bound up; and thirdly, to propose that a strong, but certainly not conclusive, case can be made for evaluative political realism as an attractive alternative to principal competing conceptions.

Commonsense realism

Essentially, this is the realism shaped by the thought and experience of E. H. Carr, Reinhold Niebuhr, Hans J. Morgenthau, Martin Wight, Sir Herbert Butterfield, Raymond Aron and indefinitely many others. According to its picture of international relations, human beings live in a world dominated by states or nation-states, the collectivity of which is variously described as a state-system, international system, an international-political system, or in some other convenient way. The most notable characteristic of such a system is that it is decentralised; it lacks a centralised political authority. This means that each nation-state is free to pursue its own interests as it conceives them. This core realist idea is expressed in the long-standing principle of national sovereignty, a legal concept that rejects the right of any external authority to control the policies of the state. Although this might give the initial impression that commonsense realism rests on the authority of certain legal rights, such is not the case. For the commonsense realist, this would be to get things the wrong way round since the reason states have the legal authority enshrined in the principle of national sovereignty is that states have the power to defend themselves against those who refuse to respect their territorial claims. If they did not have this capacity, whether alone or in combination with other states, they would not qualify as independent states and so could not be legitimately described as sovereign. In identifying national sovereignty as a property of states, the commonsense realist is effectively claiming that the state system will have a relatively anarchic character. For the commonsense realist, this has several important consequences. The most important of these is that international politics becomes a survival system in which each state has the burden of looking after its own security and well-being. Even more than in the case of the individual, the ultimate value for the nation-state is survival. But unlike the individual within society, the state is unprotected by legal institutions; hence, the state must look to its own devices – war, diplomacy, military alliances, etc. – to protect itself. The quest for survival is, according to commonsense realists, one of the significant identifying properties of international relations.

A second core belief of commonsense realism is that the resort to force in relations between states always lies in the background as a potential way of resolving disputes. The commonsense realist may tend to exaggerate the difference between the international system, with its pervasive inclination towards violence, and the relative order of domestic state systems; but she should not do so. There is over-whelming evidence that some violence exists in all political systems. And the persistent phenomenon of civil war suggests that no civilisation we have ever known in the past is immune to large-scale war. Yet, while the state may or may not possess an actual monopoly of force in society, it does, as a general rule, control the only legitimate use of force in society. Individuals and groups may wage war on each other within a nation-state but they contravene the law in doing so. This is not the case in international relations. The ultimate arbiter of whether the state will or will not resort to force against its neighbours is the state itself. History provides numerous examples of the willingness of states to resort to war in order to achieve their goals. A world government that took away from nation-states the essential prerogative of statehood – national sovereignty – might reduce the incidence of violence (though this is far from self-evident) but no such government exists nor has ever existed; the prospect of such a government arising in the near future seems very small. Given that each state must look to itself to defend its own interests, the international system is one which fosters fear, suspicion and insecurity.

This leads to a third core belief of commonsense realism, namely, that states are disposed to protect themselves through deploying balance of power strategies. As one noted commonsense realist, Martin Wight, put it: 'The aspiration for power on the part of several nations ... leads of necessity to a configuration that is called the balance of power and to policies that aim at preserving it.'[4] Stated in a simplified form, the balance of power refers to the tendencies of states to align themselves with others to promote their own interest or enhance their security.

Very roughly, this, or something like it, is the commonsense realist picture and there is, in fact, much to recommend it as the way things have been in international relations for a very long time; it is also a picture that is likely to capture a good deal of what will go on in international relations for many years to come. Although this is hardly an argument, there is here the material for a *potential* argument which could arguably serve to support the perspective of commonsense realism. However, the 'older' generation of realists did not make any such argument. Despite their penetrating insights into the power-political aspects of international politics we can regret, admittedly with all the unfair benefit of hindsight, the absence of philosophical efforts to make philosophical arguments on behalf of commonsense realism. Notwithstanding the fact that certain commonsense realists produced some schematic quasi-philosophical notions such as Morgenthau's 'six principles of a realist theory of international politics'[5] or Wight's famous 'three R's' (realism, revolutionism and rationalism),[6] the previous generation of realist thought engaged in surprisingly little philosophical analysis. This is all the more notable given the realist's official endorsement of the centrality of 'philosophy' as an indispensable feature of her favoured conception of the world.

To be fair, commonsense realists saw themselves as belonging to a single continuing and pre-existing tradition whose self-understood task is to say how things are in world politics. Such realists took as their special concern not so much the philosophical task of grounding and justifying their principles and ideas, as the moral and educative one of alerting statesmen, public opinion leaders, and the world's citizens to the menace of different sorts of totalitarianism. For these political realists, performing the task of political and moral education was a consequence of taking realism – in the practical-prudential sense – seriously. But here again commonsense realists missed an opportunity to draw from their rich moral/political heritage in order to describe their educative activity in terms of the more general categories of *theory* and *practice*. If commonsense realists had given more attention to the philosophical analysis of these and related concepts, realism might have made itself less vulnerable to the charge of 'obsolescence'. For, the analysis of concepts involves the discovery of truths that may hold good irrespective of even dramatic changes in international events.

Concessional realism

By concessional realism I mean the view which concedes a major part of the scientific empiricist's claim that theories of international politics are essentially the same as theories of nature: there is, for this kind of realist, no principled methodological distinction between theories of international politics and natural scientific theories. Concessional realists still cling to the key positivist epistemological programme of 'the unity of method'. Their position is preclusive in the sense that they believe that once the principles of scientific method have been rationally determined, there is no longer a logical basis for a discipline's determining what its methodological approach will be. Concessional realists think that there is exactly one correct methodological approach to a subject matter. By contrast, the point here will be that once the philosophical assumptions of this position are exposed to critical scrutiny, its appeal will diminish.

Concessional realism is committed to an empiricist philosophy of science. Empiricism is the foundationalist philosophy which holds that all genuine knowledge is derived from sensory observation and, when coupled with positivism, yields positivist-empiricism, as described in chapter 2. It is worth underlining here three ways in which concessional realism 'adopts' empiricist modes of thought.

First, there is the concessional realist's commitment to *formalism* in the construction and reconstruction of theories. On the empiricist view adopted by concessional realists, commonsense theories as such do not make obvious or clear descriptive and falsifiable claims about their subject matter. To determine whether the claims of theories are justifiable, they must be reformulated in formal or mathematical terms. Indeed, for the empiricist the logical structures associated with a theory are much more essential than the substantive claims it makes. The main reason for the concessional realist's formalism is epistemological. That is, insofar as international relations claims to be a rational enterprise, its theories must be supported by evidence. Hence, it should always be clear what will count as evidence and this requires, the concessional realist supposes, a formalistic presentation of the subject.

The second feature of scientific empiricism that the concessional realist adopts is *scientific naturalism*. We need, according to this view, to reconstruct our commonsense understanding of human and artefact agency out of conceptual materials that are either already available or, more likely, would be able to pass muster, in a natural-scientific depiction of nature. Thus, for example, concessional realists are disposed to modes of thought – such as rational choice theory – which provide a basis for counting human behaviour in terms which generally conform to the natural-scientific picture.[7] In the rational choice explanations popular with concessional realists, the power of human beings as agents resonates inward to disembodied reason and this seems, notwithstanding its conformity to representations in natural science, to eliminate any possible contact between intelligibility and human beings as natural animals. It is a paradox worth considering that a theory of human behaviour which claims to be within the framework of natural-scientific thinking conceives the intelligibility of human action in ways which obscure its connection with human animality. Evaluative political realism attempts to remove this distortion by adopting a more restricted naturalism (see chapter 6).

A third feature of scientific empiricism which concessional realism incorporates into its core beliefs is an *empiricist theory of meaning* such that the meaning of terms depends on the theory's empirical claims. For example, on this view, the meaning of the term 'mass' in Newtonian particle mechanics is a function of knowing its denotation or extension and its intended application within the theory. Meanings are, on this view, fixed either by convention or stipulation. The significance of meanings for concessional realists should not be underestimated: their viewpoint is a throwback to logical positivism. It was the logical positivists who claimed that meaning relations were analytic in the specific sense that they are true by virtue of their meaning and provide no information about the world: they are vacuously true. This principle of meaning underwrote an empiricist theory of knowledge, a theory according to which all non-vacuous knowledge is justifiable only by reference to sense experience. Science is supposedly successful only because it checks and justifies its claims by reference to sense experience. Thus, all cognitively meaningful non-vacuous claims about the world are supposed to be justifiable only by methods of justification that lead ultimately to sense experience.

The problem is, however, that no-one is obliged to accept these three tenets of an empiricist philosophy of science. Not only are they inconsistent with a pragmatic/realist philosophy of science, they have also all been subjected to withering attacks, many of which have come from philosophies of science generally opposed to realism. With respect to formalism, Lakatos has argued that many of the most respected theories of science were not expressed in formalistic terms at all and were not falsifiable when they were first accepted.[8] Concerning natural science, we can acknowledge the rightness of the seventeenth-century's effort to strip meaning from nature without also accepting the claim that the intelligible is equivalent to nature. Again, the conventional or stipulatory view of empiricist meaning has been undermined by Quine's frontal attack on the notion of analyticity. If one accepts Quine's arguments, there is no theory of meaning available which can support an empiricist methodological programme in the social sciences.

Where, then, does this leave us? It leaves us with an appreciation of the practical importance and significance of commonsense realism, on the one hand, while rejecting its refusal to come to terms with methodological issues, on the other. It leaves us also with concessional realism and its ill-advised acceptance of an erroneous philosophy of science grounded in scientific empiricism, on the other. Out of this tension, evaluative political realism emerges to suggest, not that we do without a philosophy of science altogether, but rather that we follow Arthur Fine in accepting a minimalist philosophy of science. According to Fine, what we need today is not another 'theory' of science to add to the junkheap of discarded theories – realism, instrumentalism, empiricism, behaviourism and so forth – which take up an essentially pro-science view but rather a new *attitude* to science. Fine rejects all previous philosophies of science on the grounds that their shared assumptions are not required; 'we thrive on less'.[9] The 'we' here refers to the attitude he favours, i.e. 'the natural ontological attitude' (NOA).[10] He describes NOA as structurally similar to minimalist art insofar as it refuses to be drawn into elaborate philosophical commitments of the sort that scientific empiricists and scientific realists would typically make. Fine counsels us 'to treat truth in the usual referential way', to adopt 'ordinary referential semantics which commits us ... to the existence of the individuals, properties, relations, processes, and so forth referred to by the scientific statements that we accept as true'.[11]

This sort of realism is closer to the commonsense realist's refusal to be drawn into philosophical discussions, say, of what constitutes science and scientifically worthwhile research. For Fine, it would be better to take scientific claims on their own terms: we don't need, and don't advance things, by telling a metastory in realist or anti-realist terms.[12] Following Fine, a minimalist pragmatic/realist philosophy of science – in contrast to positivism, the new empiricism and scientific realism – rejects the traditional view that a unified story of science needs to be told which will enable us to understand how *science as such* becomes successful. As Fine remarks 'perhaps the greatest virtue of NOA is to call attention to just how minimal an adequate philosophy of science can be'.[13] Such a minimalist pragmatic/realist philosophy of science does not buy into the scientific-realist's, the instrumentalist's or, for that matter, any other metatheoretical story about science at all. It rejects global legitimations of science altogether. This implies that the only justification which international relations requires is local. Unlike positivist-empiricism, a minimalist pragmatic/realist philosophy of science holds that only narrow justifications internal to international relations are required. This is what Morgenthau had in mind, I believe, when he wrote 'that the theoretical understanding of international politics is possible only within relatively narrow limits and that the present attempts at a thorough rationalisation of international theory are likely to be as futile as those which have preceded them since the seventeenth century'.[14] The pragmatic/realist approach avoids the science-bashing of the sort which certain poststructuralists seem disposed to make but nonetheless does not pre-empt the possibility of criticising, from within the relatively narrow limits of an historical context, the epistemological and political and cultural implications of various conceptions of a subject or discipline. Science, on this view, is a human activity and as such is not alienated from the world of human practice in the way that positivist-empiricism and concessional realism require to produce a benchmark of what is and what is not 'real' science. For the evaluative political realist, globalist justifications of science set up a false dichotomy between knowledge and activity which create the unrealistic and misguided idea of unconditional and disembodied knowledge that is supposed to represent science at its best. By contrast, the advantage of the minimalist position advocated by Fine and adopted by evaluative political realism is that it recognises the great range of knowledge which is produced by people set in complex historical relations to one another.

Now, a key feature of pragmatic/realism is that it proposes a different conception of theory and practice than that to be found either in positivist-empiricism or emancipatory international theory. In examining that conception we are moving to the heart of the matter.

Evaluative political realism: theory and practice

A distinguishing feature of evaluative political realism is that, unlike commonsense realism, it specifically articulates a unique picture of the relation between theory and practice. To help focus our discussion, let us reconsider Figure 2.1. This is intended to illustrate a key distinction between formal (A) and non-formal (B and C) modes of categorising the relation between theory and practice. We do not have to place a heavy philosophical weight on this distinction to grasp that there are significant differences between positivist-empiricism, on the one side, and emancipatory international theory and evaluative political realism, on the other, concerning the extent to which formalistic modes of thought in international relations are regarded as necessary or desirable. Positivist-empiricism may thus be viewed as an attempt to get emancipatory theorists and evaluative political realists to conceive political activity in international relations as directed towards a theoretical understanding of the world grounded in autonomous reason itself. According to positivist-empiricism, theory-offerings either satisfy identifiable logical conditions or they consist of pre-theoretical reflections ('pre-theories', 'intuitions', etc.) which, however suggestive they may be, cannot count as *theory* properly speaking. Evaluative political realism rejects this formalistic and rationalistic view of theory and replaces it with a pragmatic/realist understanding which, in giving due weight to the role of *phronesis* in making the ethical-political world intelligible, conceives theory in a more critical and reflective way.

For evaluative political realism, theory attempts to tell us how the world is; but what the world is and how we tell what is in it should not be understood in terms of the strong naturalistic models which predominate in positivist-empiricism and concessional realism. Rather, theories should be understood as conceptual capacities we deploy to do things with; they are not, as William James put it: 'answers to enigmas, in which we can rest'.[15] In helping us to say how things stand in the world, the *form* which theory takes cannot be specified in advance of its use. Different uses of theory will require different forms. In other words, evaluative political realism takes into account the *context* in which theoretical reasoning is used. If one replaced 'philosophical thinking' with 'positivist-empiricism' in the next citation, evaluative political realism would be on all fours with John Dewey according to whom '[t]he most pervasive fallacy of philosophical thinking' is 'neglect of context'.[16] On Dewey's view, theoretical reflection requires placing statements of facts within the wider context in which practical judgements have to be made. Contexts are determined by practical problems which get thrown up to human intelligence and cry out for solutions. Among international relationists, it was Morgenthau in particular who underlined the importance of context. 'The practical function of a theory of international relations', Morgenthau wrote, 'depends very much upon the political environment within which the theory operates.'[17] Morgenthau goes on to describe the 'practical functions' that a theory of international relations can perform in 'approaching political reality'.[18] Theory, on this view, is pragmatic and contextual. On the other hand, theory should not be construed as reducible to practice. When it is, theory loses its critical capacity and veers towards a frictionless world-making anathema to evaluative political realism.

Although theory is understood as a conceptual capacity designed to say how things are in the world, practice is, for the evaluative political realist, a mode of engagement with the world that derives its sense from traditions, shared capacities to see similarities and ongoing ways of life. The aim of thought about the practical is not to say how things are in a world in which human beings have no special place; it is, rather, to help us construct, in the face of genuine natural constraints, a world that will be a human world, one which gives pride of place to the social, personal and aesthetic. According to evaluative political realism, positivist-empiricism attempts to extend a model of reasoning which, though arguably appropriate to the natural world, distorts the nature of practice and its relation to theory. As Morgenthau says: 'The age of science misunderstands the nature of man in that it attributes to man's reason, in its relation to the social world, a power of knowledge and control which reason does not have.'[19] In *Scientific Man vs. Power Politics*, Morgenthau regrets the preoccupation with discovering a so-called 'science of man's political nature' which 'considers ethics as an empirical science or considers it not at all ...'[20] The extension of naturalistic forms of rationalism into the social world of political practice underwrites reverberating movements between distorting scientistic conceptions of ethics and ethical scepticism. Practice, for the evaluative political realist, need not and should not be construed either as rational action taken in one's self-interest or as productive activity hived off from practical ethics in the interest of theoretical emancipation. Rather, practice is to be conceived as an expression of intentionality in which human beings are able to grasp how things are bound up with one another as manifestations of certain states of mind and to link these with something in the context of the situation to which other human beings might respond. Such an understanding of practice may be found, I believe, in Heidegger's *Being and Time* in which the focus is on the *readiness-to-hand* of descriptions that take for granted the identity of what is perceived because they make up a world that we have assimilated and in which we are at home.[21] On this understanding, we do not *infer* what statespersons are perceiving, e.g. whether they intend to go to war; we directly perceive them as human beings whose activities are expressions of mind and language, the significations of which are the result of the readiness-to-hand of everyday life. On this picture, we avoid scepticism by circumventing the supposition that all understanding of human behaviour is derived from primitive data from which we deduce what such entities are saying and doing. Avoiding the scepticism associated with positivist-empiricism requires, on this view, being able to grasp facts directly and in ways which resonate with intelligible acting.

One way to work into a different conception of theory and practice is to draw out some of the conceptual possibilities in Aristotle's notions of *theoria* and *phronesis* ('practical wisdom'), as discernible in Table 4.1. For Aristotle, the word *theoria* was conceived to capture two different, though related, senses of the word: 'Speculation' as a kind of passive, though systematic, viewing or looking on and 'critical reflection' as the sort of thinking which is directed to practical concerns. Practice was also conceived as divided in two. On the one hand, there is the kind of practice which involves making or producing and which Aristotle

Table 4.1 *An Aristotelian conception of theory and practice*

Theory		Practice
Speculative (scientific) thought		*Poiesis* (*Techné*)
Critical reflection	Knowing-as-*phronesis*	*Praxis*
	Wisdom affecting action ——→	
	←—— Action affecting thought	

identified as *poiesis*. Because the end of *poiesis* is known prior to action, it is guided by a mode of disclosing which Aristotle called *techné*. We would call this technical knowledge or expertise. *Poiesis* attains fulfilment in the production of things or effects outside the agent; the practical knowing it produces is instrumental, a kind of *knowhow*. It seems fair to say that positivist-empiricism focuses on the way in which *theory-as-speculation* creates the conditions for understanding production in the most efficient way. Without denying the importance of this kind of knowing, the evaluative political realist's project may be understood as directed towards resuscitating the connection between *theory-as-critical reflection* and *praxis*, as discernible in the lower half of Table 4.1. The idea of *theory-as-critical reflection* is meant to capture the kind of theorising one engages in when mind and value are included in one's conception of the world from the very outset rather than as something added to a 'bleached-out physical conception of objectivity' of the sort to be found in positivist-empiricism.[22] There are three important consequences of this inclusion for our understanding of theory. First, since any conception of the world which includes mind cannot simultaneously include the mind which is now apprehending the world, our conception of the world will always be incomplete. Secondly, the world includes values, but our theorising about them can only be defended from an internal perspective which accepts, so to speak, their reality. And, thirdly, since any adequate conception of theory cannot leave behind the personal points of view whose acceptance of the theory is constitutive of its success, we are all, as theorists, practically obligated to take up a critical perspective on our views of what is salient *vis-à-vis* indefinite others. Understood thus, theory is already oriented towards practice, to the weighing of reasons about what to think and what to do, to *praxis* rather than *poiesis*.

Although *praxis* for the Greeks and Aristotle is action directed to some end, it differs from *poiesis* in important respects. In the first place, the end of *praxis* is not to produce some artefact or object but to realise some morally worthwhile 'good'. It is an activity, therefore, that is performed for its own sake. But, secondly, *praxis* is different from *poiesis* precisely because recognition of the 'good' which constitutes its end is inseparable from a discernment of its mode of expression. *Praxis* is thus what we could call morally informed or morally committed action; it involves a capacity for choice (*prohairesis*). When such a capacity for choice is acted upon it expands the scope for theory-as-critical reflection which, in turn, serves to enlarge the area of deliberative action. If this is a description of a possible process, we may be able to speak intelligibly about 'action affecting thought' and 'wisdom affecting action', as suggested by Table 4.1.

A striking difference between this understanding of theory and practice and the other views we have canvassed thus far lies in the interpretation of the shaded area where critical reflection and praxis are depicted as coming into unity by virtue of *phronesis*. The two partially overlapping circles under C (Figure 4.1) are intended to illustrate this possibility. Theory and practice are depicted as participating in the ends of the political community, i.e. faring well (*eudaimonia*), but in different ways. Practical wisdom helps the practical side of theory by conceiving action in cognitive terms, and it helps the theoretical side of practice by proposing that there is a correct conception of how to live. Nonetheless, theory is still too remote from practice because it is guided by an interest in truth for its own sake; while practice – whether as *praxis* in which activity is the end or as *techné* which relates to production – is too remote from reason, knowledge and truth. What is required, then, is a bridging concept, namely, the concept of knowing-as-*phronesis*.

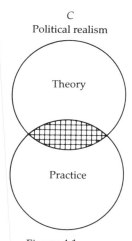

C
Political realism

Theory

Practice

Figure 4.1

The shaded area in the figure is represented as a kind of knowledge: knowledge-as-*phronesis*. For Kantians, Cartesians and Marxians, the idea that practice is a form of objective knowledge cannot be countenanced. But for Aristotle *phronesis* serves to mediate the gap between theory and practice in such a way that practice could legitimately claim to be a kind of objective knowledge, the kind that pictures ethical-political activity as answering to the demands of reason, of getting such activity right from within a specific conception of the world. *Phronesis* finds its most perspicuous employment as the intellectual virtue which guides deliberation about typical people in typical practical situations. But only those who deliberate well have *phronesis*; only those who know what it is to live well and what human beings should do in particular situations are wise. Being wise involves not only intellectual ability; no one is wise unless disposed to consider and to do what contributes to a good life. Since it is goodness of character – a practical virtue – which disposes one to the good life, no one can be wise without being good in character. 'For it is not possible to be good in the strict sense without practical wisdom, nor practically wise without moral virtue.'[23] One does not, on this view, become *phronimos* by studying some formal doctrine or theory in the modern sense. One can only become *phronimos* by doing actions which are wise and good. In the modern context this requires resistance to the reduction of *praxis* to technical control.[24] But what is the bearing of such reflections on international relations theory? First, in contrast to conceptions of theory which give theory-as-speculation a monumental role – whether to provide conceptions of the world logically homomorphic to natural scientific theories or to transform the world in radical ways – evaluative political realism puts theory-as-critical reflection into high relief. To be sure, this self-conscious depreciation of theory-as-speculation is not intended to rule out, as we shall see below, *partially* theoretical conceptions of international relations in the naturalistic mode; these are as indispensable as they are subordinate to the main game which, on the evaluative political realist view, concerns the relation between theory-as-critical reflection and *praxis*. Focusing on the main game helps to modulate the view that theory-as-speculation should automatically be the central concern of any discipline in which the question of the relation between theory and practice is itself at issue. When practice is at stake, moral-political action and ethically shaping the world in which human beings are compelled to live might well be of greater value than theory-as-speculation. For example, since any form of theory-as-speculation would be formalistic and rationalistic, it is not clear how it could be a theory *for us*, i.e. for the life that we share with others in our human groupings. The evaluative political realist's understanding of the relation of theory and practice implies, therefore, a strategic shift away from theory in the naturalistic sense of theory-as-speculation to theory-as-critical reflection in the interest of enlarging the ethical-political sphere in international relations. Such a view encourages us to understand ethical-political discourse as a linguistic practice in which reasons can be adduced and defended to support ethical claims. Such reasons cannot, of course, be offered as compelling to those who simply refuse to see *praxis* as a form of reasoned deliberation. Nothing can count as a reason for such persons. But if we are prepared to accept the idea that moral reasons exist, then we can legitimately hold that the role of practical wisdom is to generate those reasons and to provide grounds for saying why they might have to be set aside in particular political circumstances. Practical wisdom gives us a sense of what the individual case demands, of how idiosyncratic political circumstances may affect our judgements about what to do and effectively defeat our moral reasons in particular cases. We shall discuss the ethical aspects of evaluative political realism at greater length in chapter 8. (To avoid awkwardness, I shall now dispense with the terms theory-as-critical reflection and *praxis*, and use the

English words 'theory' and 'practice'. Context should enable us to determine the referent of these words.)

A second consequence of the evaluative political realist's general understanding of the relation of theory to practice for international relations is to valorise history as a way of knowing and being. Hans-Georg Gadamer brings this out with his phrase *wirkungsgeschichtliches Bewusstsein*. According to Gadamer, this means that 'we cannot extricate ourselves from historical becoming, or place ourselves at a distance from it, in order that the past might become an object for us ... We are always situated in history.'[25] But we must be careful not to allow such a view to provide a basis for thinking that theory can be collapsed into practice in the way proposed by emancipatory international relations. The barbaric and dehumanising acts of violence perpetrated by many self-identified Marxist states suggest that the emancipatory understanding of the relation between theory and practice – at least in its classical formulation – is seriously flawed. The brutal practices committed in the name of actualising *that* kingdom of ends cannot but have a chastening effect on the extent to which one is prepared to endorse a conception of theory and practice which *requires* the eventual collapse of theory into practice in the interest of emancipation. This means, in effect, that evaluative political realism endorses an understanding of theory and practice which keeps the shaded area in Figure 4.1 (representing a political order based on the conjunction of ethics and knowledge) in the background as an ideal possibility whose purpose is to shape, but not to determine, ethical-political judgement and action. The shaded area of Figure 4.1 represents a situation in which an identity between the good person and the good citizen has arisen because the good regime has been put in place and *phronesis* rules. But although phronomatics may think ethics and knowledge into identity in the notional good regime, neither they (nor anyone else) should expect notional good regimes to come into being nor use brute power to try to actualise them. Evaluative political realism recognises the dangers inherent in all perfectionist political orders and thinks that, to avoid them, we should strive for less even while we continue to register the phronomatic obligation to criticise the ways in which we are governed in terms of standards which assume that virtue is a form of knowledge. In particular, for all practical purposes, we should strive for political orders in which a creative tension is maintained between theory and practice, as illustrated in Figure 4.2.

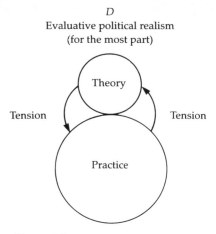

D
Evaluative political realism
(for the most part)

Theory

Tension   Tension

Practice

Figure 4.2

The leading idea behind Figure 4.2 is that, in the interest of
avoiding totalities and accepting pluralism and difference, our social
theories should be directed not towards attaining perfect political
orders – either national or international – but towards developing
those political orders in which substantive ethical life has the
possibility of expanding its reign outwards. The role of theory
envisaged in 4.2 is not to transform human life by bringing theory
into unison with practice but to use theory's critical capacities to
increase the domain of ethical consensus both inside and outside the
nation-state. This is to be accomplished, according to the evaluative
political realist, by expanding the role of democratic practices,
tolerance, civic friendship and the common good. Once we give up
the stultifying scepticism of positivist-empiricism to the effect that
we have no basis for cognitively comprehending how this is to be
done, the philosophical anxieties which force us to oscillate between
utopian transformation and uncritical approbation of the status quo
would evaporate. To be sure, evaluative political realism shares with
positivist-empiricism the idea that theory is, in some sense, a critical
tool; but it denies the instrumentalistic restriction on the human
capacity to discriminate ends into better or worse. It shares with
emancipatory international relations the thought that theory's
purpose is to achieve moral/practical ends; but it denies that theory
can eliminate itself through collective transcendental emancipation.

Theory, on this view, cannot simply be subsumed under practice; but neither can practice be deduced from theory in the way in which a particular instance of a physical law can be logically deduced from a statement of that law. For the evaluative political realist, it would be better to say that theory and practice are in constant tension with one another. On the one hand, theory is required because all political orders need critical assessments of their form of life. On the other hand, theory, conceived hyperbolically, could destroy the very foundations of practices not only in terms of which individuals and communities define themselves but also in terms of which ethical activity constitutes a form of knowledge. So practice requires independent status to constrain theory and to shape intelligible action. Evaluative political realism thinks we ought to hold on to the theory-practice tension and allow *phronesis* to mediate between them. In accepting this understanding of theory and practice, we might begin to see how we can still be realists and yet conceive the genuine possibility of an expanding moral consensus which brings more and more independent nation-states into civic relations with one another, reducing the prospect of war and the abhorrent widening of the gap between rich and poor nations. Still, the world as a whole contains communities representing such radically diverse values that our realism obliges us to concede that no conception acceptable to all of them can be constructed. In the face of this stark fact, no order of states in international politics can claim moral legitimacy; we must content ourselves with less. In particular, we must, so far as the evaluative political realist is concerned, encourage the slow process of moral legitimacy within states and the guarded hope that through the gradual spread of a cognitive conception of morality (see chapter 8 below) that law and order among states will increase. But all this needs to be done in the light of possible moral recidivism, of the possibility of moral and political tyranny and even of the possibility of a substantial net contraction of moral legitimacy in the world. There are no guarantees of human progression *sub specie aeternitatis*.

Now having said something about how theory and practice is understood in evaluative political realism, we need to examine the theoretical assumptions embedded in this conception and show how they differ from assumptions in rival conceptions. And we shall try to accomplish this by describing and defending a realist conception of the state and state-system.

5 State and state-systems in evaluative political realism

Peut-on vraiment parler de système internationale?
Philosophie et relations internationales Philippe Braillard

Introduction

In *Man the State and War* Kenneth Waltz writes: 'So fundamental are man, the state, and the state system in any attempt to understand international relations that seldom does an analyst, however wedded to one image entirely overlook the other two. Still, emphasis on one image may distort one's interpretation of the others.'[1] Although Waltz' use of the word 'image' delivers some unfortunate non-cognitive overtones, he is, nonetheless, fundamentally correct in underlining the importance of wheeling our conception of man, the state and state system into coherent line with one another at the very outset of our reflections on these subjects. Reserving our discussion of *Homo sapiens* for the next chapter, we shall focus our attention here on the state-system and the state and enunciate our first thesis for a revised and refurbished political realism.

> THESIS ONE: The state-system and the state are sortal concepts which give objectivity to international relations by virtue of the state's essential property of external sovereignty.

Thesis One stands in marked contrast with two competing metaphysical assumptions which underpin alternative conceptions of international relations from within emancipatory international relations and positivist-empiricism.

For classical Marxism (paradigmatically 'emancipatory' in our terms) there is no such thing as an 'essential property' since the world is constituted, ultimately speaking, of matter in motion: matter is the ultimate reality in space and in time. Positivist-empiricist theories of international relations hold, on the other hand, that only what is possibly observable by human beings can have ontological standing. The very idea of giving ontological place to what cannot be observed by us makes no sense to empiricists. Evaluative political realism, on the other hand, attempts to occupy a third position, *viz.*, the place which holds that a certain moderate form of essentialism is true. This view rejects the anti-essentialist idea that necessity attaches only to the way things are described and not to the things themselves. Unlike materialist and empiricist rivals, evaluative political realism maintains that notions of identity, necessity, substance and the ultimate essences of things – the idiom of essentialism – are deeply relevant to central theoretical issues of international relations, that an essentialist vocabulary of sorts can, and should, be used to revitalise political realism.

For evaluative political realism, a great deal hangs on establishing the truth (or at least the approximate truth) of Thesis One. First, establishing Thesis One will enable realists to ground an historical state-system view of international relations. Defending such a position will not only assist in resisting an implausible Heracleitian understanding of change – 'constant and ubiquitous' in the words of one international theorist – which leaves no ontological room for persistence, continuity and things that cannot change without ceasing to exist but, more importantly, it will help evaluative political realism to sustain a sharp distinction between the realist's conception of historical state-systems and the empiricist's contrasting view.[2] Secondly, upholding Thesis One may help realists resist further depredations to the concept of sovereignty. Despite persistent attacks on the concept, the evaluative political realist claims that it is as vital to maintaining a tolerable international relations today as it was in the eighteenth century. And thirdly, Thesis One, if sustained, will help realists to re-establish the eroding distinction between international and domestic politics. In the last few decades, anti-political realists – whether as functionalists, neofunctionalists, transnationalists, neoliberals, constructivists (or whatever) – have denied that there are any centrally important differences between domestic and international politics. Thesis One, however, moves in the opposite direction in implying a strong distinction between the two domains via the concepts of the state-system and the state (linked in a certain way). In so doing, Thesis

One will help to demarcate the field of international politics from other disciplines.

Process-analytic vs. historical state-systems

What a difference a system makes

In the recent study of international relations, the role of such central concepts as 'state' and 'system' have been the subject of numerous and often conflicting interpretations. A number of positivist-empiricists – Modelski, Burton, Nye and Keohane, Deutsch, Singer, Zinnes, Vasquez, Haas (among others) – have proclaimed the declining importance of 'the state' by drawing attention to certain 'system', 'structural-functional', and 'regime formation' trends, notably the erosion of traditional national boundaries, the blurring of the dividing line between domestic and international politics, and the ineffectiveness of government in many critical areas of policy. I shall call such theorists 'process-analytic system theorists'. Process-analytic systems theory embodies a standpoint in terms of which we are urged to conceive of world politics as comprising a whole range of societal systems – some basically economic, others fundamentally scientific, cultural or ideological – which have little or no relation to state boundaries, sovereignty or any other features of a traditionally realist understanding of international politics. Notwithstanding vigorous internal disagreements among proponents of this sort of perspective, there are nonetheless two central ideas which process-analytic systems theorists share: first, that there are no essential relations between the parts and the whole constituting any system and second, that our conceptual schemes for articulating the reality of world politics are relative to our interests and convenience and, in any event, largely arbitrary in the determinations they make. According to evaluative political realism, both these claims are false. But before we show this, let us say more about what process-analytic systems theory consists of.

The starting point for process-analytic systems theory is, as one would anticipate in a theory derived from positivist-empiricism, epistemological. As Dina Zinnes asks: 'how, in concrete operational terms, are we to know a system when we see one?'[3] We are told that the 'first prerequisite' of the study of systems and their changes is 'the ability to identify an international system', and Zinnes seems to think that this question presupposes an answer to the prior question: 'What is the meaning of the concept "international system"?'[4] For the evaluative political realist, one does not ask for the 'meaning' of 'international system'; indeed, this question is bound up with an empiricist semantics which needs to be replaced by a realist view according to which referring is thinking about this or that object in the world. This view also involves identifying actual exemplars which fall under the rubric of 'system' and the principles which allow theorists to individuate those exemplars. I shall indicate more fully in a moment what this entails and why it is of more than passing importance.

Process-analytic systems theory also involves an ontological commitment to the idea that our ordinary, middle-sized physical objects, bodies, artefacts of social objects are all events or processes which are in constant flux, subject to innumerable internal and external changes upon which it is impossible to put substantive limitations. On this view, all such objects are really processes: even trees, mountains and animals are, more or less, slow processes. There are no natural obstacles to change and transformation: states and state-systems are just part of the constant flow of events and processes. Although Heraclitus is the ancient source of this view, it gets support in our time from Alfred North Whitehead according to whom 'the real actual things that endure are all societies'.[5] Whitehead rejected the Aristotelian doctrine of substance and in its place he tried to establish the view that all relations are occasions or the patterned recurrence of experiences each with its own uniquely subjective form. Such occasions (which include objects and events) are nothing but patterns of relation to other occasions. If we look at the internal structure of an occasion, according to Whitehead, we do not find substance, we find process. The process is creative and its principal task is, as regards the social order, to move us inexorably from what Whitehead called 'the personal order' to the 'wider social order'.[6] The process involves several phases of integration which Whitehead described in great detail in *Process and Reality* and which, I suggest, would provide a strong metaphysical basis for the rejection of 'the state-centric view' of the state-system and its replacement by conceptions emphasising transnational processes and the like. We thus have a philosophical basis for the 'process' part of process-analytic systems theory.

The 'analytic' part refers to the commitment of such theorists to a semantics involving linguistic conventions, meaning postulates, framework principles, constitutive rules and so on. On this view, we need to replace all kind-terms with arbitrarily selected categories which constitute agreements for treating words as having a certain meaning. This is, in effect, nominalism, i.e. the view that it is through language that we group sets of particular objects and particular properties under some general heading which is, hopefully, precise and useful for quantification. The grouping itself is a disposition to respond in similar ways to stimuli perceived as similar due to the way our perceptual faculties sift the world. And the world itself is construed either as a particular or a complex of particulars in constant flux. Process-analytic systems theorists suppose that adopting such a view will yield a more fruitful conception of world politics than that which is to be found in any realist view. I shall now argue that we should reject process-analytic systems theory and accept instead the historical state-system view of international system.

Testing process-analytic systems theory

The central notion of 'systems', lies in the distinction between 'whole' and 'parts'. Suppose we apply the principle that, for any whole A, if A has B as one of its parts, then B is part of A in every possible world in which A exists. Then, if we replace the letter A with 'the international system' and the letter B with 'any arbitrary unit', what we would get as a yield is this: that in every international system the demise of any unit entails the demise of the international system. This is an extreme form of essentialism which scientific empiricists have rightly rejected; but this is not the form of essentialism which, as we shall see below, those committed to historical state-systems adopt or would adopt if they had a clear view of the alternatives. Moreover, scientific empiricists, in rejecting all forms of essentialism, have gone too far in the opposite direction of contending that there are no essential relations between the parts (paradigmatically sovereign states, international organisations, multinational corporations, etc., etc.) and the whole (the international system). For this commits process-analytic systems theory to the view that the international system could consist of any two things whatsoever, say, Deep Throat's larynx and a clay pipe. If process-analytic systems theory were correct, then *this* state-system could have been Deep Throat's larynx and a clay pipe – three things which are such that there is a possible world in which the first – *this* state-system – is made up of the second and third. Indeed, there could be infinitely many such possible worlds. In trying to imagine *this* state system, dating approximately from World War II, as being made up of

Deep Throat's larynx and a clay pipe, perhaps we try to think of them as they are, with all the particular features that they now happen to have. But if process-analytic systems theory is correct, then Deep Throat's larynx and the clay pipe could themselves have had parts entirely other than they have in fact. So the clay pipe could have been made up of a clay pipe and a piece of the Arc de Triomphe. So, in the indefinitely many possible worlds in which *this* state-system is made up of Deep Throat's larynx and a clay pipe, some of these would have been such that in them the clay pipe was made up of itself and a piece of the Arc de Triomphe, etc., etc.

It is difficult to imagine how God (or anyone else) could tell these worlds apart. Which are the worlds in which clay pipes are made up of a clay pipe and Deep Throat's larynx and which are the worlds in which they are made up of a clay pipe, a piece of the Arc de Triomphe and, say, a soap box? Note that if we follow the logic of the process-analytic systems theorist, we would have to say of a piece of the Arc de Triomphe and the soap box that they, too, could have been made up of other things. Hence, of those worlds in which the soap box is made up of Deep Throat's larynx and an old shoe, there will be those worlds in which Deep Throat's larynx is made up of a soap box and a piece of the Arc de Triomphe and something else and so on and so forth. Process-analytic systems theory appears to collapse right there into unintelligibility. For a system to be a system in any coherent and interesting sense, a certain part (or parts) would have to be necessary to it in such a way that in its absence the system would cease to exist. Hence, the claim that the identity and continuity of state-systems is a matter of the convenience of the international theorist rather than a matter of 'how the world is' need not – indeed better not – be countenanced. Let us turn now to contrast the process-analytic systems theorist view of systems with the historical state-system view.

Historical state-system view

The evaluative political realist finds great merit in the idea of an historical state-system, so brilliantly described by such redoubtable political realists as Martin Wight, R.S. Northedge, Hedley Bull, Adam Watson and Robert G. Wesson.[7] For the evaluative political realist understanding real systems – in contradistinction to those constructed empiricist systems that are generated by the dubious notion of symbolic mental representation – requires that we be able to trace a state-system's life history from origin to termination, if it has one, or from origin to present, if it does not. And this presupposes, in turn, that we have objects or entities (or something) that we can trace through temporal-spatial paths and that we can identify the persistence conditions for such entities. To be able to do this, we need to be able to take up an absolute understanding of identity. Thus, on this view, if x is the same as y, then x must be the same *something* as y.[8]

Evaluative political realists, in accepting the historical state-system view, differ from positivist-empiricists insofar as they follow the new realist theorists of reference in moving identity questions to the centre of theoretical concern.[9] So, for this sort of realist, when we use a concept to single out entities of interest to international relationists, the question will always arise concerning how we are to determine the identity conditions for these entities. To be sure, positivist-empiricists also raise the issue of identity. For example, Waltz asks: 'Given a wide variety of states, how can one call them "like units"?'[10] For Waltz, the identity problem is 'resolved' by stipulation. He writes: 'In defining a system's structure *one chooses* one or some of the infinite many objects comprising the system and defines its structure in terms of them. For international-political systems, as for any system, one must first *decide* which units to take as being parts of the system.'[11] Waltz' attempt to resolve the problem of identity via choosing a stipulative definition will not do.

In Waltz' approach to identity there does not seem to be any indication that what we say about 'like units' will depend crucially on what the units, objects or entities are. One wonders how one is supposed to take this conception of 'units'. Can we make any sense of a concept that is so general that it picks out nothing in particular? For example, what is it which determines whether international-political system Y at time t+1 is the same international-political system Y at earlier time t? From the historical state-system view, Waltz's term 'international-political system' fails to bring together specific examples by virtue of their resemblance. A similar analysis applies to Zinnes' concept of 'international system'. What, if anything, does it single out and how, in empiricist terms, does it perform this task? For Zinnes appears to want to apply the concept interchangeably to entities, units, the interactions of nations, variables and so on; but not to any particular entity. Whether the term is 'international-political system' or 'international system', such terms seem to operate as indeterminate space occupiers to denote all manner of entities just as the theorist pleases. To be sure, Waltz suggests *state* as the fundamental reference of 'unit', while Zinnes 'identifies' *nation* as the basic unit of the 'international system'; but such identifications are, and are meant to be, arbitrary. There is, on these views, no link whatever between theorist, concept and what is singled out by a theorist's conceptual capacities as basic or fundamental. For the evaluative political realist, on the other hand, international relations requires a conception of systems grounded in the idea of some *thing* persisting through change with which the mind can be in non-mysterious contact. On this alternative view, nothing has been singled out until something determinate has been singled out; and this, in turn, requires that we begin to take seriously the question of what it is for an object to count as an object which can be sorted. Let us see how this works and why it matters by referring to Table 5.1.

One may note that 'international political system' is only included in Table 5.1 as a 'possible sortal'. Process-analytic systems theorists have not deployed the concept, as evaluative political realists contend they should, to bring together specific examples that are grouped together by virtue of their resemblances. Nor has the concept been typically used to answer the central question of what its examplars have essentially in common which would warrant grouping them together. The problem is twofold: first 'international political system' picks out nothing determinate and so is in danger of picking out nothing at all. By contrast, 'historical state-system' picks out such determinate entities as the classical Indian state-system, the Chinese contending state-system, the Hellenistic state-system, the Western state-system and so forth. And 'state' – say in the world state-system of today – sorts the determinate entities *Paraguay, Nauru, Tanzania, Burkino Faso, France,* etc., etc. Since these terms pick out *something definite,* the historical state-system view would have to be regarded as epistemologically superior to any conception of systems which fails to do so. The second problem for any process-analytic system theorist is that the principle by which individuation of the term 'international political system' takes place, however, is not known. It is listed in Table 5.1, however, to mark an important point, namely, that international theorists have to face up to the ontological issue of whether entities exist or not. Whereas the empiricist attempts to bypass the issue by resorting to the dubious device of bringing entities into existence through construction, it is, for this new kind of realist, always an open question whether our concepts really do pick out the entities which they purport to pick out.

Political realism in international theory

Table 5.1 *Sortal concepts and historical state systems*

Sortal Concept	Types of Sortal	Use
International political system	Possible sortal	To individuate the international political system from other kinds of international entities, e.g. international cultural systems, international economic systems, etc., by virtue of a principle not yet known.
State-system	Indirect substantive sortal	To individuate kinds of state-systems, i.e. historical state-systems. This sortal cross-classifies to *states* whose essential property of external sovereignty tells us what the entity is, i.e. an organised collection of externally sovereign entities.
Classical Indian state-system; Sumerian state-system; Hellenistic state-system; Chinese contending state-system; Western state-system; World state-system; etc.	Restricted-historical sortal	To individuate types of state-systems in terms of specific spatial-temporal frameworks.
State	Substantive sortal	To individuate states, e.g. Athens and Sparta; Ch'u and Ch'en; France and Germany, etc., from non-state entities, e.g. mandated territories, exiled governments, political movements, etc., by virtue of their character as mixed natural and moral kinds whose one known essential property lies in their external sovereignty.
Nomocratic *vs.* teleocratic state.	Possibly restricted sortal	Possibly to individuate types of states in terms of their internal sovereignty and by virtue of a principle not yet known.

On this view, a theorist may be wrong to claim that a certain predicate individuates an entity from other entities: whether one is right or wrong is an empirical question. It would seem prudent, therefore, to regard 'international political system' as a 'possible sortal' whose capacity to individuate is to be decided by relevant experts when they have discovered the principle enabling them to do so.

The historical state-system theorist view is committed to the idea that systems and states are real objects which our natural language *individuates* or *sorts* so that historians are able to trace them as continuants. In contrast to the empiricist conception of meaning as stipulation, the historical state-system view deploys *sortal* concepts to mark off the boundaries of such real objects as states, nations, international organisations, non-governmental organisations and individuals from one another in a densely populated world of artefact, natural and moral kinds. The fundamental idea of a sortal term is that it supplies a principle for distinguishing and counting the particulars to which it applies; other general terms, while they may supply such principles, do so only for particulars already distinguished or distinguishable in accordance with some antecedent principle or method. With the notion of sortal concept in tow, an historian of state-systems can be confident that in taking up an objective viewpoint on the subject she will be tracing the same states and the same system of states from inception to demise. To be sure, the claim that state-system is a genuine sortal would have to be amplified and this would be accomplished, as envisaged by the evaluative political realist, by spelling out the activity that particular state-systems engage in. From historical work accomplished from within this perspective, we know that typical members of, say, the Western state system (in Europe roughly between the seventeenth century and World War I) conducted limited wars, shifted alliances to achieve a balance of power, increased their military capabilities *vis-à-vis* menacing neighbours and so on. This historical work would not, however, embody an adequate account of any particular historical state-system unless one could also supply some explication of what it is for a sortal to persist. That explication is provided, I claim, by providing an answer to the Aristotelian question *same what?* with respect to the state-systems that fall under the sortal.[12] But what, one may ask, is the answer to the Aristotelian *same what* question for historical state-systems? Unsurprisingly: *same states*. And what is it that the sameness of state, despite various changes of population, territory, constitution and so on, consists in? I shall argue that state has the

111

necessary property of being externally sovereign, that without this property *state*, and therefore indirectly *state-system*, would cease to exist. Once we have answered the Aristotelian *same what* question for the sortal and have traced the entity as an extension of the sortal through time, then we have settled the identity question for that entity.

Table 5.1 summarises some of these distinctions and pushes a bit further. According to the table there is a basic distinction between substantive sortals, on the one hand, and restricted-historical sortals, on the other. Although both kinds of sortal presuppose the identity of objects that fall under them, it is only the substantive sortal that answers the crucial *what is it?* question about an entity by giving its essential nature. Substantive sortals, therefore, might be said to have a privileged ontological position *vis-à-vis* restricted-historical sortals. These latter sortals only individuate their members in a specified temporal-spatial framework; they apply only to a certain phase or epoch in the history of the state-system. In the case at hand only *state-system* and *state* are sortals in the substantive sense. Of course, it is important to note an ontological difference between *state* and *state-system*. The latter substantive sortal is an indirect one in the sense that it applies both to historical state-systems and to particular named states; but it is only insofar as it applies to states indirectly by virtue of cross-classification that it can be deemed a substantive sortal at all. *State*, however, is a direct substantive sortal which individuates such entities as France, Fiji, Zambia, Thailand, etc. by virtue of its essential property of external sovereignty.

The historical state-system perspective, as adumbrated here, is, I believe, an extremely powerful one. Nonetheless, it is radically incomplete, for, as we have just seen, the validity of this conception turns on whether one can indeed show that the state has the essential property of being externally sovereign. This is the subject of the next sub-section.

Sovereignty and necessity

The place of sovereignty and state in recent international theory has been widely regarded as problematic. Some theorists have argued that the sovereign independence of the state is increasingly giving way to interdependence. From this perspective, sovereignty tends to be viewed as obsolete, or at the very most, as an idea that should be relegated to a distinctly secondary status in the current understanding and description of international relations. Vasquez sums up this attitude by noting that 'the geographical nation-state map of the world [does] not adequately capture the linkages and transactions that shape world society and are unaffected by state boundaries or notions of sovereignty'.[13]

Along somewhat different lines, Richard Ashley claims that the sovereignty discourse of political realism is a farrago of internal contradictions which can – and ought to be – deconstructed into textual/ global discourse.[14] And R.B.J. Walker dismisses the very idea of sovereignty as an artefact of the territorial state whose usefulness and reality have ended.[15] The very idea of sovereignty for more extreme anti-realists is either just plain myth or something, at the very least, that has to be 'radically demoted'.[16] Even those more sympathetic to classical versions of realism, e.g. 'utopian realists' who accept the existence of states, hold that states are withering and that sovereignty 'is disintegrating'.[17] For evaluative political realists, such views are egregiously theoretical: theory is used to depreciate sovereignty but fails to explain why sovereign states have continued to increase in number, and develop internally, right down to our own time. Evaluative political realists, by contrast, agree with Hedley Bull according to whom the essence of world politics today lies in 'the existence of independent political units acknowledging no political superior ... claiming to be sovereign...'[18] Despite persistent attacks on the very idea of sovereignty, the realist claims that it is as vital today as it was in the eighteenth century.[19] Although evaluative political realism recognises that rejection of state sovereignty often plays a capacious role in a larger political agenda, it holds that a failure to make certain important distinctions may also be at work. The most important of these distinctions is also due to Bull. He writes:

> On the one hand, states assert, in relation to this territory and population, what may be called internal sovereignty, which means supremacy over all other authorities within that territory and population. On the other hand, they assert what may be called external sovereignty, by which is meant not supremacy but independence of outside authorities.[20]

Bull's distinction between internal and external sovereignty is of vital importance. However, the evaluative political realist also contends that if realists in general are to resist the challenges of the anti-realist, this distinction needs to be understood within the context of a realist conception of the world. In particular, it has to be grounded in an understanding of necessity in terms of which our knowledge of the essential properties of an object constitutes empirical knowledge. This idea may seem dubious at first since it goes against the grain of the dominant Kantian idea, firmly rooted in positivist-empiricism, that all necessity is linguistic. The dubiety, however, has been reduced somewhat by virtue of some innovative ideas about modality developed by two American philosophers: Hilary Putnam and Saul Kripke. To grasp the bearing of their views one first needs to bring the traditional empiricist perspective on necessity into visibility.

According to traditional empiricism, all statements belong to one of two categories: (a) the analytic/*a priori*/necessary category or, alternatively (b) the synthetic/*a posteriori*/contingent category. And this will mean, of course, that for the empiricist all necessary truth will be analytic. On this view, the truth of analytic statements is held to be solely a function of their meanings; and these are obtainable by consulting dictionaries. Extra-linguistic reality is irrelevant to their truth. This, in turn, makes them necessarily true or necessarily false in all counterfactual situations or possible worlds. The truth of synthetic statements is held not to be completely determined by their meanings; hence, one needs to consult extra-linguistic reality. Their status would therefore be logically contingent in various possible worlds. An important consequence of this distinction is that statements of necessity, being merely verbal, are not about extra-linguistic reality. Necessary truth, on this view, applies only to language.

Although this empiricist view has long been accepted, a new realist theory of reference has made it quite problematic. Hilary Putnam, for example, has argued that 'once we have discovered the nature of water, nothing counts as a possible world in which water doesn't have that nature ... it isn't logically possible that water isn't H_2O'.[21] Saul Kripke has maintained a similar thesis regarding gold, claiming that if gold has the atomic number 79, then it necessarily has the microstructure of that atomic number.[22] On the Putnam/Kripke view, the necessity of claims such as 'Water is H_2O' lies in a combination of speakers' intentions and the contingent discovery that the entities ostended possess a physically significant microstructure. Moreover, the Putnam/Kripke view thoroughly undermines the empiricist distinction, alluded to above, according to which all necessary statements are analytic. One knows that necessarily all bachelors are unmarried if one knows the meaning of the relevant terms, on the empiricist view. But for the new theory of reference the modal status of statements is not at all automatic: sometimes statements about objects turn out to be necessary (as in 'Water is H_2O'); on other occasions they may turn out to be contingent. There may be a wealth of *essential properties* that things possess that we never dreamt of when we learned the meaning of the terms for those things. Necessary truth – and the correlative notion of essential properties – might lie in the world, to be discovered only *a posteriori*.

According to the evaluative political realist, we can apply this general result to Bull's distinction between external and internal sovereignty. Deploying the new realist theory of reference, evaluative political realists are prepared to say that since without external sovereignty France would cease to exist, external sovereignty is an essential property of France and every other state. An essential property of an object is the property that object must have to be the object that it is. And what property would that be for the object *the state of France* if not the property of being externally sovereign? To be sure, France has other properties – accidental properties such as the property of having citizens who speak a certain natural language, the property of having the highest per capita consumption of alcohol in the world, the property of having multinational corporations operate on its territory, etc., etc. – but its essential property is external sovereignty; for, unless there is a locus of ultimate decision which distinguishes one group of people from another, there can be no state.

If state equals external sovereignty in all circumstances in which we can imagine states to continue to exist, then the state is necessarily externally sovereign. Given this condition, it does not follow by ordinary logic alone that an essential property of an object holds of the object necessarily. However, if we allow the thesis of non-contingent identity, as I believe we should, and assume that *necessity* distributes over entailment, then it would indeed follow that a property essential to an existent holds of it necessarily. If this is correct, then it is patently absurd to hold that a state should exist and yet not be externally sovereign. Being externally sovereign is the only necessary property of a state; a state is nothing if not externally sovereign. To be sure, a lot more would need to be argued to accept this as a 'proof' of some sort since it depends on assumptions which we have made no real attempt to sustain here. Yet, it does provide a basis for accepting a long-held view about states and external sovereignty which should go some way towards dispelling the idea that the very idea of sovereignty is thoroughly obsolete and indefensible.

We can also sustain the idea of the necessity of the state's external sovereignty by considering necessity of origin. The idea of considering origins has long been associated with realist views. For example, F.S. Northedge summed up a chapter entitled 'Origins and Growth of the System' in *International Political System* with the following observation: 'We are concerned with the process of birth, not so much for its intrinsic historical interest, but as a means of defining what the international system is and what constitutes its principal properties.'[23] One reading of this passage is that the essence of the international system is grounded in the necessity of its origins.

Such an idea may be supported by applying Saul Kripke's notion of necessity of origin.[24] For just as Kissinger could not have come from a different sperm and egg from which he did come, so France – *this* France – could not have come from an origin different from its actual origin. Whatever France's origin turns out to be, it will be *that* origin necessarily. For suppose France to have come from a different origin, say, that of Sri Lanka. Consider a possible world in which this is the case. Then it is surely compossible with this supposition that in the same possible world France is co-present with that world and develops into what it is today. Which of these individuals, however, has the greater claim to be France? Clearly the latter individual since it offers a basis for understanding France as an entity identical to itself and its origin and therefore as a persisting object. But what is it to be a persisting object *vis-à-vis* other persisting objects at origin? If France's origins are necessary to France's being identical to itself and this is true of all other states as well, then the property which is common to all states at origin is their being physically separate and independent of one another, i.e. their external sovereignty.

The main reason for developing an essentialist basis for sovereignty is not to glorify the state, still less is it to ground a so-called 'state-centric' view of the international system. The purpose here is to provide a basis for treating the state as a moral agent which has obligations and is morally accountable for its actions. On the evaluative political realist view, states are distinct from one another and members of a moral community; they are moral persons. That is why it makes sense to regard states as having external sovereignty as an essential property; to be externally sovereign is to be a person with the power to act intentionally and thus to have duties and obligations. To be an agent that participates in morally accountable relationships for which they are responsible, one first has to be externally sovereign, i.e. an entity identifiably independent of other entities. In this sense external sovereignty involves actions which need not be ascribed to human beings alone. In ordinary language we often say of states: 'France believes that a Palestinian state should be created' or 'Cambodia ought to be free of foreign intrusion' or 'Italy desires a negotiated settlement in Somalia'. Intentional language is often used to describe and to predict the behaviour of collectives and so there would be nothing odd in associating it with the behaviour of states. Once we have established that the state is externally sovereign, then it would be possible to describe events involving, say, the United States, France, Nauru, Colombia, etc. as intentional actions. In doing so we shall be able to hold states responsible for what they do, whether they act in morally reprehensible or morally generous ways.

Internal sovereignty

Some theorists of international relations imply that external sovereignty is inextricably bound up with internal sovereignty. As Alan James marks the point: 'The one goes along with the other, and the absence of one means that the other is absent, too. Their intimate interdependence reflects the unitary nature of the sovereign condition.'[25] Evaluative political realists, however, resist attempts to articulate a completely general principle of internal sovereignty. Different constitutional forms have different and not necessarily commensurable values. Sometimes a constitutional form is evaluated in terms of the goals of a particular group and sometimes it is evaluated in terms of the fairness of its rules and procedures. Different types of constitutions may fit different ways of life in different environments depending upon the resources available, climate, the distribution of capacity in the territory and so forth. On this view, evaluative political realism is not committed to any view of internal sovereignty which involves attributing to all states a single overriding goal or purpose: the commitment is to pluralism not monism. Using Michael Oakeshott's analysis, the evaluative political realist thinks it illuminating to distinguish nomocratic political orders, characterised by non-instrumental, purpose-independent rules, and teleocratic political orders directed by the thought of actualising some overriding goal such as freedom or justice.[26] On the teleocratic view, history is immanently construed as a rational process in which the highest good can be realised. Historical ends serve as foci to bring together the actions of individuals, aggregating and collectivising them. History would then constitute a process where the synthesis of freedom and nature would occur. Understood in this way, the teleocratic political order would be endowed with an obvious moral superiority over any nomocratic political order; or, it would embody a process whose end-state would be logically constitutive of moral progress. At the end of the process there would stand a world community consisting of one single homogeneous state or, possibly, a world community of states of some sort. The comprehensive good for human beings, on this view, cannot be regarded as the satisfaction of private pleasures but is intimately bound up with the good of others. We are what we are by virtue of our membership in a community of shared meanings. Moreover, the political community, on this view, is not merely an aggregate of isolated individuals but is at least partially constitutive of what it is to be a human being. For the evaluative political realist, the very idea of a teleocratic political order in the sense described is thoroughly rebarbative of the way things are, or should be, in international politics. To partially justify this view it is useful to consider certain ideas developed by Robert Nozick in his brilliant and resourceful book, *Anarchy, State and Utopia*. Think, Nozick says, of the following list of names:

> Wittgenstein, Elizabeth Taylor, Bertrand Russell, Thomas Merton, Yogi Berra, Allen Ginsburg, Harry Wolfson, Thoreau, Casey Stengel, The Lubavitcher Rebbe, Picasso, Moses, Einstein, Hugh Hefner, Socrates, Henry Ford, Lenny Bruce, Baba Dam Dass, Gandhi, Sir Edmund Hillary, Raymond Lubitz, Buddha, Frank Sinatra, Columbus, Freud, Norman Mailer, Ayn Rand, Baron Rothchild, Ted Williams, Thomas Edison, H.L. Mencken, Thomas Jefferson, Ralph Ellison, Bobby Fischer, Emma Goldman, Peter Kropotkin, you and your parents.

With respect to this list of names, Nozick poses a series of highly pertinent questions:

> Is there really one kind of life which is best for each of these people? Imagine all of them living in any utopia you've ever seen described in detail. Try to describe the society which would be best for all these people to live in. Would it be agricultural or urban? Of great material luxury or of austerity with basic needs satisfied? What would relations between the sexes be like? Would there be any institution similar to marriage? Would it be monogamous? Would children be raised by their parents? Would there be private property? Would there be a serene secure life or one of adventures, challenges, dangers, and opportunities for hedonism? Would there be one, many, any

religion? How important would it be in people's lives? Would people view their life as importantly centred about private concerns or about public action and issues of public policies? Would they be single-mindedly devoted to particular kinds of accomplishments and work or jacks-of-all trades and pleasures or would they concentrate on full and satisfying leisure activities? Would children be raised permissively, strictly? What would their education concentrate upon? Will sports be important in people's lives (as spectators, participants)? Will art? Will sensual pleasure or intellectual activities predominate? Or what? Will there be fashions in clothing? Will great pains be taken to beautify appearance? What will the attitude towards death be? Would technology and gadgets play an important role in society? And so on.

Nozick's comments are pertinent and incisive:

> The idea that there is one best composite answer to all these questions, one best for everyone to live it, seems to me an incredible one. (And the idea that, if there is one, we now know enough to describe it is even more incredible.)[27]

Now consider the following list of states:

> India, Norway, Burkino Faso, Nauru, Pakistan, Greece, Vanuatu, Paraguay, Lesotho, Fiji, El Salvador, Finland, Libya, Chile, Suriname, Kenya, Israel, Guatemala, Nigeria, Afghanistan, Djibouti, Iraq, Western Samoa, United States of America, Yugoslavia, The United Arab Emirates, Turkey, St. Christopher-Nevis, South Africa, Panama, Nepal, Antigua, Malta, Laos, Haiti, Belgium, Bangladesh, Iran, your own state and that of your parents and grandparents.

Don't Nozick's questions, appropriately adjusted for the life history of states, apply *a fortiori* to any proposed community of states? Isn't it just as incredible to imagine that there is one best composite answer to the question of 'how states should live' than for how individuals should live in their communities? As with the case of individuals, we are also faced here with the epistemological issue of how we could even conceive of acquiring enough information about states and the state-systems in which they act to propose a common overriding goal for both. In its place the evaluative political realist proposes that we accept the idea that states now, and in the future will continue to, seek a diversity of 'goods' which we have little reason to believe can be fully integrated and harmonised with one another. For the goods which the evaluative political realist sees as being advanced by political orders are such diverse ones as a life of self-mastery, self-expression, active pursuit of knowledge, a willingness to accept moral responsibility, a concern for human flourishing (especially of the neighbour one knows and respects) and so forth. Surely, we have no reason to think that these goods (and many more) can be unified into a single overriding end or purpose. And if this cannot be made a reasonable goal, then the task of the statesperson, as realist, will remain as it has been in the past, namely, to make judgements and to undertake actions for the good of the community both in their individual and collective capacities; and most importantly, to mediate the differences between individual and collective goods when they stand, as they so often do in international relations, in irreconcilable conflict. This points up a crucial difference in realist and anti-realist views of the state.

For the evaluative political realist, the state would point to possibilities of, and promote work towards, reconciliation between conflicting groups within society. The nomocratic state's role, then, would be to try to ensure that group differences did not become irreconcilable. But could this role be carried out if in the name of change – a change to what we cannot really describe fully – constant intervention from outside powers is considered a right, presupposed by the notion of change itself? And could this task of the state be achieved in the face of constant intrusions from other cultures embodying radically different historical experiences viewed from the perspective of radically different sovereign forms? Affirmative answers to these questions would certainly strain our credulity. And so the evaluative political realist believes it appropriate to support the 'older' political realist's resistance to attempts to transform the world into a global order without boundaries of authority and purpose. What we are left with, tragically perhaps, is a pluralist world of evolutionary change involving political dilemmas, moral conflicts, disruptions, instability, hard compromises – all constrained and restricted by the thought that 'the state is externally sovereign' is a necessary truth.

Implications of the historical state-system view

We shall explore two implications of the historical state-system view which we have been elucidating, extending and justifying:

    (i) The dominance of the state-system by the state; and
    (ii) The avoidance of ontological reductionism.

The grounding of the historical state-system view in the essentiality of

the external sovereignty of the state helps to sustain the realist understanding of 'international systems' as systems which are paradigmatically dominated by the activities of states. Other institutions do have
roles to play, but there seems no escape from the idea that since the
very existence of state-systems depends on the continued existence of
states within them, realists need no longer shrink from their commitment to a state-dominated understanding of world politics. To be sure,
from the fact that states are, and ought to be, the primary focus of
international relations, it does not at all follow that the international
stage is not peopled by other sorts of actors. However, as long as there
are state-systems dominated by the activities of states that are necessarily externally sovereign, we would seem to have a strong basis for
expecting state-systems to exhibit certain characteristic features. First,
we should expect state-systems to be dominated by security concerns.
Since state-systems have states as their essential members and states'
external sovereignty consists in maintaining independence from other
states and institutions, we should expect states to be vigorous in
protecting themselves against encroachment by their neighbours.
When each state has external sovereignty necessarily, each state has to
be prepared to use force to maintain its territorial integrity. However
banal it may be to restate the point, security is a primary characteristic
of states. Secondly, we would also expect some sort of mechanism such
as the balance of power to be a prominent feature of any state-system's
general activity. Since there is always the possibility of the strongest
power in the system 'rolling up' the rest, thereby threatening the very
existence of the state system and the states that depend upon it, one
would expect weaker states to form alliances to protect themselves
against stronger states. Thirdly, in a state-system dominated by states
whose external sovereignty is a necessary feature of what they are, we
should anticipate seeing a large degree of consistency in the actions of
the states themselves. Whether states are monarchical, socialist, Shi'ite,
democratic, or whatever, *raison d'état* can be expected to reign supreme
and ideology, though significant, will be of secondary concern. De-
clarations to the contrary notwithstanding, states can be expected to
act to protect their interests, their ways of life, their customs and their
cultures.

The historical state-system view also offers up the prospect both of
avoiding a radically implausible atomistic reductionism and of not
succumbing to the blandishments of radical holism. Atomistic reductionism is the view that every manifestable piece of human behaviour

is a causally determined outcome of the existence of a finite number of events over which the individual has no control. Atomistic reductionism is a very crude form of the *genre* and Waltz' famous polemical attack on it appears warranted.[28] It does not follow, however, that we must accept the kind of radical deterministic holism embodied in Waltz' account of system in which individuals are construed, whether expressly or not, as total prisoners of systemic structures. The historical state-system view adheres, contrary to Waltz, to a form of methodological individualism which nonetheless manages to avoid reductionism. To be a reductionist, it is at least necessary to hold that commitments expressed in one kind of vocabulary and which give rise to certain metaphysical, epistemological or linguistic problems can be avoided by employing a different kind of vocabulary – the reduced vocabulary. The historical state-system theorist is not at all a reductionist in this sense. He does not hold a positive theory which says in effect 'let us reduce all social vocabulary to individualist vocabulary'. The historical state-system view, as analysed here, holds rather that the debate between methodological collectivists and methodological individualists can be resolved by using the notion of sortal concepts. Such sortal concepts as *state-system* and *state* individuate real objects: we can describe them, trace their life-histories and analyse their impact on international affairs. Nonetheless, it does not follow from this that we can treat social objects such as the Western state-system and France as 'over and above' human beings. In fact, nothing whatever follows from claims about the existence of social objects that would help to sustain the thesis of methodological collectivism that all social objects can, in principle, be potentially harmonised with one another if we take up a suitably configured holistic viewpoint. In effect, the historical state-system view says that the identity conditions of entities are determined by what the entity is, and since state-system and state sort different entities, they will have different principles of activity associated with them that will constitute formidable barriers to any projects for their integration.

To appreciate the historical state-system view, one needs to distinguish it from the more orthodox methodological individualist position which holds that only individuals are real. Some 'older' realists expressed just such a viewpoint. For example, there is Herbert Butterfield's worry that 'certain basic ideas, such as that of "the state", tend to be puffed up, so that they acquire the dignity of philosophical concepts and eternal verities. When we use words like "the state", "society", or "Germany", it is safest to remember that, in the last resort, they represent just so many people.'[29] In the historical state-system view, Butterfield's position, though not without merit, is misleadingly expressed. For one thing, a state may act to form commitments which are authoritatively independent of the views of any 'representative' or group of people. For another thing, a state may, without implying methodological collectivism, certainly have interests which go beyond the personal interests of individual representatives. The idea of sortal concepts helps us to put claims concerning state interests in the right perspective by construing them initially as ontological questions dependent on our capacity to individuate objects in the world. By treating state-system and state as sortal concepts which pick out (when they do) continuing objects in the world, the historical state-system view can render these objects their ontological due without exaggerating their moral significance – that is, without 'puffing them up' and giving them a morally privileged position of some kind.

Support for this general perspective is to be found independently in Pettit and McDonald's *Semantics and Social Sciences*.[30] The authors concede what needs to be granted to methodological collectivism while nonetheless maintaining that methodological individualism is fundamentally correct. In particular, Pettit and McDonald accept the validity of the claim which many methodological collectivists have pressed against their opponents, *viz.*, that it is logically permissible to refer to groups (e.g. tribes, cities, nations, states, etc.) since doing so enables social scientists 'to express truths that we could not express just by reference to individuals'.[31] We have already stated above that it is important to be able to refer to states as persons – indeed *moral* persons because we want to be able to hold states morally responsible for their actions. However, this does not entail any form of methodological collectivism as traditionally understood. Pettit and McDonald refer to this form of the methodological collectivist's claim as 'the expressive autonomy of institutions'.[32] It is a claim consistent with the idea of sortal concepts, for the methodological collectivist thesis denies the view of those who hold that anything that can be said by referring to groups can equally well be said, if only at greater length, by referring to people who make up these groups. By means of this concession, Pettit and McDonald distance their position from untenable forms of methodological individualism.

Despite this concession, Pettit and McDonald insist – quite rightly from the point of view of historical state-systems – that there is an important sense in which institutions such as the state are not autonomous; that is, that terms referring to institutions do not, according to Pettit and McDonald, increase our 'explanatory resources'.[33] Such terms, though they may be employed, are not necessary when providing causal explanations of events. On this view, the fact that we are able to say more by talking about institutions is not as important as the fact that we are not able to explain more by doing so. The methodological implication of this is 'that nothing on the social front is explicable in any way if it is not capable of being individualistically explained',[34] a view consistent with the general tenor of Butterfield's remarks above and with commonsense realism. If this view is correct, then the historical state-system theorist will be able to accept the idea that our talk of state and state-system is logically legitimate and enriching without having to accept the deterministic holist's thesis that we must explain activity in international relations by providing macro accounts of social phenomena. For the historical state-system theorist, macro accounts would have to be supplemented by explanations which render social events individualistically intelligible.

One upshot of this analysis is that it will help to sustain the views of 'older' realists concerning the nature of historical explanation. On this view, we render historical accounts intelligible not by providing a macro-level explanation but by providing more individual detail. This view is represented, for example, by Herbert Butterfield who wrote:

> In the last resort the historian's explanation of what happened is not a piece of general reasoning at all. He explains the French Revolution by discovering exactly what it was that occurred; and if at any point we need further elucidation all that he can do is to take us into greater detail, and make us see in still more definite concreteness what really did take place.[35]

Echoes of this view may be found in Michael Oakeshott's *Experience and Its Modes* wherein it is claimed that 'the method of the historian is never to explain by means of generalisation but always by means of greater and more detail'.[36] And G.R. Elton argues in *The Practice of History* that history deals with datable events and not with laws or generalisations as such.[37] Since process-analytic systems theorists manifestly do not offer such accounts, their accounts are, from the point of view presented here, ontologically suspect.

Conclusion

In the early sections of this chapter, I argued that the evaluative political realist's conception of theory and practice as constituting a tension is superior to alternative conceptions. I then went on to argue in favour of a realist understanding of state-system and state, though on far more abstract grounds than is customary among realists. The main reason for the high abstraction is that the anti-realist challenge requires that we push the level of argument up to the point where salient differences make themselves perspicuous. The content of the abstract argument, in its dual reliance on sortal concepts and a certain moderate form of essentialism, shows that there is *au fond* a vast gulf between realism and anti-realism concerning state and state-system. This difference has been largely ignored owing to a pervasive tendency in the discipline to avoid 'philosophical' arguments. There seems to be a strongly held anti-philosophical belief that debates between realists and anti-realists are essentially vacuous, irrelevant both to the practice of international politics and to its theoretical, i.e. scientific development. This idea owes a good deal of its inspiration to a Humean and positivistic distrust of metaphysics and is backstopped by the repeated insistence that international relations must help to resolve the pressing problems of the world. But one of the most important spin-offs of this pervasive idea, process-analytic systems theory, has been a marked failure; its claims have been excessive, generally hollow and are now generally ignored. The idea that there may be general laws of systems from which one may eventually derive laws or significant generalisations useful for prediction increasingly appears to be the scientistic fantasy which political realists have always claimed it to be. By contrast, a striking feature of the historical state-system view lies in its theoretical modesty. Unlike general systems theory, this view asserts no desire to discover the general theory of systems from which laws pertaining to the international system may be derived. Unlike Morton Kaplan's version of systems – comparative systems – it does not claim to provide an 'explanation sketch' of change in the international system.[38] Unlike Waltz, it does not claim to provide a structural model 'useful' for explanation at the macro level. Unlike Richard Rosecrance, it does not claim to be able to discover the conditions of stability for an entire historical epoch. In comparison with such grandiose claims, those advanced by historical state-system theorists might appear to be laughingly modest. The historical state-system view claims that state is essentially externally sovereign; it claims that it is possible in principle for the historian to trace the life-history of time-differentiated but identical units. To some critics it might seem retrograde (and indeed immodest) to employ the vocabulary of substance, essence and kinds to defend the historical state-system view in international politics. My response is simply that I know of no other way to bring out the necessity that exists in the world and, in particular, in world politics. The claim that the state is necessarily externally sovereign rests upon the state being such that it is impossible to envisage it having any property whatever unless it has that property. If there were no necessity to a state's sovereignty *vis-à-vis* other states, the persistence of arbitrarily good exemplars (e.g. France, Nigeria, Singapore, etc.) through time would be quite inexplicable.

In this chapter, I have tried to spell out why I believe an appeal to essences is indispensable to a true understanding of realism and its distinctively different understanding of the world, as that is discernible, in particular, in the historical state-system view of international politics. But having described the evaluative political realist's conception of state and state-system, we must now show how it 'fits' with our second thesis, that is, a theoretical conception of human nature which is distinctively different from the thin theory of the self offered by the positivist-empiricist.

6 Evaluative political realism and human nature

> However much I may trust my neighbour I am averse to putting myself completely at his mercy.
>
> Lord Cherwell, adviser to Winston Churchill

Introduction

> Square held human nature to be the perfection of all virtue, and that vice was a deviation from our nature, in the same way as deformity of the body is. Thwackum, on the contrary, maintained that the human mind, since the Fall, was nothing but a sink of iniquity, till purified and redeemed by Grace.[1]

It would be difficult to improve upon Henry Fielding's description as a summary of the terms in which 'idealists' and 'realists' have attempted to shape the concept of human nature for international theory. According to idealists (in their stereotypical form anyway), human beings are fundamentally benevolent and generous by nature; their capacity for moral improvement and an expanding altruism know no constraining limit. The exponents of this position – the position of Square – will readily admit that people often act in selfish ways. Even Kant, who is regarded (somewhat unfairly) as the representative of the idealist view *par excellence*, allows that human selfishness manages to insinuate itself into situations which call for altruism and benevolence; but for idealists this selfish behaviour is to be accounted for by bad social conditions, or institutions which bring economic pressures of a dehumanising sort to bear on people, or which otherwise alienate them from others. Once people have been freed from the artificial conditions and false values of our present social structures and institutions, their innate altruism and love of one another will come to the fore.

Traditionally, the 'cash' value of the idealist's conception of human nature for the study of international politics has been directed to devising notional social structures which would permit the continual enlargement of the other-regarding capacities of human beings and their altruistic propensities. It hardly needs pointing out that there are many international relationists who accept, or otherwise presuppose, this picture of human nature and its consequences for understanding international relations, despite various qualifications and the changing fashion in which the details of the picture have been filled out.

By the seemingly inevitable contrast, we have the traditional realist position – the position which Thwackum represents in a somewhat extreme form – according to which human beings are radically selfish and lust for power regardless of the consequences for others. The exponents of this perspective will grant that people sometimes appear to act in unselfish ways but this, they say, is only a smoke-screen; behind the outward show lies the incurably selfish individual driven in a vainglorious waste of power-lust in action. The excessive quantity of sheer self-concern which permeates all human relationships points up the overriding need for social organisations – and in particular the state – whose most compelling task is to achieve some sort of control, however uneasy and temporary, over the individual's assertive selfishness. Thomas Hobbes (not so unfairly) is often regarded as the most distinguished representative of this school of thought. One consequence of such thinking is the familiar power-dominated emphasis on military security, state sovereignty and *raison d'état*.

If this were the full story of the debate between idealists and realists, we would certainly be well advised to follow Kenneth Thompson in passing 'beyond' idealism and realism, even though such action might risk giving aid and comfort to those who think that all debates between Squares and Thwackums, idealists and realists, Marxists and anti-Marxists, postmodernists and their detractors, are empty of content and unproductive – indeed quite thoroughly misconceived.[2] Given such a backcloth, however, we need to raise two questions. First, is there a concept of human nature which encompasses some common universal traits that may play a fundamental role in accounting for certain features of international relations? Second, is there a view of human nature which, though it avoids resonating the heavy moralising so salient in the Square-Thwackum debate, nonetheless leaves room for ethics and morality in its conception of international relations? This chapter contends that we can answer both these questions in the affirmative if we bring certain naturalistic facts about human beings (qualified in important ways) into contact with a certain understanding of persons. On this sort of realist view – an evaluative political realist view – biologically based facts about human beings are only part of what is required for understanding international relations; we also need a concept of the human being which is not biological, namely, a concept of the person (or self) as a moral agent with a point of view on the world. Whereas biologically based facts wait upon empirical science to uncover the characteristic features of *Homo sapiens*, the concept of the person already contains within it the raw materials which constitute what it is. This leads straightaway to our second thesis for a refurbished form of political realism.

> THESIS TWO: Human nature consists of two components
> (related in a certain way): animal and person.

That political realists have been traditionally committed to *some* concept of human nature will hardly come as a surprise to international relationists familiar with the writings of Thucydides, St Augustine, Machiavelli and Hobbes, or of such modern realists as Morgenthau, Butterfield, Niebuhr and Isaiah Berlin. In particular, international relationists may well be familiar with this famous statement by Morgenthau: 'Human nature, in which the laws of politics have their roots, has not changed since the classical philosophies of China, India, and Greece endeavoured to discover these laws.'[3] It should also be noted that Herbert Butterfield devoted an entire chapter of *Christianity and Politics* to the notion of human nature, and that Reinhold Niebuhr regretted the 'excessively optimistic estimates of human nature' with which the 'democratic credo' had been associated.[4] Isaiah Berlin, a profoundly important realist, went far towards summing up the traditional realist view when he wrote that the 'ideas of every philosopher concerned with human affairs in the end rest on his conception of what man is and can be'.[5] For many years, this realist view was dismissed as philosophical speculation rather than scientific fact; but recent scientific research in evolutionary biology and cognate disciplines, coupled with the increasingly evident failure of positivist-empiricism to achieve its self-declared goals, suggest the need to re-evaluate this judgement. In pursuing this route I am fully aware that certain feminist theories of international relations (among other) regard appeals to biologically based facts as manifestations of patriarchical thinking of precisely the sort which feminism needs to overcome. There is merit in this complaint and I argue below that if we conceptualise the relationship between the biological and non-biological correctly, we can obviate the difficulty. According to the evaluative political realist, we can – and should want to – avoid the sort of robust naturalism which evokes the complaint in the first place. On the other hand, we cannot legitimately construct a conception of human beings which transcends the biological altogether. More about this below.

The idea of a common human nature has, of course, an ancient lineage; it is bound up with some deep philosophical questions concerning rationality and change. Plato and Aristotle both believed in a common human nature and located it in human rationality. Although they recognised that what human beings observe is constantly changing, they also held that there is a limit and an order to these changes. Plato had one way of explaining this limit and order, but the difficulties of relating everything to forms is too well-known to rehearse here. Aristotle avoided Plato's difficulty by introducing the concept of a 'final cause' – that for the sake of which things happen. What makes the idea of a final cause so ingenious is that it allows for a distinction between the human and the non-human within a single order of nature; nonetheless, the idea of final causes is itself problematic and arguably not recoverable from the wreckage of defunct and discredited teleological theories of nature. So the problem for evaluative political realists may be described as how, in eliminating the metaphysics of final causes, they can carve out a conception of themselves and the species to which they belong in which they participate in the natural order of things but without such participation leading to a reductive naturalism which has no place for the concept of human beings as rational persons.

I shall argue that the route to such a conception requires the idea of the human being as a biological entity and a mental symbol-using being with moral status, i.e. a person. Notwithstanding the threat of reductionist scientific naturalism, we can no longer reasonably accept an understanding of international theory and practice which attempts to transcend biology. Competition is real; kinship, if understood as rooted in certain biological imperatives, imposes special claims on human beings; war, insofar as it is bound up with biological needs, is likely to remain a persistent feature of international politics, and altruism will, quite probably, often take the 'low' biological form of reciprocal altruism. On the other hand, there is strong evidence to show that human beings show affection towards members of their group, especially to children, have no particular inclination to kill others, not even 'hostile' strangers, and are inclined to cooperate with other members of their species (as well as with other species) on a range of activities. These 'insights' from ethology and evolutionary biology will help in the effort to re-establish contact with nature (as understood by the Greeks, e.g. in opposition to mechanism) and with human beings as a natural kind. It is equally important, however, that these ineliminable natural features of *Homo sapiens* not lend themselves to some reductionist thesis of the sort to be found in some versions of biopolitics and 'pop sociobiology'. For another feature of human beings – also ineliminable – is that they are persons and as such endowed with moral agency as well as certain capacities of deliberation and choice. They are self-focusing beings engaging in what Charles Taylor calls 'strong evaluations' of one another's moral and political activity.[6]

The strategy of this chapter will be to outline a view of human nature consisting of two components: animal and person. The aim is to establish that we can combine naturalistic facts from biology and a philosophical concept of the person to yield a non-reductionist, yet coherent, conception of human beings. To be sure, the end result of the argument will not be to determine the 'essence' of human nature, whatever that might come to, but rather to develop a contextual understanding of the subject that helps us to make contact with a range of issues and problems relevant to international relations.

The animal component view of human nature

Avoiding extremes

For the evaluative political realist, acquiring a proper conception of *Homo sapiens* entails assiduously avoiding two extremes: constructivism and naturalism. Constructivism – whether in the form of logical positivism, existentialism or postmodernism – refuses to recognise that the human being *is* a natural kind and, like other natural kinds, has palpably real properties discoverable by natural science. On the other hand, naturalism – at least in its extreme forms – refuses, quite wrongly, to countenance facts about personality, of what it is to be a person, in contrast to an animal, endowed with certain psychological needs and capacities that have to be satisfied in certain ways if human beings are to flourish. For the evaluative political realist, constructivism and naturalism represent failures to see that there are two sortal concepts at work here. To identify a human being as *an animal* is to say of it that it has evolved according to the principles of natural selection; that it is vertebrate, mammal and a member of the order primate; that there is both continuity and non-continuity between it and non-human animals; and that there may be certain limits which being a member of the natural kind *Homo sapiens* puts on the possibility of achieving certain political communities. By contrast, to identify something as *a person* is to judge that the entity has reasons, sensations and emotional states which permit it to engage in certain psychological and moral relations with others of its kind, that human beings are innovative and creative beings whose relations with one another need to be guided by friendship and community. To say that something is a person is to say of it that it can hold values, adopt plans about its life and that it has rights.[7] To avoid naturalism and constructivism we require both these sortal concepts, keeping in mind that one and the same thing can be an instantiation of different sortal concepts. In what follows I shall first describe some of the central features of *the animal component view of human nature*.

According to this view, members of the natural kind *Homo sapiens* have internally based, i.e. culturally and genetically mediated, tendencies to be in cooperative competition with other members of their kind. By cooperative competition I mean that animal groups have been genetically and culturally selected to cooperate with human beings with regard to certain tasks and under certain conditions and to compete with them with regard to certain other relations. In the former category we would list hunting and gathering, agricultural production, bringing up children, grooming and so on. In the competitive category we would list competition for females, food, shelter, and agonistic behaviour to potentially aggressive foreigners.[8] Cooperative competition, and the ever present potential for conflict which goes along with it, has survived because it has been evolutionarily successful. Evolutionary theory tells us that natural selection – whatever the ultimate mechanisms which create it – produces differential survival and reproduction. Since human resources are finite and since each individual is naturally inclined to produce as many descendants as possible, some considerable competition, even in the midst of expanding cooperative behaviour, will be selected for. On this view, human beings will tend to use their positions of wealth, power and prestige to produce more progeny and hence will be self-compelled to compete with other conspecifics for a finite set of resources. Even when human beings are cooperating with others, their putatively unselfish behaviour may often be self-advantageous. For the evaluative political realist, this way of giving content to the idea of a common human nature has certain distinct advantages.

First of all, in its unmistakable insistence on a scientifically based understanding of human nature this view avoids, as some older theories of human nature did not, the drawbacks of a theory grounded in a philosophy of psychological egoism. According to the usual version of such a philosophy, all human beings are *motivated* to act in terms of their self-interest, however much they may appear to do otherwise. But however attractive such a theory might have been to 'older' realists, psychological egoism is conceptually befuddled and will not bear critical examination. Political realism should not saddle itself with tautologous attempts to explain all human behaviour in terms of self-interest. Nonetheless, there is still a place for self-interest when understood in terms of the now familiar idea in evolutionary biology that possessing certain genetic materials may yield advantages for certain related groups. The main difference between psychological egoism and the animal component view is that whereas the former says that individuals must be *motivated* by self-interest, the latter position holds that motivation is irrelevant: self-interest is a natural feature of the evolutionary development of normal adults whatever their psychological motivation. An evolutionary theory of self-interest, backed as it is by the theory of natural selection, provides a more solid basis for a realist's conception of an interest-guided international politics than does any philosophical theory of psychological egoism.

A second advantage of the animal component view of human nature is that it connects up with a tradition of realism that stretches back to such recondite thinkers as Aristotle and Thucydides, moves forward through Machiavelli, Hobbes and Spinoza and makes intimate contact with realists of our own time. That tradition distinguishes itself by virtue of its attempts to find a space for reason in a moderate, non-reductive naturalism. The two most significant thinkers in this tradition are Aristotle and Hobbes. Aristotle believed that human beings, like non-human animals, are political animals because group members engage in functions that all can do together. Nonetheless, human beings are different because their common work involves the complex task of maintaining the structure and organisation of the city-state:

they are best suited by nature to be city-state dwellers because they weigh reasons in deciding what to do. Aristotle's view that humans are natural beings because they are biologically and rationally disposed to engage in differentiated cooperative activities in the city-state is part and parcel of the rich tradition upon which the evaluative political realist wishes to draw; but it is not the only view from which she gains sustenance.[9] For although Thomas Hobbes developed a view of human nature which conflicts with Aristotle's on many key points, there are certain features of his position which are also relevant to developing a revised understanding of realism.

Hobbes believed that although human beings might become cooperative, they were not naturally so. A 'war of all against all' arises in the natural condition because human beings are naturally in conflict with one another. The desires of different people are in conflict because the supply of the many commodities they want is insufficiently large to satisfy those desires. Sometimes two people will want exclusive access to the same particular object such as a piece of property; sometimes they will seek power and glory and take pleasure in conquering others. But since human beings are generally concerned about their long-term survival and well-being, they will, if minimally rational, take prudent measures to ensure their future condition. In the case of conflict between individuals and groups, force and the threat of force are the *lingua franca* of their relationship; even when not employed, coercion always lies in the near background as the ultimate basis for resolving conflicts that cannot be won by guile and wit. People and groups of people *vis-à-vis* other groups of people value their own survival and well-being more highly than the survival and well-being of others and act accordingly.

Although there is much here which evaluative political realists may be able to retain for a revised version of human nature, the evidence available from evolutionary biology suggests that Hobbes's premise that human beings are asocial cannot be sustained. As Roger Masters remarks: 'No living primate species studied by ethnologists is totally asocial ... there is no question that *Homo sapiens* has always been a social animal; debate centres, rather, on the kind of group that was characteristic at various periods of hominid evolution.'[10] Nonetheless, Hobbes's view was not totally biologically misplaced, for it underlined the deep importance of competition among human beings for valued human resources.

In general, the animal component view of human nature attempts to

134

bring these two great political thinkers into closer contact with one another than traditional political philosophy would normally endorse by working them into a centre from extreme interpretations of their views. On the one hand, evaluative political realism sides with Aristotle to the effect that human beings are social (or, better, *political*) by nature. As such, human beings are naturally suited to live in political communities and to take up, where possible, an attitude of care, concern and friendship towards one other.[11] But the sort of political communities which Aristotle considered – small city-states of 40,000 or so – gives us no explanation for why human beings are suited, if indeed they are, for modern states, governments and bureaucracies. Here Hobbes' emphasis on self-interest and competition may be quite correct, that these are both the source of the demise of the more generous cooperative spirit found in small city-states and the central problem which states must constrain if they are to avoid self-defeating wars and maintain sufficient stability to further knowledge, science and the arts. Hobbes' emphasis on the disorder created in communal life when self-interested human beings seek competitive advantage over others for limited resources, and the subsequent need for laws which will constrain this disorder, is as indispensable to the animal component view as Aristotle's conception of the natural co-operativeness of human beings (which doesn't at all preclude them from being competitive and disruptive). More importantly for our present concerns, the idea that human beings are cooperatively competitive in the sense indicated receives support from evolutionary biology.[12]

Moreover, in bringing the thoughts of these two thinkers into closer contact evaluative political realism obtains a greater grasp on the distinction between internal and external sovereignty as discussed in chapter 2. For there is an important inference to be drawn about international relations from both Aristotle's and Hobbes' views: that human beings concern themselves more with people inside the state than they do with people outside the state. Of course, their explanations differ for this: for Aristotle, justifying this distinction would involve highlighting the moral concerns which people have for their fellow citizens but not for those outside one's state (except insofar as it impacts on one's own concerns); whereas for Hobbes the difference would be explained by pointing out that the covenant agreed upon by members of one community leaves anyone outside it beyond the pale of law and justice. One might be inclined to accept Aristotle's view that people in one city-state lack sufficient concern for people outside the city-state because civic interest is lacking. Alternatively, one might accept Hobbes's idea that as long as those in control of governments are subject to no higher power to restrain and control them and have no special concern for the people in other states, they remain in a condition of potential hostility to one another even if there are no open hostilities. Some older realists such as Reinhold Niebuhr have tended to accept the Aristotelian notion and supported the idea of inherent human sociality. 'Man is endowed by nature', Niebuhr said, 'with organic relations to his fellowmen; and natural impulse prompts him to consider the needs of others even when they compete with others.'[13] Other realists have been inclined to agree with Hobbes' view. But whether one accepts Aristotle or Hobbes, the idea that lies behind the animal component view is that evolutionary biology can illuminate the tensions and strains in these opposing political philosophies by throwing refracted light on their differences and, by so doing, engage issues that bear upon international relations.[14]

The third advantage of the animal component view of human nature is that it brings out a sharp contrast with the positivist-empiricist conception of international politics in which the provenance of conflict is held to be cultural, psychological or societal, requiring no reference whatever to the biological inheritance of human beings. On such a view, as Tang Tsou has observed, 'serious political conflicts and struggles for power' are 'considered accidental or unnecessary events ...'[15] Nor is this positivist-empiricist idea innocent of practical implications; many theories of international relations are derived from just such assumptions as these, including functionalist and neo-functionalist theories, many versions of systems theory, and the socio-psychological theories of John Burton. Problems of international relations, Burton says, 'do not arise necessarily out of the aggressiveness, hostility, or other characteristics of people and nations ...',[16] but this is not because human beings have other traits or characteristics that counteract these, but rather because '[s]ocial relations are perceived relations. Friendship, cooperation, hostility, envy, anger and aggressiveness are attitudes that are perceived by individuals and groups.'[17] Since conflict, on this view, is a matter of 'perception' and 'attitude' and not in the least internal to human beings, it can presumably be controlled from some rational point outside it and replaced by attitudes 'appropriate' to our situation-relative, historical circumstances. The leading assumption undergirding this idea is that agonistic behaviour – and the pain and cruelty that goes along with it – can be radically diminished once one takes up a genuinely rational scientific perspective. The 'downside' in such a view is that it offers untold opportunities for political, social and economic manipulation of individuals which an understanding of human beings as living creatures firmly rooted in their biological nature would help to block. For in insisting upon the animal component view of human nature one is effectively placing conceptual barriers to the decomposition of the self into functional attributes as a preliminary to their eventual incorporation into systemic frameworks designed by global engineers. So in accepting the animal component view one is also accepting the useful idea that men, women and children cannot be identified without making essential reference to their being members of a natural kind, of being sentient, of having a certain shape, and of constituting forms of biological life which may put them in cooperative competition with other members of their kind.

And the fourth advantage of the animal component view of human nature is that it points us in the direction of a theory which one is not expected to accept on some philosophical basis alone (although as our references to Aristotle and Hobbes suggest, there *are* philosophical bases and they *do* lend additional credence to the theory); rather, it suggests a theory partially sustainable *a posteriori*, on the basis, that is, of empirical evidence and theoretical argumentation.[18] In particular, the animal component view is grounded in the theory of natural selection which is, on any account, an impressive theoretical construct for the human sciences.[19] The theory of natural selection says, among other things, that competition is a major driving force in the evolutionary process. Competition, on this view, was not invented by Thomas Hobbes, Adam Smith or Milton Friedman to justify capitalist modes of production and class oppression: competition is real. It arises naturally from the need to protect necessary resources from the depredations of extrinsic phenomena, from what Darwin called ' "the hostile forces of nature": weather, shortages, predators, parasites and diseases'.[20] Competition for food, shelter and sexual competition for mates implies that organisms that compete effectively will be better represented in the next generation than their rivals. Contrary to positivist-empiricism and emancipatory international relations, evaluative political realists accept natural selection and its clear implications for human beings, viz., that they, too, are competitive. To be sure, as Mary Midgley has correctly pointed out, to say of human beings that they compete with one another for resources is not at all the same thing as saying that they are *basically* competitive.[21] As noted above, ethology and other studies in evolutionary biology make clear that human beings are cooperative as well as competitive. Hence, it seems better to say that human beings are evolutionarily constrained to be cooperatively competitive, that this form of competitiveness manifests itself in different ways in different cultures, and that it should be given due weight as a factor that limits divergence between cultures. In saying this one would not have to be committed to any 'deterministic' theory of human beings but only to the theory that natural selection, shaped in various ways by human cultures, acts on human beings. If one objects that even this view has insufficient scientific warrant, consider the alternatives. Either human beings are exempt altogether from the constraints of natural selection or natural selection does not act on the individual level. Neither of these alternatives seems warranted.

These, then, are some of the advantages of the animal component understanding of human nature. Given their far-reaching implications, one should note that this view is supported by empirical and theoretical evidence, although, as we shall see, the evidence is neither conclusive nor always persuasive. It is important to remind ourselves that evidential support is not proof. We should always bear in mind that there is no such thing, as many positivists have supposed, of interpretation-free evidence; evidence is always such in the light of theoretically infused background assumptions which, practically speaking, can never be fully displayed. Moreover, all judgements are fallible. No judgement, even when based on extensive evidence, can gain much authority simply by being asserted. Keeping these qualifications in mind, let us examine three categories of evidence – Leap, Early-Man and Theoretical – to see what kind of support can be given to the animal component view of human nature.

Leap evidence

By this term, I mean the sort of evidence which we adduce on the basis of our observations of non-human animals and attempt to apply to human beings. Although the gatherers of such evidence understand that there is some sort of gap between human beings and non-human animals, they also contend that leap evidence generates analogies which, if carefully deployed, may be a source of insight into human behaviour. Above all, we must avoid inferring, on the basis of animal studies alone, that human beings are naturally aggressive, naturally territorial, naturally friendly, and so forth. One cannot ignore the fact that organised social activity in the form of the sharing of culture and language has shaped human life in certain non-random ways. On the other hand, one must resist the idea that organised social life is thoroughly autonomous from the biological, for the demands of the biological contribute to the significance we give to organised society. In general, organised society is the outcome of a continuing process of biological evolution, inseparable from it and incomprehensible without it. So although there are undoubtedly important discontinuities between non-human and human animals, it nonetheless seems reasonable to believe that the study of the higher vertebrates at least could reveal some significant continuities useful for understanding the context of human action.

With this as backdrop we may now ask whether non-human animals are naturally social. It will not be sufficient to argue that since animals live in groups they must be social, for group living, though a necessary condition of sociality, is not a sufficient condition. The answer offered by modern evolutionary biology is that despite the significant drawbacks associated with group living in terms of increased competition and so on, there must have been, for group living to have evolved, a range of benefits. In the case of non-human animals, two major selective pressures may be cited as 'incentives' to group living: protection from predators and resource exploitation. Defence against predation appears to be important for an enormous range of animals high on the phylogenetic scale, including bank swallows, ostriches, musk ox, geese, marmites and prairie dogs.[22] Group living may also enhance the capacity to gather food. For example, groups of birds seem to be more successful in finding food, and therefore in increasing their fitness, than isolated individuals. Moreover, when food is plentiful in the non-human world, the frequency of aggression declines, presumably because the gains involved in winning contests are not justified by the costs in terms of time, energy or risk of further reproductive potential in fighting.[23] The key point is that one does not have to hypothesise 'sociality' to account for a propensity towards group living: non-human animals may live in groups because it enhances the genotypic fitness of their relatives and near-relatives.

But what is it that explains the competition and conflict that is evidently so rife within the non-human world? The simple answer is that since members of the same species share the same requirements for food, defence from predation, shelter, mates and so on, they must, when resources are limited, contest for them or suffer reduced genotypic fitness. Aggression evidently does indeed take place between spotted hyenas in intergroup encounters.[24] Wolf packs that are strange to one another frequently engage in agonistic behaviour which ends in death.[25] Hawlin monkeys, Hanuman languars, toque monkeys and chimpanzees also display considerable intergroup antagonism. And one particularly interesting study reported that despite a lack of aggression *within* groups of Ceylon grey languars, aggressive troop-to-troop encounters were actively sought.[26] In the face of all this (and much more) deadly intergroup conflict, it seems implausible to hold with Lorenz that conflict performs a 'species-preserving function'. An alternative explanation is that aggression tends to take place in the non-human animal world when the genotypic advantages exceed the disadvantages. Traits which enable animals to engage in conflict behaviour can spread through the population even if they diminish average reproductive success. A relative increase in competition and conflict between groups is likely to take place, on this view, when the value of direct competition (in terms of access to resources and so on) is greater than the potential gain from cooperation with other group members.

But now the hard, yet obvious, question: To what extent does this very widespread degree of intergroup conflict in the non-human animal world apply to the world of human animals? There are many arguments that could be brought to bear to resist the application of these findings to human societies; and some of the arguments are cogent. After all, there does seem to be a perfectly good sense in which human animals differ from non-human animals, i.e. non-human animals seem to lack an objective conception of other sentient beings and thus a sensitivity to their concerns and interests. This might make non-human animals more aggressive, particularly in the face of severe resource deprivation, but it is not at all clear that it would completely undermine the claim of important continuities between human and non-human animals. It would surely not warrant any claim to transcend certain biological imperatives as such. Of course if leap evidence were all the evidence an investigator could ever adduce for her claims, the realist's interest in biology would evaporate quite quickly. Leap evidence only gains credence when combined with two other types of evidence to form a structured, interrelated and mutually supporting web of evidence and understanding: early-life evidence and theoretical evidence. It is to these other types that we now turn.

Early-life evidence

By 'early-life evidence' I am referring both to paleontological evidence concerning 'how things were' for our early ancestors and anthropological evidence concerning relevant activities of extant preliterate societies. Now, it is a commonplace that prior to the establishment of the first cities roughly 6,000 years ago, early human beings were hunters of large game and lived in small nomadic bands, usually of kin-related individuals. However, as Richard Alexander has trenchantly argued, the group-hunting hypothesis cannot account for 'the organisation and maintenance of recent and large human groups'.[27] As group size increases beyond a certain point, a group's relative efficiency in capturing and killing large game declines; hence, there are practical upper limits on the size of hunting groups. What, then, accounts for the rise of large-scale organisations, leading eventually to those huge conglomerations we call nation-states? States of millions of people are unique in human history and cannot be explained by any 'man-the-hunter' hypothesis.

As alternative, Alexander advances the idea that 'at some early point in our history the actual function of human groups – the significance for their individual members – was protection from the predatory effects of other groups'.[28] Early life was, on this view, a brand of warfare, a hunt in which people were treated as prey – deceived, ensnared and forcibly run to ground just as in a chase. To protect themselves, individuals would have joined groups which, despite their costs, were worth it in the biological sense of enabling them to enhance their reproductive success. Alexander calls this 'the Balance-of-Power hypothesis', and it is easy to see why a term from the lexicon of international relations is appropriate in accounting for the rise of large states. For suppose we have three non-kin related societies A, B and C. And suppose two societies A and B are in competition with one another for food, shelter and other resources necessary to survival and differential reproduction. Then if, say, A makes an alliance with C in order to conquer B and succeeds, it will have significantly expanded its relative resource base. Those societies in the past which learned how to engage successfully in balance of power politics would have been naturally selected for and have expanded from smaller groups to larger groups. The guiding thought here, in any event, provides biological content to Martin Wight's incisive observation: 'The idea of balance arises *naturally* in considering any relationship between competing human units, groups or institutions . . .'[29]

Another kind of evidence that needs to be examined under this rubric is derived from the study of war, sex and power in preliterate extant societies. The study of these societies tends to capture selective forces more readily than postliterate societies because environmental influences would not have had a chance to work themselves into their cultures and ongoing forms of life. A good example of such evidence is to be found in attempts by certain biological anthropologists to render their principles consistent with what we know about primitive war. In a well-known article, William Durham argues that primitive war represents something of an embarrassment to non-biological anthropology 'which has tended to believe that human societies are functionally integrated systems well adapted to their environments'.[30]

On the basis of a carefully designed research project examining the Mundurucu head-hunters of Brazil, Durham was able to support the hypothesis 'that people fight wars when they stand to gain individually and in terms of their reproductive success'.[31] So we have here an example which supports the realist's traditional claim that warfare is a natural, if regrettable, feature of human activity whose legacy stretches back to our ancestral past. Since natural selection depends on environmental factors, this goes no way towards showing, of course, that warfare cannot be eliminated from human cultures in the future.

In another anthropological study of great interest, Napoleon Chagnon found that individual Yanomamo Indians engaged in a host of activities, many of them political in character, to enhance their inclusive fitness. Contrary to the more traditional anthropological emphases, Chagnon found that such practices as kinship behaviour, marriage alliances and village fissioning made 'sense in a sociobiological context'.[32] In the remote corners of Brazil and Venezuela, there are '150-odd villages' each of which 'is an autonomous political entity'.[33] These political entities engage in constant warfare – it is 'endemic' and often intense among them. To reduce its harmful consequences, 'political alliances' are formed with neighbouring groups for mutual assistance in the event of 'raiding' from 'common enemies'. Alliances are particularly important for smaller villages which 'are more vulnerable targets of raids from larger villages and less capable of mounting an effective, long-term pattern of raiding'.[34]

For our present purpose, it is useful to point to two implications of Chagnon's study. First, it suggests the potential power of the biological theory of inclusive fitness to illuminate phenomena of interest to international theorists such as intergroup conflict, warfare, coalition-making and the splitting of groups. Secondly, the study demonstrates the capacity of the realist's lexicon of international politics to describe and analyse fundamental relationships between autonomous units in conditions approximating a Hobbesian state of nature, *viz.* where no legal sovereign serves to moderate independent action in the villages' self-interest.

Of course, this evidence is controversial but it *is* based on empirical research and carried out in ways which empiricists have insisted constitute prerequisites for knowledge acquisition. Citing such evidence is important because, contrary to what has often been said, political realism is not anti-scientific, at least not in the revisionary form advocated here. What evaluative political realism resists is not science but a variety of empiricists' claims, including the claim that there are laws *at the proximate level of human activity* which determine how people behave. Such a claim, and the research programmes that go along with it, is unjustified and unwarranted. Empiricism in this sense is, essentially: a complete failure.[35] But the absence of law-like explanations at the proximate level does not entail their absence altogether. It could be that the laws which 'apply' to human behaviour are partially biological in character, as some realists have maintained.[36] They might also be remote, which could help to explain why they do not appear to have much impact on quotidian international politics. However this may be, we have shown at the very least that there is an evidential basis for the animal component view of human nature and, in particular, that intergroup aggression, conflict and competition are salient features of our ancestral past. Many of the arguments supporting this claim have important implications for issues in international relations, for such research findings would indeed, contrary to what Quincy Wright maintained in 1955, 'set limits to the possibilities for reconstructing world society'.[37] However, since evidence about early man and preliterate societies may be heavily discounted because it is remote from the circumstances in which culture is said to play a decisive role, it seems desirable to cite evidence in which this drawback is absent, i.e. theoretical evidence.

Theoretical evidence

By 'theoretical evidence' I am referring to those arguments that offer abstract, general or analytical solutions to conceptual problems. Such problems abound as much in current international theory as in evolutionary biology but those whose focus is primarily on international theory may profit from drawing certain connections between the two. One of the most important of these problems concerns 'altruism', a concept whose role cannot be ignored in any realist understanding of ethics in international relations.[38]

The central problem of altruism for Darwinian biology is easy to state. If nature is a struggle for existence, as Darwin maintained, how could altruism have evolved? A large range of common phenomena in the animal kingdom needs explaining here. For example, if an animal makes a loud call on the approach of a predator, the alarm-caller might draw attention to itself, thereby increasing the likelihood of its being devoured by the predator. Of course, by sounding an alarm the alarm-caller increases the probability that others will survive. It may well have enhanced others' fitness, but only at the expense of its own. But why? Should not animals, in their struggle for existence, attempt to enhance their individual fitness? And if they do not, should we not expect the trait for altruism to disappear since the altruistic individuals would be putting themselves at greater risk?

W. D. Hamilton developed an ingenious explanation to account for this apparent anomaly. He argued that the tendency to self-sacrifice could be selected for if it was helpful to those who shared the individual's genetic material. This is kin-selection, the genetically based tendency to assist one's relatives. According to the theory, the decreased fitness of altruists can be more than compensated for by the increased fitness of relatives who are the beneficiaries of the altruism. That is, natural selection considers *inclusive fitness* – the fitness of the individual and her close relatives – and not the reproductive success of individual organisms as such; it acts on the genotype which the organism shares with her relatives.

Kin selection theory and international ethics

There are two applications of kin selection theory to the ethics and morality of international relations which may be cited here as illustrations.

144

The first area of application lies in suggesting the deep implausibility of robust forms of globalism. For kin selection theory says, in effect, that patterns of kinship will be crucially important to human societies, that the characteristic differences that divide the species into different groups are not only the result of environmental influences but of cultural/genetic inheritance and that, consequently, certain institutional objectives that 'go against' this inheritance may be forever beyond human realisation. Such institutional objectives – *the world state, world peace through world law* in the older formulations; *world society as cobweb*,[39] *global redistributive justice*,[40] and the *anarchy\text problematique*[41] in some newer renditions – have been variously argued; but they all seem to rest, despite interesting differences, on the assumption that the primordial conflicts animating human groups can be expected (or simply made) to disappear, that human society, by extending globally under a certain dispensation, can become rational and scientific. But now, paradoxically, there seems to be some scientific basis, rooted in kin selection theory, for suspecting such claims. If the formation of kinship groups is itself rooted in the biological ubiquity of conflict and competition, globalism of a strong *genre* appears to be deprived of a scientific or rational basis: it is bound to fail because it presupposes 'an indiscriminate, species- or population-wide altruism' for which, as Alexander says, 'no evidence ... has been reported for any organism'.[42]

A second possible contribution of kin selection theory goes deeper: it suggests the possibility of shifting back to a form of realism in international politics in precisely the area in which realism has appeared to be most vulnerable. For in recent years realism has been subjected to apparently withering attacks for its *immoralisme*, for its failure to recommend foreign policy action from what Marshall Cohen has called 'the moral point of view', roughly a non-partisan, impartial view from nowhere.[43] Although the conceptual grounds of the moral point of view, given its implicit reliance on naturalism, has become increasingly problematic, the general idea assumes an important distinction between moral and non-moral ideals in terms of which no weight is to be given in one's moral judgements – except as obstacles to overcome – to non-moral ideals. But for the evaluative political realist, any conception of morality in international politics must give sufficient weight to non-moral ideals, for these may very well be in conflict with – and not just additional to – our favoured moral ideals; and this claim gets some unexpected support from kin selection theory. For example, kin selection theory implies that someone who loves his children, i.e. is willing to 'invest' in them in the appalling jargon of sociobiology, will be acting in terms of the internal imperatives of inclusive fitness. Such a person might have great difficulty in reshaping his desires to meet the demands of an impersonal, moral point of view which requires, say, that he invest instead in famine relief for strangers that will make them marginally better-off. Nor perhaps should he have to. Since it is widely held among moral theorists that moral action has to meet the standard of 'ought implies can', kin selection theory, if veridical, provides strong grounds for rejecting moral doctrines that refuse to give sufficient weight to non-moral goals and interests – including the non-moral interest that underlies replication of one's own genetic material by giving preference to one's children.

The key point here is just this, that there is a basis in evolutionary theory for the realist's idea of the incompatibility between the moral point of view and personal and community ideals. Whereas the moral point of view, as Susan Wolf says, involves the recognition 'that one is just one person among others equally real and deserving of the good things in life', a person's or a community's viewpoint presupposes the saliency of that person's or community's particularity – the saliency of the kind of life it would be best for *these* individuals or *these* communities to live.[44] The moral point of view involves pressure towards impartiality; the realist perspective, by contrast, comes with a 'built-in' emphasis on each person's or community's or state's particularity or difference. Once we have accepted the idea of genuinely competing points of view, we will have effectively undercut the thesis that the moral point of view has an inherent superiority over other points of view. For the evaluative political realist, the point of view of loyalty, of prudence and of the individual or the community striving for self-actualisation, should not be given short shrift compared to the generalism of the moral point of view. For whatever may be said in favour of the moral point of view in constraining human selfishness, greed and social irresponsibility (and these certainly need constraining), there is a deep incompatibility between the demands of the morally ideal and the requirements of non-moral interests – part of which may be grounded in the genetic interest of individuals in their inclusive fitness – which leads evaluative political realists to reject privileged claims for the moral view from nowhere. Here kin selection theory may be viewed as independently backstopping a prior philosophical claim with theoretically based evidence which lends additional weight to a revised realist conception of international relations.

Criticism of this project

On the basis of this highly selective review of three classes of evidence, it seems fair to say that enough material has been assembled to give some credence to the animal component view of human nature. But here we reach a difficulty, for it might be said that evaluative political realism, in seeking support for its views in the findings of evolutionary biology and sociobiology, is effectively trading on a politically biased pseudo-science, whose theories are no more than 'just-so stories', i.e. speculative, unscientific accounts of complex phenomena that offer little prospect of genuine knowledge and which, more importantly, promote a particularly nasty political ideology. Criticism of this sort is too extensive to be ignored, and some of it comes from distinguished biologists.[45] Let us first consider the claim that sociobiology lacks scientific credentials.[46]

The main difficulty with this part of the criticism lies in the failure to indicate the theory of knowledge or science that is being assumed or presupposed. A positivist philosophy of science holds that to obtain genuine knowledge in a complex scientific discipline there has to be a clear distinction between observation and theory, that theory must be falsifiable through experience or experiment, and that reality is essentially immediately given, hard and inert. An alternative philosophy of science, popular with many recent international theorists, looks to Thomas Kuhn for support. On a Kuhnian view, there is no binding algorithm to determine the correctness of theory-choice for any pair of theories relative to a given body of evidence. For the Kuhnian, all standards of theory-choice are paradigm related: there is no such thing as a paradigm-free choice of theory. Moreover, one has to admit, according to this view, that a choice of one theory over its rivals will be influenced by non-cognitive factors such as pressures from within a scientific community or a theory's aesthetic, cultural or social value.

Choosing between these two philosophies of science poses a dilemma: if we accept an essentially positivist philosophy of science, then sociobiology could perhaps be legitimately dismissed as a mere pretence to knowledge. There are certainly no decisive tests that will enable researchers to confirm sociobiological hypotheses concerning, e.g. kinship. The problem, however, is that the stories told by cultural

147

anthropologists (and the derivative stories told by those political scientists who use or presuppose them) would *a fortiori* also have to be dismissed as mere pretences to knowledge. Notoriously, their theoretical offerings, however persuasive to their proponents, cannot pass muster in terms of positivist standards of scientific validity.[47] If, however, we replace a positivist philosophy of science with an essentially Kuhnian one, as some international theorists recommend,[48] then it would seem that sociobiology could well be regarded as one of the most innovative, puzzle-solving and revolutionary paradigms now available in international relations! As indicated above, this dilemma can be outflanked by the evaluative political realist if she refuses to be drawn into accepting a global philosophy of science. But in that event contemptuous dismissal of evolutionary biology and sociobiolgy would be off the mark.

Nonetheless, this would still leave the problem of how to avoid succumbing to the materialist and reductionist underpinnings of one version of evolutionary biology: sociobiology. To escape this, the evaluative political realist needs to reconfirm her commitment to a commonsense explanatory framework which is uncompromisingly anti-reductionist. On this view, any reductionist-cum-materialist explanation scheme of the sort proposed by Wilson,[49] Rosenberg,[50] or (in political science) Glendon Schubert[51] or Roger Masters[52] drastically *underdetermines* our ordinary explanations of human beings who have reasons, form plans and projects and who, most of the time, act in a variety of imaginative and essentially unpredictable ways. On this alternative view, the study of international relations is ineliminably bound up with an explanatory framework which makes liberal use of such concepts as belief, intention and desire. Using such concepts to describe human activity presupposes the idea of a subject in some degree of control of her thoughts and actions; biological imperatives cannot alone *explain* such thoughts and actions.

Within the commonsense framework which the evaluative political realist regards as ineliminable and non-revisable, the role of sociobiology would, therefore, have to be considered a restricted one. Sociobiology may assemble naturalistic evidence which supports (or fails to support) the commonsense view of human nature; it can invent concepts such as kin selection and reciprocal altruism to illuminate moral issues in international relations and it can, perhaps, offer a better understanding of why ethical sensibilities may become 'thinner' as one moves outward from the family to the larger community of the nation-state and 'world society'. But sociobiology cannot *replace* the common-sense framework of explanation in which more or less reasonable human beings act in terms of beliefs, desires and intentions marked out by an inner world of reality. For the evaluative political realist, the main role of sociobiology is the different one of grounding the idea that there is something internal to human beings which shapes and influences what they are and which precludes certain options from practical consideration.

Let us now consider the claim that sociobiology ought to be rejected as politically odious because it attempts to sustain reactionary and male-dominated solutions to political problems. If one does not agree with these judgements, there appear to be two good ways of dealing with them: denying the claim or deconstructing sociobiology. Evaluative political realism encourages both these strategies. First, it agrees with Roger Masters' counterarguments.[53] Against the male-dominance charge, for example, Masters argues that difference does not imply dominance.[54] Against the reactionary charge, Masters argues that such a claim may have had some substance when environmental determinism grounded 'equality before the law', but modern evolutionary theory removes this problem. 'Insofar as the phenotype is simply a "vehicle" for genetic replication, no individual can claim to be "naturally" superior in all respects. None of us can know which genes will turn out, in future environments, to be essential for continued human life.'[55]

Although Masters' arguments are valid as far as they go, they display a certain political naiveté concerning the relation between science, understood as a privileged rational perspective on the world, and politics, conceived as power. Masters simply assumes that international relations can be studied in neutral scientific terms which imply no commitment to reactionary modes of thought and practice. Of course a neutral non-political scientific understanding of genetics and evolutionary biology may be possible and, with certain qualifications, contribute to a theoretical understanding of international relations. But there is, the evaluative political realist argues, no such thing as a neutral political practice based upon that understanding. Genetic and evolutionary biology (like all natural sciences) underdetermine our conceptions of political practice (including ethics). Since human beings have different political beliefs which they are fully prepared to promote, genetic knowledge, too, can be expected to be deployed for political purposes. For the evaluative political realist, neutrality is a false and unattainable ideal: there is no conception of human nature, the self or international politics which is, or can be, neutral in the required sense. All political arrangements, notwithstanding their alleged neutrality, comport contestable beliefs from which one cannot both stand apart and deploy for understanding political activity. Instead of trying to neutralise politics or separate them from the purposes which give them life, evaluative political realism aspires to open spaces for pluralism, for alternative perspectives and alternative forms of life. In working towards these objectives, evaluative political realism has no interest in defending sociobiology as politically neutral; it attempts to deconstruct it, that is to displace but not to discard. Evaluative political realism displaces sociobiology and evolutionary biology from their point of origin in a robust scientific-naturalist understanding of knowledge by denying that the deliverances of such knowledge can be politically neutral and 'engineered' for practical application to social and political life. In any case, evaluative political realism can hardly be said to be in the business of defending socio-biology. How could it? Evaluative political realism rejects the robust scientific-naturalist account of knowledge whose truth sociobiology presupposes. Evaluative political realism is in the business of de-fending a certain revised version of political realism. In working towards that goal, Evaluative political realism wants no truck with racism, anti-feminism, or reactionary politics. This is one reason why it holds that something more than a biological concept of human nature is required.

The person component of human nature

The human animal as person

From the fact that human beings are members of a natural kind and are animals, it does not follow, as some reductionists think, that human beings are not persons. As we have already remarked, one and the same thing can be instantiations of many different sortal universals. The main reason for starting with the animal component view of human nature was to underline the necessity of understanding human beings as inextricably bound up with their nature as animals. We can now draw back from that claim to see the equally important need for carving out a role for human beings as persons, i.e. as beings who reflect and become intentional agents.

In a neglected passage of Morgenthau's classic work on international politics, *Politics Among Nations*, there is an effort to balance a conception of the human being as a natural kind with a conception of the human being as a person; however, the effort is largely inchoate and needs to be reformulated and made perspicuous. 'Beneath the interminable contentions and conflicts of politics', Morgenthau wrote, one finds

> an irreducible minimum of psychological traits and aspirations which are the common possession of all mankind. All human beings want to live and, hence, want the things necessary for life. All human beings want to be free and, hence, want to have those opportunities for self-expression and self-development which their particular culture considers to be desirable. All human beings seek power and, hence, social distinctions, again varying with the particular pattern of their culture, that put them ahead of and above their fellow men.[56]

I designate this level of understanding of persons *Beta*. I claim that it is the *primary level* of personhood, that the wants invoked here are *primary wants* and that they express psychological needs and capacities which are universal. We can add to Morgenthau's list such facts as that we admire, fear, hate, envy, get angry at certain people; that we are sometimes happy and at other times unhappy; that we experience joy and grief; close relationships with some people and distant relations with others. We want our lives to be regulated so that we get what we like and avoid what we dislike. We are thus prepared to adhere to certain ethical rules, norms and conventions. We want to make use of our reflective capacities to learn from the past and to plan for our future. We have views, whether expressed or not, concerning: family, birth, death, success and failure, sexual relations, authority; and we want our lives to correspond to our views. Although different societies may have different ways of meeting these psychological needs, no society can do without them altogether.

By contrast, we have what I shall call the *secondary level*, designated *Alpha*. Morgenthau again: 'Upon this psychological foundation, the same for all men, arises an edifice of philosophical convictions, ethical postulates, and philosophical aspirations. These, too, might be shared by all men under certain conditions, but actually they are not.'[57] Goods at the Alpha level depend on cultural, social and personal variability. The wants that persons articulate at this level are *secondary wants*; they express what a person is naturally inclined to desire immediately and spontaneously in terms of the culture, customs and history of the community in which he or she lives. While primary wants are the same for everyone, secondary wants vary. The concepts used for understanding primary wants are thin and universal; those deployed at the secondary level are thick and local. For the evaluative political realist, it is important to represent the knowledge available at the secondary level as local knowledge, i.e. practical knowledge which shapes the wants and interests of people within a particular community. Such knowledge should be understood in contradistinction to the universal knowledge available, at least in principle, at the primary level of personhood.

Alpha level

At the level I am calling Alpha, we have the *secondary self*, a concept, as I envisage it, closely related to Charles Taylor's idea of *the person as agent*.[58] The secondary self is best understood as a creature which takes up a first-person perspective on the world; and there seems no good reason to believe that all the different points of view in that world will yield to convergence of method or description. Since to be a person is to be a creature for whom it is *like* something to be that creature, descriptions of persons will always be subject-dependent. This is the idea of the person for whom, as Taylor puts it, 'things matter, who are subjects of significance'.[59] To attribute subject-dependent properties to persons is to see them, in contrast with non-human animals, as endowed with a comprehensive subjectivity whose perceptual capacities reach out to the world around them. Descriptions of personal activity at this level will involve, among other things, invoking the capacities of persons *from within* their collectivities and institutions – their religious groups, their families, their kinship systems, their political parties and interest groups, their nations and their governments. For persons are not only strategic, rational and calculative creatures responding to their immediate environments, they are also emotional, memory-endowed beings bound to particular local loyalties, solidarities and passions which shape and articulate their conduct *in their world*. The moral and political claims that persons make, individually and through their social and political institutions, often come into conflict with the moral and political claims of persons from different families, kinship systems, tribes, nations and states. It is these conflicts which constitute a good deal of the subject matter of international relations.

A person cannot live without some culture, without thick concepts which give meaning to human projects, without idiosyncratic ways of going on. Within each nation-state one can expect to see ways of life which require specifically different types of behaviour, different personal relationships, in different social and historical contexts, employing different embedded concepts concerning religion, rightness, justice, welfare, friendship, loyalty and so forth. And it seems plausible to believe that a good part of the knowledge we obtain of persons as agents embedded in social and political orders will be not observers' knowledge but participants' knowledge – knowledge obtained by taking up the attitude of a *native* in one's judgements irrespective of whether or not one has actually 'gone native'.

Consider, for example, the difficulty of trying to understand as an observer what was going on in Indonesian foreign policy under Sukarno without grasping the nuances of meaning in 'Pantja Sila' (in Bahasa Indonesia). In English this phrase is usually rendered as 'Five Principles' which, though not an 'incorrect' translation as such, fails to resonate the religious notes in the original. 'Pantja sila' is derived directly from the Hinayana *Pancha-sila* and suggests the Five Pillars of Islam which invoke certain mandatory practices for every good Moslem. When Sukarno used the term in speeches, he was evidently not referring to what any non-believing observer would refer to in using the term 'Five Principles'. The neutral, non-believing observer cannot refer to what Sukarno referred to because the term invokes certain religious beliefs whose truth, *ex hypothesi*, such a non-believing observer could not accept. So the term 'Pantja Sila' in the sense of 'Five Principles' will not pick out the same things as Sukarno picked out and the observer, we are supposing, has no other term which will enable her to do so. For the observer to refer to the same things as Sukarno, she would either have to accept, or imaginatively suppose, the possible truth of at least some of its religious beliefs. If she does not and if she regards as false and mistaken the whole religious discourse which Sukarno sounded in using this term, her judgements concerning the value and significance of Sukarno's speech of 1 June 1945 proclaiming 'Pantja Sila' as the basis for Indonesia's foreign policy would quite probably have been dramatically different from, and inferior to, local judgements; and so would our understanding of Sukarno and his significance as a political leader. And if we cannot, via observer's knowledge, grasp the simple speech-acts of Indonesian political leaders, it seems unlikely that we should be able to understand post-war Indonesian foreign policy.

The key point for our present purposes is that if we accept the general validity of the distinction between observers' knowledge and participants' knowledge (as I think we must) and if we also regard participants' knowledge as necessary to the task of uncovering the significance of things for the secondary self, then we would have no reason to think that the knowledge assembled at the Alpha level of description and analysis could ever be universalised across nation-states or other important cultural and institutional entities. At the Alpha level no perspective has sovereignty *qua* point of view, nor is there any transhistorical, transcultural description of the world which can make commensurable all competing points of view. How, for example, could the various forms of political excellence to be found in Islamic states, and in terms of which people define what is to count as knowledge, be fitted into the contrasting understandings to be found in Christian secular states? There does not appear any way to combine such knowledge, without loss, into a general, cross-cultural body of knowledge. Similarly, there do not appear to be any publicly available institutional norms for settling all arguments between people with different historical experiences and cultural backgrounds. What would settle an argument, for example, between those who say that adherence to Islamic law is, and must remain, the ultimate determinant of the Good and those who deny this? At the Alpha level, knowledge of what human beings are like as such has to be replaced by what Tanzanians, Japanese and Swedes and so on are like, described not from some perspective that transcends them, but from the participant's own perspective, i.e. the historical, cultural and societal position they actually occupy. At the Alpha level conduct within the community is shaped by thick concepts and local knowledge. Since communities are shaped by different thick concepts and local knowledge, the potential for conflict between communities will be ever present.

Beta level

At this level of the person component of human nature, we suppose there to be mental concepts constituting a network of *contextual a priori* truths for the study of international relations.[60] There is an important sense in which human beings have objectively identifiable interests (within a certain context) that do not depend directly on cultural or social norms or practices. Although we recognise the enormous diversity of human beings in human cultures, we also appreciate the constancy of mental state across cultures, of those 'psychological traits and aspirations,' as Morgenthau put it, 'which are the common possession of mankind'. In focusing on these objective features of human beings we tend to see them, as Taylor says, as strategic creatures who conceive of an array of possibilities among which they must choose.[61] At this Beta level, persons are essentially planners who, in responding to their environment, lay out certain possibilities, attentive to calculating their value in terms of goals and the possibilities of attainment. In describing and analysing human beings in terms of strategic concepts and categories, we would quite naturally attempt to capture the facts of the self, i.e. truisms about our human psychology. These will include such matters as understanding how the past experience of persons affects their lives, their preferences, their projects and their concern about members of their own species. There are objective facts about human beings which we gather systematically using appropriate methods. And although different cultures will use different methods there is always the possibility of convergence over time at the level of community inquiry.

Bringing the person component into contact with the animal component level

Below the psychological we have the animal component level of human nature which, as stated above, displays human beings as shaped by evolution, biological imperatives and natural selection. Since natural selection just is differential reproduction of alternative genes (alleles) in a population, it necessarily involves cooperative competition. Such competition, to be sure, need not be direct or fierce; but in the case of human beings, there is strong evidence to suggest that ancestral members of the kind organised themselves into groups to fight, to kill and even, on occasion, to consume other members of their kind. A contrasting aspect of differential reproduction is altruism (in the biological sense): it is generally directed either towards relatives or is reciprocal in character. Given the indispensability of this component of human nature, the prospect that altruism will attain the predominance required for anything remotely resembling universal brotherhood, or even some very much more attenuated moral order, seems remote.

Also at this level concern will be directed towards what human beings need to survive as opposed to what they need to flourish. Here facts of the body will be the heart of the matter. The structure of the human body as well as motor and sensory capacities will constrain and shape the kinds of social and psychological relations human beings can have and will feed back into the other levels.

This sketch of the relationship between the various components and subcomponents of human nature or self provides the kind of complexity which the Evaluative Political Realist thinks is required not only to capture political activity in international relations but to retard the growth of reductionism and scientism. Its form is meant to be no more than suggestive of what a more fully developed theory would need to deliver.

Avoiding dualism and reductionism

But, one might ask, what is the nature of the relation of the personal and animal components in this realist understanding of human nature? First of all, we know that the relation will be a contingent and not a necessary one. If the relation were like that between water and H_2O or heat and molecular structure in which we could not sensibly envisage the two components separately, we would have to conclude that the relation was a necessary one. But we can conceive, and talk intelligibly about, the personal component independently of the animal component; hence, the relation is contingent. Secondly, we know also that the relation is one in which underdetermination holds; hence we know that indefinitely many facts about persons could fit any given set of mental states. Thirdly, we know that the person component is not reducible to the animal component. To be a person means, *ex hypothesi*, to be a creature possessing mental traits; but the possession of such traits is not a necessary feature of being an animal.

Now, it might be thought that these conclusions lead to dualism and thus incorporate the usual difficulties of that conception of the relation of mind and body. Two such difficulties may be cited here. There is the problem of explaining just how the mind is related to one's animal body and the world around it. And, secondly, there is the problem of explaining how natural selection could be fit into a dualistic framework. For, implicit in the idea of natural selection is the thought that mind somehow developed from matter as matter became organised under the pressure of natural selection. Are we to suppose that only physical bodies evolve and minds, having always existed in their present form, became somehow coupled with animal bodies at some time in evolutionary history? The absurdity of the idea is patent. In reflecting on evolution we seem compelled to suppose that mind somehow came from matter in a way that dualism would regard as unacceptable.

The way out of these difficulties is to eschew dualism and to insist on a certain form of the claim that the mental supervenes on the physical. Let me explain. In recent philosophy of mind, it is often claimed that one state of affairs, set of conditions or properties supervenes upon another. The general idea is that some states of affairs change as a consequence of a change in some more basic subvenient states of affairs. On this basis one could then hold that a change in the properties of persons is constrained; they cannot vary irrespective of changes in the more basic genetic properties of the natural kind *Homo sapiens*. Thus, reductionists might attempt to claim that descriptions of persons are replaceable by subvenient descriptions of neural mechanisms and genetic structures, that descriptions at the personal level are mere epiphenomena destined to be replaced by underlying physically based generalisations and statistical laws. The trouble with this claim is that there are many different kinds of supervenience not all of which lend support to reductionist arguments.

For instance, it is important to distinguish logical supervenience from factual supervenience. Concerning the latter, empirical science tells us that colours are actually supervenient, i.e. no two surfaces can differ only in colour. That was an empirical and not a conceptual discovery; but we know that a parallel argument concerning the relation of personal and animal components cannot go through. For, as we have just seen, to be a person is to be endowed with mental traits of various kinds which animals need not possess. But this was not a discovery made *a posteriori* on the basis of empirical data; rather, it came about *a priori* on the basis of nothing other than our ordinary, commonsense grasp of psychological concepts. So the supervenience in question is logical not empirical. Logical supervenience involves the claim that the properties of a thing cannot vary independently of any simultaneous variation in its subvenient properties. The logical reductionist claim might then be that necessarily if there is such a thing as underlying physical properties to a set of psychological properties, then anything else which is like those underlying properties is a being with those psychological properties as well. This would appear to be a strong argument in defence of a reductionist strategy. However, even if we grant this, it would not rule out possible worlds in which there are both things with the underlying physical properties and mental things supervenient on them which are not physical properties. Hence, even if we grant the claim of logical supervenience, it would not enable anyone to infer that a person is reducible to animal components whose essence is determined only by genetic and evolutionary facts.

If the foregoing argument is correct, it has at least one important methodological implication, namely, that we shall no longer have a basis for bypassing commonsense psychology in our descriptions of human conduct in international relations. For, even if evolutionary biology proved to be correct about the underlying genetic basis of human behaviour, we know that the irreducibility of the mental to the physical will entail an ineliminable indeterminacy in our assumptions about specific attribution of mental states to human beings. Since our commonsense explanations of human behaviour are governed by the condition that the agent be represented as intelligible to himself and others, we shall presumably no longer be tempted to suppose that naturalistic facts at the animal component level can force us to eliminate our commonsense descriptions of what human beings say and do.

Implications for international relations

Apart from the implications considered elsewhere, there are two additional upshots of this second thesis for a revised realism. First, our schema offers a route to avoid radical relativism of the sort to be found in the views of many international relationists from Quincy Wright to Richard Ashley and R.B.J. Walker. Evolutionary biology and cognate disciplines oppose every form of cultural relativism which holds that all truths about human activity (assuming there are any) are relative to the culture in which the activity takes place.[62] This sort of cultural relativism might even agree with Jean-Paul Sartre's assessment that there is no such thing as human nature. But, as we have just seen, there is a solid biological basis for accepting the commonsense view that human nature exists and that it serves to limit cultural divergence. But although there is good biological evidence for stating that human nature exists, we have no grounds for supporting Morgenthau's statement that human nature 'has not changed . . .' On the contrary, the appropriate conclusion to reach on the basis of evolutionary biology is that although human animals have a nature, it is complex and changing.[63] Nonetheless, the implication of the 'older' political realist's view – that human nature involves conflict and cooperative competition – is overwhelmingly supported by evidence from evolutionary biology.

A second upshot of these considerations for the study of international relations lies in the resuscitation of the realist idea of the *primacy of foreign policy*, understood in terms of how the heritage of different nation-states shapes the views of statespersons. This idea, rooted in von Ranke's notion of historical individuality,[64] arises through our interpretation of the person component of human nature. At the Alpha level of personal activity, we can expect political leaders to act in ways which are shaped by the tradition and history of their society *vis-à-vis* their competitors. If our analysis of persons is correct, then we have undercut the ground for holding that particular states, and the different ways of life and culture they represent, can be integrated into one another into a world state or some similar universal institution. Hence, under these conditions, we should treat states as independent life forms (keeping always in mind that states are comprised of individuals) from within which one tries to understand and explain the activities of other states similarly understood. Since there is no impersonal, detached absolute perspective from which to view other people, societies or their foreign policies, we have no choice but to describe them from where we actually are, i.e. from within our particular historical, cultural, institutional configurations. This creates the risk of parochialism, the fear of being conceptually trapped within the confines of the culture into which one happens to be born; but the risk is exaggerated. In accepting personhood we are not obliged on this account to give up an objective understanding of human beings; for, as we have shown, there is a Beta level of personhood which is objective and cross-cultural. So we can describe and analyse ourselves not only at the Alpha level of different cultures and ways of life, but also at the Beta level of persons consisting of 'universal' facts of the self, keeping in mind that Beta level descriptions are necessarily distant from the ineliminable commonsense descriptions of international relations gathered at the Alpha level. From the evaluative political realist point of view, we are encouraged to deploy all three levels – animal, Alpha and Beta – in our descriptions and explanations of human beings engaged in activity in international relations, remaining mindful of the need to grasp the limits of each.

Conclusion

In chapter 5 we argued that the state-system is a sortal concept whose main task is to differentiate kinds of state-systems and states. We also argued that the state is a real entity whose essence consists in its external sovereignty. In this chapter, we have advanced the thesis that human nature is best understood as consisting of the two sortal concepts, human animal and person, where the latter is taken to be supervenient upon, but logically distinct from, the former. But now this raises the following question: Is there any reason to believe that these several entities, each with different associated principles of activity, can be integrated into some universal whole in the way required to sustain belief in the possibility of world order?

Viewed from the realist perspective and the substance ontology that goes along with it, an affirmative response here would have to be seen as some sort of massive delusion. It would, for example, neglect a fundamental feature of a realist ontology, namely, the separateness of persons and states. To emphasise this separateness is, in effect, to see their relations as embodying an ineliminable tension, *viz.*, that between individual persons and persons organised collectively into states. If this tension is ineliminable, then we also seem to lack any rational basis for revolutionary reform of the present international system of states which would be directed to something approximating a world order. A system of sovereign states might then be seen as the best means, all things considered, for attaining the reasonable goals of cultural difference, stability of possessions, observance of agreements, and freedom from arbitrary violence. States act in terms of their objective interests while persons act as they will, constrained only by their underlying natures as animals.

Also, the realist idea of human nature, as adumbrated here, might help to restore contact with a moderately naturalistic neo-Aristotelian ethics whose most important feature is that it has not lost all contact with what human beings are *as such*. To bring out the importance of doing so, consider the following passage which suggests, in a vivid way, one possible consequence of trying to do without it. Richard Rorty writes that 'when the secret police come, when the torturers violate the innocent, there is nothing to be said to them of the form, "there is something within you which you are betraying. Though you embody the practices of a totalitarian society which will endure forever, there is something beyond those practices which condemns you". This thought is hard to live with.'[65] Indeed it is, and it has been one of our tasks to propose a theory of what human beings are in their biological constitution in order to circumvent it. For a neo-Aristotelian understanding of ethics and politics carves out a place for human beings in something independent of human will and decision. Having secured this ground in the animal component view of human nature, we were then able to move on to the high country of what is involved in conceiving of ourselves, not only as animals, but also as persons who live in communities. Since bringing together the animal and person components of human beings should help to avoid the twin dangers of relativism and nihilism, there is a good deal at stake in efforts to sustain Thesis Two. That much more would need to be done to show its truth only suggests the complexity and difficulty of establishing questions which relate to human nature. Failure to raise such questions because they are in the 'too hard' basket can only impoverish what we think we know and how we act in international relations.

7   Evaluative political realism and historical realism

> Faithfulness to the truth of history involves far more than research, however patient and scrupulous, into special facts ... The narrator must seek to imbue himself with the life and spirit of the time ... He must himself be, as it were, a sharer or spectator of the action he describes.
>
> Francis Parkman

Introduction

It is a remarkable, though often unnoticed, fact that such realist thinkers as E.H. Carr, Sir Herbert Butterfield, Martin Wight, Hans J. Morgenthau, Friedrich Meinecke, George Kennan, Kenneth Thompson, Raymond Aron (among others), despite a variety of other differences, shared a deep sense of the many ways in which international politics is bound up with historical concepts, categories and methods. As one self-identified 'older' realist has put it: 'No school of thought or "theory" concerned with international relations is closer to history ... than is political realism.'[1] Continued insistence on the intimate connection between history and political realism is both necessary and desirable; nonetheless, for the 'newer', more self-conscious political realist we have been calling evaluative political realist this kind of declaration effectively ignores a central yet obvious question: which conception of history? There are different understandings of history and since they have conflicting implications, it is incumbent on the evaluative political realist to identify the main features of her conception of history. So the leading question here is this: is there a conception of history which captures the realist's point of view in international relations and which, as it turns out, may be regarded as superior to

162

rival conceptions of history? Evaluative political realism affirms that there is and that it is best identified, though with some trepidation, as historical realism.[2] A word of caution needs, however, to be entered: historical realism, as here conceived, is not necessarily committed to theses advanced by philosophers using its name. Historical realism, for example, should not be construed as 'stubbornly non-philosophical'.[3] Historical realism is here understood, rather, as a conception of history committed to the idea that historians can describe past events and actions as they actually happened at a particular time and place. In this respect, the historical realist purports to establish what named individuals or collectivities – Alcibiades, Talleyrand, Kissinger, France, Japan, Panama, Kenya, etc. – did and suffered, of the events in which they were involved and the actions they performed – not by comparing the historian's account of the past with the past (which is impossible), but by showing that the historian's claims to knowledge form a coherent whole such that it would be appropriate to say of these claims that they are true or possibly true. But although historical realism is committed to the idea that at least some historical statements may be *true*, i.e. correctly describe actions and events which have actually occurred in the past, it is no part of this position to contend that actions and events are a matter of the way things are in themselves utterly independent of human conception. At the same time the historical realist rejects the idealist notion which holds that what-there-was in the past is that which we can now *construct* in the way novelists compose their fiction. On this view, the 'reality' of the past itself is up to historians: they construct past actions and events themselves. The historical realist rejects this on the grounds that it engenders a conception of the past which is arbitrary and from which it is impossible to learn anything about human action in the present.

Historical realism – the evaluative political realist's conception of history – also generates non-vacuous differences between its position and rival viewpoints. For example, for the orthodox materialist, the world is constituted, ultimately speaking, of matter in motion: matter is the ultimate reality in space as well as time. The positivist-empiricist holds, on the other hand, that only what is possibly observable by human beings can have ontological standing. The very idea of giving ontological place to what cannot be observed by us makes no sense to empiricists. Evaluative political realism, on the other hand, occupies a third position, *viz.*, the place which, in avoiding deep metaphysical commitments, holds that the social practices of the natural sciences

differ from those in the human sciences and require different conceptions of knowledge. The conception of realism envisaged by evaluative
political realism is close to Heidegger's, as understood in Hubert
Dreyfus's illuminating commentary.[4] Historical realism accepts Heidegger's view that '[s]cientists work within a social practice that
neither they nor philosophers can transcend ... scientists suppose they
... *can* discover the truth about nature as it is, independent of scientific
practices'.[5] Since we have no basis for doubting the suppositions of
natural science, we can then say that science is an enterprise for
securing knowledge of objects and properties in nature.

The primary aim of natural science, on this realist view, is to
provide us with reliable and accurate descriptive information about
the true make-up of a physical reality that is not of our making and
whose existence and nature are largely independent of our cognitive
endeavours. Our understanding of the physical world, then, may be
grasped in absolute terms. To understand human beings and their
institutions, however, we cannot ask questions solely from the absolute perspective that the physical sciences take up; we must also –
indeed mainly – deploy an historical/cultural perspective which
makes room for the points of view which subjects themselves have on
what they are doing and why. In international relations we need this
latter perspective precisely because the entities with which we deal are
so different from physical entities. Since international relations concerns human beings who, as argued in chapter 6, are not only animals
but persons who are self-aware and who express themselves in shared
languages, there is no escape from recognising the personal points of
view which they, in belonging to various institutions (states, multinational organisations, non-governmental organisations, cultural communities, ethnic and racial groups, individuals and so forth),
represent. However much one may strive to express – sometimes
inchoately – an absolute, impersonal conception of the subject, the
ways in which self-interpreting human beings with points of view
characterise the world in which they and others act constitute an
ineliminable feature of historical realism. Since neither positivist-
empiricism nor emancipatory international relations make a place for
such characterisations, we have identified yet another basis for saying
that 'the debate' between evaluative political realism (understood in
this context as historical realism) and its two principal rivals is neither
theoretically nor practically vacuous.

Although the historical realist has many other objections to empiri-

cist and reductive materialist rivals, we have said enough here to state
our third thesis for a refurbished political realism.

> THESIS THREE: History is best studied from a human
> perspective which is practical, actional and objective in a way
> consistent with being a human rather than a physical science.

My strategy for supporting Thesis Three will be to show how the
human perspective on history brings practical, actional and objective
components together to form a coherent whole. There is no implication
in this strategy that some ultimate ground for the understanding of
history will have been located. The task here is the self-consciously
limited one of providing materials for edifying conversation on this
devastatingly important subject.

Historical knowing as theoretical and practical knowing

According to Hans Morgenthau, 'politics, domestic and international,
is susceptible to a radically different kind of understanding from that
which is appropriate to the world of nature'.[6] The different kind of
understanding alluded to by Morgenthau is, I believe, a species of
practical, commonsense knowledge of the sort to be found in life and
history and given due weight and significance by historical realism.
The idea that insofar as human beings are embedded in history a
different sense of knowing is involved in understanding them stretches
back at least as far as Giambattista Vico. In Isaiah Berlin's evocative
reconstruction and interpretation, Vico is seen as carving out a sense of
knowing which is the sense in which I know what it is to be poor, to
fight for a cause, to belong to a nation, to join or abandon a church or a
party, to feel nostalgia, terror, the presence of God, to understand a
gesture, a work of art, a joke, a man's character or that one is lying to
oneself'.[7] Berlin goes on to say that one knows such things:

> in the first place, no doubt, by personal experience; in the second
> place because the experience of others is sufficiently woven into our
> own to be seized quasi-directly as part of constant intimate commu-
> nication; and in the third place by working (sometimes by a conscious
> effort) of the imagination ... This is the sort of knowing which
> participants of an activity claim to possess as against mere observers;
> the knowledge of the actors as against the audience, of the 'inside'
> story as against that obtained from some outside vantage point;

knowledge by 'direct acquaintance' with my 'inner' states or by sympathetic insight into those of others.[8]

For Berlin, in any case, this sense of knowing is 'neither deductive, nor inductive (nor hypothetico-deductive), neither founded on a direct perception of the external world nor a fantasy which lays no claim to truth or coherence'.[9] The suggestion (which links up with our discussion in the previous chapter) is that, as human beings ourselves, we can understand the inner world of human creatures as objects of experience in reality. Derived largely from the exercise of our conceptual capacities as agents in the everyday world, this knowledge is used, in the form of imaginative insight, to establish the full significance of the actions and creations of history. On this view, human beings have conceptual capacities which permit them to enter into one another's thoughts and feelings instead of remaining mere observers of them. Berlin calls this a 'species of self-knowledge of activities of which we, the knowing subjects, are ourselves the author, endowed with motives, purposes and a continuous social life, which we understand, as it were, from the inside'.[10] He contrasts such knowledge with the inferior variety we obtain of inanimate and sub-human phenomena: 'we can perceive and describe a table, a tree, an ant, accumulate information about their behaviour, establish laws but what we still cannot tell is what it is like to be a table, a tree, an ant, in the sense in which we know what it is not merely to behave like but to be, a human being'.[11] By positing a comprehensive subjectivity structured by our conceptual capacities, we can acknowledge the possibility of a form of knowing that is different from our knowledge of nature while still keeping in mind the indispensable thought that human beings are animals.

This conclusion is partially supported by Thomas Nagel's philosophical analysis in 'What Is It Like To Be A Bat?'[12] Here, we are told that for any organism like ourselves in having conscious states, 'there is something that it is like to be that organism – something that it is like for the organism'.[13] In opposition to any form of scientific empiricism or naturalism, someone who holds firmly to the view that certain states just are ways it may be like to be an organism of a certain kind is suggesting the absurdity of investigating such states by a science accessible to creatures who may be unable to experience them. Any shift to 'greater objectivity – that is, less attachment to a specific viewpoint – does not take us nearer to the real nature of the phenomenon: it takes us further from it'.[14] To take up the attitude of, say, positivist-empiricism, an attitude which craves 'the view from nowhere' in Nagel's felicitous phrase, is to attempt to treat the mental as the analogue of a centreless concept of space for physical objects and this, on Nagel's position, is incoherent.

Interestingly enough, Nagel's conclusion is consistent with the view of a philosopher who was more directly concerned with history, R.G. Collingwood.[15] For Collingwood, natural science, entrenched as it is in a world of abstract universals, concerns itself principally with the 'outside' or physical aspect of an event from a point of view which, if deployed in history, would deprive the inquiry of just the sort of perspective which would make it intelligible to us as human beings. Any conception of historical understanding which cannot make a place for first-person perspectives that are also accessible to third-person conceptualising will fail to capture the content of our commonsense understanding of the world's reality. Natural scientists and their naturalistic followers in the social sciences are oriented in their training to treating commonsense ideas with disrespect; but, in regard to their use in historical studies in particular, they have no entitlement to do so.

Depreciation of commonsense is in effect a carryover from the seventeenth century, an era of great scientific advance which tended to look to mathematics and the natural sciences as the supreme models of knowledge and, correspondingly, to devalue the cognitive qualifications of commonsense and history. Descartes, for example, was one of the most eminent philosophical representatives of the attitude that consigned history to an inferior position in the scale of knowledge.[16] He likened historians to the writers of romance and considered history as hardly worth the interest of serious minds, since it lacked rational standards, was credulous and accepting of untrustworthy narratives. He believed that 'antiquarian' scholarship occupied itself with trifles useless to human life. Vico reversed this judgement and Berlin and other realists have sided with Vico and against Descartes. On this sort of realist view, knowledge of the past is indispensable to understanding ourselves as self-interpreting animals who are required to make ethical-political choices.

These claims of historical realism stand in marked contrast to the positivist-empiricist tradition which contends that the best form of reason is not conceptual understanding bound up with practice but theoretical thinking in and for itself. Positivist-empiricists regard practical reason as an unsatisfactory substitute for theoretical reason. One hastens to add that positivist-empiricism is partially right in holding that we need to retain *some* distinction between theoretical and practical reason, particularly as against those conceptions of history which propose the eventual collapse of theory into practice. For the historical realist, theory and practice can never be identical. Theoretical reasoning, for example, tends to be directed to truth and to structures which preserve truth through change while practical reasoning tends to be oriented to what one should do and not to truth *per se*. However, it is also important to understand that there are structural similarities between theoretical and practical knowing which make any strictly dichotomous separation between them ill-conceived. For example, knowing a proposition to be true implies that one believes the proposition and this is certainly analogous to what goes on in practical knowing. Knowing how to negotiate with the representatives of other states, for example, normally follows from having understood the purposes and aims of negotiation and this, of course, involves understanding what negotiators reasonably believe about the nature and character of negotiation. So reasonable belief seems to be involved in both theoretical and practical knowing.

There is another important structural similarity. Learning to perform a complex skill such as negotiating is essentially a matter of learning how to reason practically and teaching someone to execute a certain purpose is similarly a matter of instructing him in the ways of practical knowing by means of rational directives, of acquainting him with rational procedures and showing him how particular ends are logically related to specific means. The 'logic' involved here is the logic of practical inference in which a valid conclusion is a piece of reasoning undergone for a deliberate purpose. So just as evidence and logic have to be employed to acquire knowledge of 'how the world is', so too these tools of reasoning have to be used in making practical inferences to acquire practical knowledge.

The practical characteristics of history may be considered from the perspective of language as well. Since language is a storehouse of meanings, any human activity that involves language will present historians with pre-articulated interpretations of what the activity they are trying to understand is all about; hence, the historian's interpretations of those actions must be ones which agents themselves may be supposed to have understood. From this it follows that historians must be in a position to reconstruct the practical aims, interests, intentions, desires and beliefs of the agents themselves if they are to understand the sequence of events in which agents have been involved. But in reconstructing beliefs that agents have about their society or the events in which they have been involved, historians will also bring their own social theories to bear and consequently, theory in history will have a dialectical and reflective character. That is, it will consist of historians' beliefs, the beliefs of historical agents and the attempt to mediate the differences between the two when conflicts arise.

But there is still another important sense in which historical knowledge differs from 'scientific' knowledge, as construed at least by robust naturalism. Historians normally make value judgements concerning the objects they study. Although one might attempt to argue that it is not logically necessary that historians of international relations make moral judgements concerning, say, the causes of war, alliance making, the world environment, third and fourth world poverty, the appalling conditions of women in many states and so forth, it would be a particularly empty kind of history which refused, on so-called 'scientific' grounds, to offer such judgements. For example, consider an historian who examined Hitler's role in exterminating Jews: it would certainly be quite natural for her to use the contrastive language of good and evil to compare Hitler's behaviour with, say, Winston Churchill's. Moreover, as William Dray has argued, even the historian's use of causal language which, for the positivist-empiricist must be value free, is normally charged with value. In analysing an article by the diplomatic historian Norman Graebner on the causes of the Mexican–American War, Dray remarks that Graebner's language 'belongs not to the language of science but to the language of morals'.[17]

Dray argues, quite successfully, that despite Graebner's effort to hive moral language (and the judgements it comports) off from the generalisations he offers, his language remains studded with evaluation.[18]

We may sum up these reflections on practice in history by noting that for historical realism *practical knowledge* exists; it is not an oxymoron like 'jumbo shrimp'. Of course, the kind of knowledge which becomes available to us when we deploy our conceptual capacities in acting in the world will not be scientific knowledge; rather, it is the kind of knowledge that we gather up because we are historical beings who have reasons for acting the way we do and memories for storing them. Such knowledge is accumulated practical wisdom and the historical realist unabashedly calls upon it in citing the lessons we learn from history, including, most importantly, the lessons that we learn concerning the limits of historical knowledge itself. Learning the lessons of history in this sense will warrant a certain sceptical attitude towards utopian schemes for a new enlightenment generated by conceiving history as transcendent and directed towards a transcendent good. It will mean learning the lesson that we have no valid organic perspective in terms of which to integrate conflicting interpretations of the world. And it will mean learning that there is no finitude, no *Aufhebung*, no metanarrative to ennoble the everydayness of conflict and tragic dilemmas. The historical realist's major compensation for incorporating these somewhat depressing lessons into her conception of the world lies in the recognition of the harm she avoids in resisting the temptations of monism and in appreciating anew the pluralism of an intractably palpable past. We turn now to examine the actional component of historical realism.

History and human action

In describing and explaining historical events and actions, historical realists make constant appeal to such concepts as intentions, desires, interests, wants, beliefs and reasons. This suggests that historical realism is committed not only to preventing the elimination of the gap between theory and practice, but also to an actional perspective on the past. For example, Morgenthau famously recommended that:

> we put ourselves in the position of a statesman who must meet a certain problem of foreign policy under certain circumstances, and we ask ourselves what the rational alternatives are from which a statesman may choose who must meet this problem under these circumstances (presuming also that he acts in a rational manner), and which of these rational alternatives this particular statesman, acting under these circumstances, is likely to choose. It is the testing of this rational hypothesis against the actual facts and their consequences that gives meaning to the facts of international politics and makes a theory of politics possible.[19]

Although Morgenthau uses the word 'rational' here, it would have been closer to his intention, I believe, if he had used the word 'reasonable' or one of its cognates. For what Morgenthau was alluding to, on my reading, is the possibility of intentional explanations, i.e. in which we explain behaviour by making it intelligible, or by showing how it makes sense, in the light of an individual's desires and reasons (including reasons concerning the contextual circumstances in which she is required to make choices of certain kinds). Although commitment to an actional perspective on history and international relations has many ramifications, we shall focus here mainly on how reasons explain historical actions.

What though are actions? For the historical realist, there is a decisive difference between actions and bodily movements, namely, that actions are voluntary and normally explicated by discovering the agent's reasons. This is not to deny that there exists a broadly causal element in the citation of reasons for actions; but only that causes operate differently from the way they do in purely physical contexts. When someone performs an action she does what she does at will. She puts something into motion and it is she who does it. When physical movements take place such as a rock tumbling over a mountain ledge, the change that is effected is one that is a causal consequence of something else that happened. The difference between actions and bodily movements is decisive in that it shifts attention *from* what is in movement *to* the mover and the mover's reasons for action. It is the agent, often acting in terms of certain intentions, who brings about certain changes with the understanding that such changes go beyond purely physical movements. Very often the action involves a shift from what may be directly observed to what is not publicly observable, a feature of action which raises, from an empiricist perspective, sceptical worries.

The idea that action is best construed as reducible to bodily movements, or some analogue thereof, plays a very large role in positivist-empiricist approaches to international relations. In presupposing the need for programmes to reduce actions to physically observable events, positivist-empiricists appear to be motivated largely by the desire for a uniform understanding of causality and scientific objectivity. Motor responses or bodily movements constitute the behavioural terms in which we are supposed to define the causal role of a person's mental state. For positivist-empiricists, the goal here is to be able to specify the functional (causal and probabilistic) relations between mental and bodily states as picked out in a vocabulary of physical inputs and outputs. For example, Karl Deutsch claimed that the occupants of causal roles can come to be identified with physical states of the brain.[20] The only effects of a person's actions relevant to her psychology, on this view, occur at the surface of her body and the inner states which cause actions can be described without alluding to the world she inhabits. Since an agent's psychological states can be, in principle, fully and scientifically captured by observing her overt behaviour, any appeal to the historical or political context in which the agent moved would be otiose. Descriptions of people's mental states need to be comprehensively decontextualised if they are to be made available for uniform scientific description and explanation.

The historical realist, on the other hand, rejects this essentially physicalist viewpoint, replacing it with a humanistic concept of human action. In so doing the historical realist relies on a number of arguments to support the idea that identifying human action requires the application of criteria that are different from those used to identify physical movements. First of all, the criteria for the application of terms relating to bodily movements are not the same as those for the performance of actions signified by those bodily movements. Thus, for example, the same bodily movement is involved in the three different actions of signing a cheque, giving an autograph and authorising an agent to do something on one's behalf. Obviously, the criteria appropriate for determining whether certain bodily movements took place bear no resemblance to the criteria that would have to be invoked to determine which, if any, of the above-mentioned actions actually took place.

Secondly, the predicates appropriate to answering questions about human actions are of a different logical order from the predicates appropriate to answering questions about bodily movements. Thus, if someone were to ask me why my hand moved when touched by a hot flame, the appropriate answer would include reference to conditioned reflexes, muscles and nerves. If someone were to ask me, however, why I moved my hand, an appropriate answer would make reference to my reasons, goals, intentions or purposes. Also, as a corollary to this, when the question concerns why I moved my hand, I possess a special, though not absolute, authority in answering which stems from my usually being in a better position than anybody else to know the reasons, purposes, goals, etc. that motivated my behaviour. When the question, however, is why my armed moved, I have no special authority in answering the question, and must defer to the expertise of the special sciences.

Thirdly, when I refer to an action that I did (or tried to do), there is no room for the further question, how do you know? Raising such an epistemological question has point only where the relevant criteria that are appealed to can be placed along a sliding scale indicating varying degrees of certainty. Where self-knowledge of my own present actions is at issue, my knowledge is not one of degree. Where bodily movements are concerned, however, since objective observations by myself or others are always in place, so too are varying degrees of knowledge. Hence, the question, 'how do you know?' retains its appropriateness.

Fourthly, where I talk about a proposed action, using the future tense, the statement that I make should be classified as the expression of an intention and not a prediction. Even where I want to make a prediction about my behaviour, knowledge of my intention forms the prior step which makes the prediction possible. Where bodily movements are concerned, however, the notion of intention is completely out of place, and the language of prediction alone suffices. One can make safe predictions about a person's bodily movements without any knowledge of their intentions.

Fifthly, and most important, historians often explain (or purport to explain) an action by alluding to agents' reasons why they acted as they did in the circumstances in which their actions took place. Following Collingwood, William Dray, for example, undertakes to show, against the positivist-empiricist tradition in particular, that human actions can be explained without recourse at any point to universal causal laws. As Dray puts it, rational explanations are the historian's reconstruction 'of the agent's calculation of means to be adopted toward his chosen end in the light of the circumstances in which he found himself'; and hence 'to explain the action we need what considerations convinced him that he should act as he did'.[21] Where the person is shown to have done the reasonable thing because it was the reasonable thing to do, this can be said to constitute an explanatory end to that particular historical question. Admittedly, the historian will not always know what would have been the reasonable thing for a person to do but, in that event, she must make a considered judgement, i.e. rely on reflective deliberation. In offering an explanation, the historian is, in effect, comparing the reasonableness of what different persons have done with her own reckoning of what would have been reasonable under the circumstances. She need not claim to be omniscient, but she cannot avoid making a judgement of the reasonableness of the persons whose past actions she is trying to explain.

But what if we encounter a situation in which some of the central beliefs agents had about their alternative possibilities were in some way unreasonable? It may be that their possibilities were more or less numerous than they believed, or that they found possibilities attractive or unattractive because they ignored readily available features whose acknowledgement would have inclined them in another direction, or that they were deceiving themselves, or that their beliefs were caused by anger, fear, fantasy, spite or envy. In such cases, knowing the reasons agents gave will not be enough for understanding the significance of their actions. The search for understanding, then, must go beyond these reasons and explore the question of why there is a discrepancy between what the agents believed about their possibilities and what it is actually reasonable to believe about them. By understanding why the agents were unreasonable, we may come to understand the significance of their actions, even though that significance may have been hidden from the agents themselves. But how, more particularly, do these considerations lead to explanation in cases of the sort that international relationists would be interested? To understand this we need to understand the logic of practical inference.

Practical inference and intention

The idea of practical inference stretches back to Aristotle's theory of the practical syllogism in *de Motu Animalium* and *de Anima*. In these works, Aristotle says that the first premise of a practical syllogism tells us that such and such a kind of person should do such and such a kind of act. The second premise informs us that this is an act of the kind meant and a person of the type intended. The conclusion follows by logic alone. This simple yet powerful idea has been shaped into a far more complex structure by G.H. von Wright whose practical inference schema looks like this:

  I   The agent intends to bring about a certain end E.
 II   The agent believes (in the sense of deliberates) that unless he does action A in time, i.e. no later than time T, he cannot achieve E.
III   At time no later than T, normal conditions prevail:
(a)   The agent is not prevented from acting.
(b)   He has not forgotten about the time.
(c)   His intention is still in effect; he has not changed his mind, etc.
 IV   Therefore, the agent undertakes the doing of A.[22]

Von Wright contended that his general schema was a candidate for a formal model of explanation in history and the social sciences and the historical realist is sympathetic to this claim. In applying von Wright's schema to history, however, certain adjustments have to be made and certain supplementary materials added. In trying to explain an action in the past, historians already know that the action has occurred; hence, premise III no longer needs to be determined. Historians only need to determine the intention-premise and the belief-premise. Taken together such premises (I and II) state the reasons why historical agents acted as they did. At this point a diagram (slightly modified from von Wright) might be useful:[23] What needs noticing here is that this is not really the practical inference model described above but a new schema, one which is applicable, in particular, to historical study. The practical inference schema moved from premises to conclusion in a straightforward manner; whereas the schema we are now considering – let us call it 'the interpretive schema' – moves from situational facts (or what von Wright calls 'motivational background') to practical premises, where the agent's intention is affected by his perception of these facts, and hence to the action done.[24] As the schema suggests, practical inference reasoning is 'a reasoning of transitions':[25] a movement from situational facts to practical premises to action conclusions.

As example of the use of this schema, von Wright cites the role played by the assassination of the Austrian archduke at Sarajevo on the outbreak of World War I. Von Wright's main point is that between the assassination which is the cause of the event (the *explanans*) and the outbreak of war which is the effect (the *explanandum*) there is no general law at work but rather a complex series of actions, each one of which provided a motivation for the next action and ultimately for the last in the series, the outbreak of the war itself. The general overall link between explanans and explanandum is causal but, nonetheless, practical inferences incorporating intentional explanations are still required to move us from a situational fact (e.g. the assassination at Sarajevo) to a particular action, which then constitutes a new situational fact for yet another practical inference culminating in further action and so on. The practical inference constitutes actual assessments by historical persons of the aims and interests of the parties which had a stake in Balkans' politics: they are links in a chain which provide motivations for further actions. Thus, the assassination provided Austria with a 'rationale' for presenting Serbia with an ultimatum and this in turn motivated Russia to mobilise its forces. Since Serbia was allied with Russia, this generated the resolve the Serbians needed to refuse to comply with the ultimatum: the Austrian declaration of war ultimately followed. And so forth. To be sure, there is no implication in

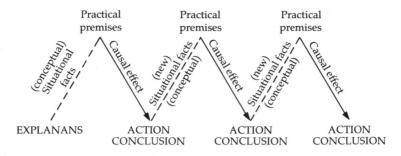

Figure 7.1

von Wright's views that historians actually follow or should follow
this schema in their historical research; the point is rather to uncover
the logic of what historical realists like Morgenthau are claiming to use
when they recommend that historians put themselves in the place of
historical persons to give meaning to the 'raw material' of foreign
policy.

We are now prepared, in a way that von Wright did not make
explicit, to examine the character of the links between situational background and practical premises, on the one hand, and practical premises
and action conclusion on the other. As to the former link, we hold that it
is conceptual rather than causal. This is one reason why we cannot
follow either positivist-empiricists or poststructuralists in banishing
agent intention. On our picture, situational facts, e.g. the assassination
of the archduke, exert a rational influence on an agent's thinking such
that an intention to act takes shape in the practical premises of an
historical explanation. The conceptual capacities of the agent who is
engaged in experiencing situational facts rationally link them to a wider
reality and create an intention to act or not to act. The historical realist
does not deny that many intentional explanatia include causal claims;
the historical realist says rather that such causal claims have to be
understood through the agent's rational thoughts about them. The key
point is that behaviour which is to count as intentional action must be
linked to practical premises in a certain way, namely, as brought about
for reasons which make the agent's actions reasonable. Beliefs and
wants alone are not sufficient to account for an action; intentions must
be appealed to as well if the historian is to make intelligible the events
she is examining. In revealing intentions historians are putting events
and actions into a context of intelligibility and meaning.

Intentions play a causal role as well. Consider, in this connection, the link between practical premise and action conclusion. Evidently this link is a causal one. Intentions here play a causal role in the production of action in the same way in which beliefs that the premises of an argument are true play a causal role in the production of the believer's belief in the entailed conclusion. When someone practically infers an intention to do A here and now because he believes that doing A here and now will ensure that E will occur and he intends to make E occur, this intention and the instrumental belief play a causal role in the inference making: they enter intrinsically into his act of bringing about his intention. Actions entail, as a necessary condition of their occurrence, that the agent should take account of the content of the intention; and intentions, in turn, bring about events as their object and consequently have a causal role in linking practical premises and action conclusion. So although intentions do not causally suffice for intentional action, they are necessary to what does causally suffice: the events which are objects of the agent's doings. Intentions, then, play a dual role: they make intelligible why an agent is motivated to take a certain course of action to resolve the situation in which he finds himself, and they play a causal role in producing the events which the historian's narrative tries to capture. On this interpretation, one can understand perhaps why von Wright might want to call his schema quasi-causal: it permits both a conceptual and a causal role to an agent's intentional states.

Understood in this way, the theory of action helps to clarify the logic of Morgenthau's methodological prescription of putting oneself in the position of a statesman who is faced with a certain problem and who has to make a rational decision as to which alternative is the most reasonable one, all things considered. As analysed in terms of von Wright's schema, this would not involve re-thinking or re-enacting the actual thoughts of the statesman – a procedure which historical realists would, quite rightly, regard with derision. It involves an historian's attempt to uncover the situational and motivational facts which form the bases of practical premises whose descriptions of agents as intentionally bringing about certain events explain action conclusions. Note also that there is no implication in Morgenthau's recommendation that historians or international relationists should attempt to do this through intuition and without evidence. To avoid any possible false implication of this sort, it would seem advisable to understand Morgenthau's recommendation as a practical inference, that is, as an argument with premises and action conclusion. The premises will render an action understandable only if the action conclusion follows from true premises. But the only way the premises of practical premises can be determined to be true is on the basis of evidence concerning the situation in which the statesman found himself and his own motivations and intentions. Any suggestion that political realism is 'intuition without evidence' is a red herring.

We can sum this up by saying that for the historical realist such concepts as intention, purpose, wants, desires, reasons and so forth cannot be banished from our historical accounts of international relations without distorting and misrepresenting historical actions and events. This is one reason why historical realism rejects the strident anti-humanism that is so much a part of both positivist-empiricism and poststructuralist international relations. An important feature of the latter is to claim, following Derrida and Foucault, that intentions are, and should be, eliminated from whatever conceptual apparatus we use to understand human beings.[26] The position identified here is meant to move in the opposite direction but nonetheless avoids – as one should – a Cartesian cognitive model of human action. The heart of the historical realist's view lies in the assumption that history is composed of agents who *sometimes* intentionally *try*, and sometimes *succeed*, in bringing about certain happenings and states of affairs. We must now raise the question of whether history is, as the historical realist claims, at least partly objective.

The absolute conception of the world

Thomas Nagel's position

An appealing and dramatic way of bringing out what is at issue in claims to objectivity is to postulate an 'absolute conception of the world'.[27] This is a conception of what there is in the world independently of our experience. It is a conception of the world extracted and detached from the various points of view which people have of it. This externalist approach to reality tells us about the way things are in themselves. By postulating an absolute conception of the world, the realist would then be in possession of a framework which would evidently ratify one of his fundamental principles, namely, that much of our natural scientific activity investigates a mind-independent world, a world of trees, electrons and quarks, of people who actually exist and of events in the past which actually happened. For the historical realist, the idea that historians use the absolute conception of the world – the model appropriate to acquiring physical knowledge – to obtain knowledge of international relations, however, is anathema. To avoid this result the historical realist urges us to adopt some of Thomas Nagel's important philosophical conclusions on the incompleteness of reality. In doing so the historical realist will be using a framework that will enable her to consider the limits of historical objectivity.[28]

An important feature of Nagel's position is that he accepts, consistent with the commitments of historical realism, the deep value of natural scientific theory for our understanding of physical objects while rejecting all versions of a physicalist understanding of the human sciences. In particular, Nagel denies any sort of identity relation between robust naturalism and the intelligibility of reality. For although our 'understanding of the physical world has been expanded enormously with the aid of theories and explanations that use concepts not tied to a specifically human perceptual viewpoint', Nagel holds, quite rightly, that 'there is more to reality than what can be accommodated by the physical conception of objectivity'.[29] That 'something more' turns out to consist of subjective viewpoints. When these are given appropriate place within an objective, but non-physicalist, conception of the world, what we get as a yield, according to Nagel, is an *Incomplete View of Reality* (IVR). The incompleteness arises because objectivity and subjectivity are in a tension, one upshot of which is to make the world unintelligible.[30] But contrary to what rationalistic views of the world might lead us to suppose, this is 'no cause for philosophical alarm, because there is no reason to assume that the world as it is in itself must be objectively comprehensible'.[31]

In *The Limits of Objectivity* Nagel draws a tight connection between *IVR* and the possibility of accommodating mind and value in a non-physicalist, but nonetheless objective, conception of the world. He suggests, for example, that we have good reason to suppose the possibility of representing our subjective experiences in general terms, viz., in terms of what he calls 'subjective universals – some instances of which one is familiar with from one's own experience'.[32] The possibility here alluded to is of thought stretching beyond verifiable experience, a notion which Nagel locates in an unequivocally realist and 'pretheoretical' conception of the world 'which permits us to go some way beyond our experiences and those exactly like them'.[33] Now, if we are able to form a general idea of a perspective on the world that goes beyond our verifiable experiences, as Nagel suggests with persuasive examples that I shall not reproduce here, then in applying this idea to ourselves it should in principle be possible 'to analyse our experiences in ways that can be understood without such experiences', i.e. in an objective fashion.[34]

For historical realists, there are good grounds for retaining *some* notion of objectivity in our understanding of human beings. There is an important sense in which human beings have objectively identifiable interests (within a certain context) that do not depend directly on cultural or social norms or practices. Although we recognise the enormous diversity of human beings in human cultures, historical realists also appreciate the constancy of mental states across cultures. As indicated in the previous chapter, people have primary wants and are makers of future plans; they lay out certain possibilities and clearly calculate their value in terms of goals and the possibilities of attainment. And there seems no reason why our descriptions of these activities cannot be 'objective' in some prosaic understanding of this word.

From objective conception to subjective experience

As Nagel quite correctly points out, in taking up any such objective viewpoint 'something will inevitably be lost'.[35] Just as Isaiah Berlin holds that there is no such thing as a world without loss, so Nagel contends that a completely objective standpoint will deprive us of the specific qualities that make up the subjective point of view. In particular, we shall not be able to know what it is like to be a bat or a statesperson (if we are a physicist) without characterising that animal's point of view. And this in turn implies that any objective conception of the world will be incomplete: 'no objective conception of the mental world can include it all'.[36] So any attempt to form a true conception of reality 'must include an acknowledgement of its own incompleteness'.[37] Since we have imagination, the incompleteness of reality will not hinder us from conceiving 'of experiences we have not had'; however, it 'may not allow us to detach the concept of mind from a human perspective'.[38]

But if the human perspective is a personal one and involves essentially the idea of competing points of view, there will be no transhistorical, transcultural description of world politics that can include all competing points of view. 'Reality', Nagel says, 'is not just objective reality.'[39] To be true to reality, so understood, we must make a place both for a limited objectivity and those ineliminable subjective features of it which allow us to penetrate to the inside of events.

Support for this conclusion is to be found in Colin McGinn's *The Subjective View*.[40] McGinn contends that a physicalist world makes no place for indexical modes of thought – those represented by the use of 'I', 'here', 'now' – because they articulate a point of view on the world. Such a point of view is possessed by a psychological subject whose judgements would be partially reflective of that point of view and hence, to that extent, recalcitrant to any absolute conception of the world. So the question for the evaluative political realist is whether we can make sense of the mind's evident capacity to be directly and cognitively aware of space, time and itself (in the form of introspection) which does not involve thinking of these items in indexical terms. If the answer is an unequivocal 'no' (as seems likely), then we have yet another basis for restricting the scope of what Nagel calls 'the view from nowhere'.

To sum up the argument concerning the IVR principle: when we try to envisage a world devoid of subject-related properties and indexical modes of thought, we are bound to fail. How are we to conceive of what such a world would be like without conceiving of what it would feel or look like? And how would it be possible to think of a world stripped of indexical modes of thought, of *I, here* and *now*? It is hard to take exception to Nagel's contention that '[m]ost of our experience of the world ... belong[s] to our individual points of view'.[41] Once we concede the idea that our viewpoint on the world is mostly a personal one, necessarily involving primary and secondary qualities as well as indexicals, then it would seem that no conceivable perceptual experience of the world can fail to include subjective features of it, i.e. our conception of the world can't be fully objective in the way that the scientific empiricist, for example, requires to make sense of his project for history. And this view has a certain fallout. For we now seem to face the opposite difficulty of saying whether there are any grounds for rejecting historical scepticism. Since the various *mises en perspectives* which historians employ cannot be integrated into a single, valid universal perspective, there would seem to be no basis for saying which perspective is true, right or correct. Is there any ground for saying, as Raymond Aron evidently wanted to, that a partial form of objectivity can be achieved in historical study, or must we, rather, agree with Richard Ashley and 'the New Historicism' that all writing of history is a form of fiction that has no legitimate claim to truth, warranted assertibility or correctness?[42] To push beyond these disputes what is needed, in my view, is an account of historical narrative which makes contact with rule following. It is to this task that we turn now.

Narrative, rule following and objectivity

Despite the voluminous literature on narrative and narrativity, international theory has not, in general, come to grips with understanding international relations as narrative. This is not the place to try to fill this gap. Nevertheless, it is also clear that historical realism needs to develop a conception of history which makes it less vulnerable to charges that political realism is rooted in structuralist categories inimical to historical change, without at the same time falling into the swamps of radical historicism in which all claims to 'truth', 'reality' and 'objectivity' are disguised forms of power/domination.[43] A conception of history as narrative might help here and in two ways: first, such a conception permits claims to truth and, second, it makes a certain form of objectivity possible by virtue of rule-following.

Historical realism and historical truth

In certain formulations, the idea that history is best understood as narrative has seemed to require rejection of the thought that historical narratives strive to be, and can sometimes attain, truth. For example, according to Louis Mink there is no basis for defending any historical narrative's 'claim to truth by any accepted procedure of argument or authentification'.[44] Moreover, with the rise of poststructuralist philosophies of history, the way has evidently been cleared for embracing a conception of history for international relations in which truth, reality and reference get no purchase whatever. On the extreme version of the poststructuralist view there would be no basis for distinguishing revisionist accounts of the Holocaust which say that it never took place from accounts which identify it, quite properly, as one of the most important ethico-political events of all time. History, for the extreme poststructuralist, is arbitrary; all interpretations have an equal chance of being true but there is no way of telling whether one account is 'more' true than any other. Let us consider how an historical realist might argue against someone who also holds that narratives cannot be true, a position usefully identified as the 'no-truth view'.

Suppose a no-truth-viewer argues that there is no prospect of our determining whether the realist idea that 'states in the seventeenth and eighteenth centuries acted in terms of their interests' is true. For an historian to have some hope of succeeding in establishing this claim, she would have to have access to earlier discourses about the state's role and function many of which, let us suppose, would take the form of narratives. The no-truth-viewer might say that critiques of earlier narratives about the state show the self-cancelling or self-subverting character of those earlier narratives. The no-truth view might then attempt to show that such claims were ideological or, perhaps, that they were in the service of power/domination which controlled the earlier narratives. But to get any genuine argumentative leverage on the topic at all, the no-truth viewer would have to presuppose that the earlier narratives had *potential* access to the truth about the state's interests which earlier narratives were evidently unable to grasp just because their writers were in the grip of ideology or power/domination. For this to be the case, moreover, there must have been enough that was determinate in the meaning of the earlier narrative to give it purchase on the object in question, i.e. the state's interests. Otherwise, the object that the no-truth-viewer picked out would not be the object of *that* text but of some wholly different one. But then access to that determinate meaning cannot be accounted for in terms provided for by the idea that interpretations are arbitrary. Furthermore, it would hardly be possible to withhold a similar acknowledgement in the case of a past author whose text the no-truth-viewer wanted to analyse. This need not involve accepting the knowledge-claims of the narrative historian who lived and wrote in the past, but it is at least to accept that some part of her statements either refer or fail to refer and that they must be judged to be true or false. Without the possibility of such claims, we would become vulnerable to implying a form of relativism such that it would be possible to live in radically different worlds in which anyone could mean whatever they wanted to mean.[45] Since this sort of relativism is incoherent, the idea that a narrative about the past, to be about *our* past, can be a narrative about what really happened in the past and might therefore be true has not become obsolete. Insofar as this analysis has merit, historical realism, in adopting it, need not accept any view of narrative which assumes that it has nothing whatever to do with truth.

Rules, rule-following and objectivity

In *The Idea of a Social Science* Peter Winch argued that rules generate epistemological worries concerning objectivity in the social sciences, but few philosophers of history have been inclined to follow up Winch's insights.[46] Interestingly enough, Winch accepts the idea, in terms strikingly similar to Morgenthau's above, that 'the investigation of society is on quite a different logical footing from the investigation of nature'. Unlike Morgenthau, however, Winch derives this conclusion from philosophical arguments concerning the role of language in social life. For Winch, as for Wittgenstein, learning a language involves participation in social practices. One's very categories of meaning are logically dependent for their sense on the intertwining of practices and language. To learn a language is to be involved in a practice in which the speaker comes to grasp the rules which govern the use of concepts and how social practices are made intelligible because of the rules they embody. To act, to be doing something, is to be committed to a context in which it makes sense to speak of actions being correctly done or not. According to Winch, all meaningful behaviour – all behaviour which has a point – is rule-governed. Despite a large critical literature opposing Winch's views, his position has not been successfully refuted. Nonetheless, it needs to be supplemented.

The most important property of being rule-governed is followability. W.B. Gallie has worked out a valuable account of what it is to follow a story.[47] To understand what a story is, according to Gallie, is to know what it is to *follow* a story – to know what, in general, the features of a story are which make it *followable*. He argued that this feature was similar to what made a game followable. Following a story, like watching, say, a cricket match involves surprises and contingencies – which side will win, for example, and whether the teams have played well or badly. What we are doing effectively in watching a game is following a series of events and actions across their contingent relations in terms of certain explicit or implicit rules and conventions which make them intelligible. We understand such events and actions, Gallie said, as leading to an irreversible conclusion without, however, necessitating it. By the same token, an historical narrative does not demonstrate the necessity of events and actions but, rather, makes them intelligible by imbricating them in a narrative. It is followability which enables us to make intelligible to ourselves and others what is going on, say, in picking out salient features of diplomatic negotiations, in understanding the different religious practices that shape actions in international politics and in interpreting the role of judicial decisions promulgated by the International Court of Justice. In simple and well-defined cases, followability involves the capacity to apply (or follow) rules; following a rule involves knowing its point and this means that acting in accordance with a rule presupposes a context of meaning within which the rule must be set. In history, followability is a matter – at least in the simplest of cases – of being able to understand how a series of what would otherwise be unconnected actions and events link up with one another. Followability in history minimally implies that a true or correct story of how actions and events connect up with one another can be told. Followability does not imply that the events and incidents in the story need to be predictable; on the contrary, stories admit of surprises, fortuitous happenings, twists and turns – in a word contingencies – for these are of the very nature of what it means to be a story.

It is important to stress the close relationship between followability and contingency because these two concepts will help us to distinguish the aims of history from the aims of the natural sciences, and without compelling us to give up all claim to objectivity in historical studies. In natural science one searches for laws, for necessary and sufficient conditions, for closure of systems, etc., i.e. for the elimination of contingencies. Of course, the natural scientist may have to accept contingencies temporarily but only until the appropriate laws have been discovered. An historian, however, who tries to eliminate con-tingencies may be depriving herself of just those features of the situation which will make her account a story of related events; for contingencies, as Oakeshott puts it, 'help us to see how other things actually worked out as they did'.[48] Contingencies are bound up with our answering the question of what historical episodes mean.

But what is it that makes certain contingencies acceptable or admis-sible to a story and not others? Gallie argues that this is virtually equivalent to the question 'what makes a particular story followable?'[49] But now we are in obvious danger of circularity with our two concepts. To break out of it Gallie encourages us to explicate 'followability' in terms of what it means to follow a game. To follow a game we have to grasp its rules. And here we make contact, however tenuously at first, with a certain familiar idea concerning the nature of international politics, viz., that it is 'a game' played mainly by states in terms of certain 'rules' the principal object of which is to 'win' certain valued things such as territory, economic strength, political power and influence. Viewing matters in this way materially captures a great deal of what goes on in quotidian international relations, as any reader of Thucydides' *Peloponnesian Wars* or Henry Kissinger's *White House Years* and *Diplomacy* will readily appreciate.[50] But this is not the aspect of rules with which we are concerned here. Rather, we wish to focus on those features of rules which will help us see how historians of international relations make judgements concerning what is to count as 'going on in the same way'. It is precisely because rules are identifiable entities which people can, and often enough do, follow and which historians can retrace and make perspicuous that we can legitimately speak of historical objectivity. I shall call such rules, for mnemonic purposes, following-rules.

Unlike Morton Kaplan's 'essential rules', following-rules are not constitutive in character: their purpose is not to define those abstract features of an international system without whose presence the system would cease to exist.[51] The task of following-rules is to help one to grasp practices which evolve and change, sometimes in unexpected ways, so that historians can work back from 'what is going on' to 'what went on'; hence, following-rules form a context of pastness for present situations and undertakings. Following-rules identify a major portion of history's *res gestae*, those recorded survivals from the past which historians piece together to form a coherent historical description. They are to be found in codified and quasi-codified form as customs, social rules, maxims, plans, warnings, instructions, advice and commands that constitute the raw materials for reconstructing past events and actions. Following-rules are also embodied in uncodified sets of practices: of ordering, intuiting, explaining, intending, interpreting and so on. In recognising that historical agents develop independent dispositions or inclinations to extrapolate from one situation to another, we are able to characterise their descriptions of human actions as 'potentially objective'. If there were no following-rules, it would be hard to see how we could choose between alternative historical descriptions of human action at all. There would be no way of saying that a particular description of past human action conforms with the way things were for X or Y.

Following-rules apply to virtually every aspect of international politics: security, foreign trade, laws of the sea, diplomatic bargaining, the practices of multinational corporations and so on. Following-rules help to foster consensual judgements on what happened and what action X or Y performed in the past: consensus is possible because it is derived from a shared language the understanding of whose following-rules enables historians to make objective claims about what went on in the past. Insofar as following-rules embrace explicit reference to past cases, they enable historians to pick out patterns of relationships and so give continuity and shape to what would otherwise be a chaotic jumble of historical material. For example, the rule that statesmen should 'act in terms of their national interests' or the rule that statesmen should 'not engage in appeasement policies' will help historians to know where to look for facts concerning the activities of an important class of individuals. This is no accident. International relations deals with social institutions which shape group and individual relations. If the behaviour of groups and individuals were not to a very large extent governed by commonly recognised rules, people would not know what to expect of others. Without following-rules there would be no organised social life and no history of states or state-systems or other group entities. But since there are histories of these entities, the bare possibility of objectivity in international relations appears to exist. We need not – indeed better not – try to go beyond that bare possibility to uncover a supposed *foundation* for objectivity in international relations since we have no reason to think that there is one. In any case, if objectivity is construed as rule-following, as we urge here, we need not regard narrative histories of international relations as lacking objectivity or truth. Narrative historians can follow what X and Y did because they understand how human agents go on from one activity to another; that is all one requires to defeat radical subjectivism. In this respect historical realists accept what Wittgenstein said about grasping a rule:

> There is a way of grasping a rule which is *not* an *interpretation*, but which is exhibited in what we call 'obeying the rule' and 'going against it' in actual cases ... Hence there is an inclination to say 'every action according to the rule is an interpretation'. But we ought to restrict the term 'interpretation' to the substitution of one expression of the rule for another.[52]

So if one discovers actual cases in which statespeople did not 'act in the national interest', the historian can say that they went against the rule. There is no compelling need to say that such cases require historians to hold that history is nothing but interpretation.

Now the sceptic has available several sorts of challenges to the claim that history finds its objectivity in following-rules. We cannot examine all of these here. Let us consider, however, what might be thought to be the severest challenge. Such a position might maintain that although history finds its appropriate conception of objectivity in following-rules, one would still need to draw a contrast between those disciplines where standards of assessment are reliable and rational and those where they are not. Surely, the sort of standards of rational assessment to be found, one might say, in mathematics will show history to be a very poor second at best insofar as practices of historical objectivity depend on shared rules in a way that the kinds of practices found in mathematics do not. But this argument will not go through in the light of Wittgenstein's discussion in *Philosophical Investigations*. According to Wittgenstein, understanding mathematics depends on possessing a set of attitudes which constitute good reasons for drawing a particular inference. Although Wittgenstein did not explicitly say so, it may be argued that there is no essential difference, in this respect, between history and mathematics.

One might think that historical agreements will differ from mathematical agreements because, when there are disagreements in the latter, one of the disputants must have engaged in self-contradiction, plain error or deviant understanding. By contrast, in an historical dispute, there is, the sceptic might allege, an additional possibility, one on a different epistemic level from these others, i.e. a mere difference in attitudes. But Wittgenstein's example of the woodsellers who calculate the price of wood in a manner that may seem odd or even unintelligible to us – say, in terms of the *area* covered by a pile irrespective of its *height* – shows that there is nothing sacrosanct about our mathematics.[53] For someone can have a different attitude from us to mathematics but, notwithstanding the divergence, this places us in no position to convict her of a mistake, self-contradiction or a disagreement of meaning. If we say that Wittgenstein's woodsellers merely differ in attitude from us, does this rob our mathematics of objectivity? If not, why should parallel reflections on the differing attitudes, say, of Marxist and non-Marxist historians force that conclusion on us in the case of history? Put this way, the problem with completely impersonal standards of objectivity which make no room for different attitudes toward the subject is that the standard which it claims history fails to meet is of the same sort that mathematics would fail to meet it as well. But mathematics is generally regarded as the paradigm case of an objective discipline and so the sceptic's argument clearly fails. In the face of this Wittgensteinian point, it is difficult to find a clear sense in which the practice of historical judgement could be said to depend on attitudes in a way that mathematical practice does not, and in such a way as to deprive historical judgement, but not mathematics, of its objectivity.

This response seems to establish enough of the anthropocentric character of objectivity to allow the historical realist to cope with some of the cruder forms of scepticism and reductionism. The historical realist would not, in any case, advocate trying to transcend general forms of human salience and the human point of view. Recognising the inherent limitations of following-rules, historians of international relations will see themselves as embedded in time and unable to take up a point so completely outside it that an objective foundation can at last be determined. And so it is the human viewpoint which the historical realist must ultimately rely upon to give meaning and content to his conception of history. This viewpoint permits historical realists to identify entities such as states and state-systems in space and time; it permits them to be consistent with themselves and with the following-rules of international politics; and it permits them to have a concept for bringing evidence to bear on their historical assessments. In addition, it permits them to conceive of experiences they have not yet had and to understand imaginatively the way in which statesmen have viewed their situations. All this could be developed to show that the historical realist's understanding of history will resist the cruder forms of subjectivity and incoherent forms of relativism sometimes attributed to it. But it will not allow the realist to have a conception of history which severs history's connection to a human perspective. If this is correct, then one must grant that there are limits to the objectivity of history; nonetheless, recognition of those limits will not entail a radical subjectivism. It means, rather, that historical realism gets the sort of objectivity which the subject matter requires.

Conclusion

If it were possible to sustain a thesis by identifying some of its salient features and contrasting them implicitly with what alternative positions offer, then perhaps enough would have been said here to sustain historical realism. Alas, it is not. In a more extended treatment, one would need to develop a series of arguments concerning the relation of mind and action. Without such arguments Thesis Three cannot be sustained. Nonetheless, Thesis Three seems to have obtained a measure of plausibility and that will have to suffice for our present purpose.

8 Evaluative political realism as moral realism

And unawares Morality expires.
                                        Alexander Pope

Introduction

In the nineteenth century, scholars, practitioners, students and interested citizens construed the subject of international relations as paradigmatically bound up with morality and ethics. But with the rise of logical positivism and logical empiricism in the philosophy of science and some associated doctrines, many people apparently became convinced that the intimate connection between morality and the study of international politics constituted an obstacle to a scientifically valid understanding of the subject. Support for their rigid separation was to be found in the dominant epistemology of the time which contrasted the kind of knowledge said to be available in scientific inquiries with that to be found in ethics in such a way as to depreciate ethics, or to make it, at best, a 'special' study outside the purview of mainstream 'empirical' international relations. The implications of this view may be gleaned from a passage in a well-known text in international relations written in the 1960s:

> Science and scientific words relate to only one kind of knowledge, and not to any other kinds of knowledge that may exist. They do not relate to alleged knowledge of the normative – knowledge of what ought to be. Science concerns what has been, is, or will be regardless of the 'oughts' of the situation.[1]

If 'science' is the domain of 'what has been, is, or will be' and morality consists of 'what one ought to do' where the sort of knowledge involved is 'alleged', *prima facie* that would seem to leave morality with hardly anything to do. So far as positivist-empiricists are concerned, this is as it should be since unlike scientific statements, normative statements have no truth-value.

Now according to evaluative political realism all views which attempt to dichotomise science and ethics, facts and values, the descriptive and the prescriptive may be usefully thought of as falling under a single rubric: 'non-cognitive ethics'. Although non-cognitivism is a multifaceted idea, for our purpose here it may be construed as supposing two things: a strict dichotomy between facts and values and the belief that moral judgements have no truth-value. For non-cognitivists ethical statements cannot be shown to be true or false because how things really are in the world is independent of value experience: there is nothing in the world – no moral objectivity – which our ethical statements can be true of.[2]

Non-cognitivism is bound up with empiricism and with the belief that international relations is, or can become, a science logically homomorphic with the natural sciences. By contrast, evaluative political realism rejects moral non-cognitivism, notwithstanding its dominance in shaping the post-war study of international relations. The particular form of non-cognitivism which is of interest to us here is the neo-Kantian variant which is strenuously at odds with evaluative political realism. Neo-Kantian non-cognitivists see moral reasoning as consisting of five features, namely, that moral reasoning is obligational, universal, impartial, prescriptive and rational. It is obligational: neo-Kantian moral theory is driven by the need to discover ways of getting moral agents to do their moral duty. It is universal: it is meant to apply to all subjects which fall under the scope of its moral principles. It is impartial: since all agents are equal no privilege can be given to any particular agent's position. It is prescriptive: sets of rules determine which actions must be performed in which circumstances. And it is rational: the agents who engage in moral reasoning are purely rational beings. Understood in this way, it is not hard to understand why positivist-empiricists have been attracted to neo-Kantian non-cognitivism, i.e. it poses no threat to the leading positivist-empiricist idea that science is the realm of observation and ethics is the realm of 'the normative', of the 'ought-domain' logically self-removed from empirical knowledge. Given this dichotomous distinction, scepticism concerning claims to moral knowledge seems quite compelling. For what, the positivist-empiricist would want to know, is the property which we ascribe to people when we say that they ought to perform *this* or *that* act? There does not appear to be anything observable in the world which has the property of 'oughtness'. Whatever epistemic status ought-statements turn out to have, they will not be a source of knowledge which can arise, in the positivist-empiricist view, solely from observation of properties to be found in the world.

In recent international theory, neo-Kantian non-cognitivism exhibits a deep concern and interest in the search for rational principles and moral rules concerning obligation, human rights, promises and commitments, peace and equality, and so on. Notwithstanding the value of these subjects, evaluative political realism rejects neo-Kantian non-cognitivism in international relations on the grounds that its understanding of moral reasoning either falsifies our moral experience or that it fails to account for a range of moral phenomena which are of decisive importance for understanding the relation of ethics to international relations. According to evaluative political realism, neo-Kantian non-cognitivism is formalistic, generalistic, utopian and fundamentally misguided in trying to provide a *foundation* for international ethics. Effectively, neo-Kantianism makes two fatal manoeuvres. First, it derives the practice of morality from theoretically understood experience. As such, morality comes to be viewed as a formalistic system, a code of imperatives or rules or principles addressed to moral agents, totally distinct from the practically understood interests, desires and conventions of real men and women in real political societies. Secondly, neo-Kantian non-cognitivism theoretically translates the practical interests of men and women into exceptionless universal principles whose 'thinness' patently fails to capture the local knowledge of value in the world. The cure for both these fatal manoeuvres lies not in rejecting neo-Kantian non-cognitivism *tout court* but in attenuating it by building on a cognitive conception of morality and ethics whose sources are to be found principally in the Aristotelian ethical tradition. The evaluative political realist's goal is to bring non-cognitive aspects of moral life into closer contact with cognitive features and to do so without having to give up an essentially pluralist perspective. This brings us to our fourth thesis for a revised realism:

> THESIS FOUR: International politics is inextricably bound up with an ethics which is cognitive, dilemmatic and pluralistic.

My strategy for defending the truth of this thesis will be threefold: first, to carve out a place for a form of moral objectivism in which at least some moral judgements may correctly be held to be true or false. This will be done via a re-examination of the fact–value issue. Second, to argue for a partially objective understanding of moral dilemmas. And third, to provide some rudimentary materials for defending a pluralist, rather than an absolutist or relativist, view of moral judgements.

Three features of soft moral realism

For the evaluative political realist, non-cognitivism is an erroneous understanding of ethics or morality which should be rejected and replaced by a version of moral realism which we shall call 'soft moral realism'. The 'hard moral realist' accepts the idea that moral facts hold for everyone irrespective of culture and other relativities and this view, for reasons to be brought out below, does not provide a plausible account of the different human goods (and conceptions of human goods) that exist across cultures.[3] By contrast, soft moral realism accepts the following ideas about morality: that the Weberian fact–value thesis is false because some moral statements can sometimes be said to be true; that the existence of moral dilemmas pose special problems for neo-Kantian moral theories; and that moral pluralism is true. Let us consider, on behalf of evaluative political realism, these three features of soft moral realism.

The fact–value distinction in international relations

The attempt to maintain a science pristinely protected from the vagaries of practice was one of the important motives behind the acceptance of a rigid distinction between facts and values. The classic source of that distinction is to be found, of course, in David Hume's famous disjunction between 'the is' and 'the ought'. By the same token, Max Weber made a seemingly equivalent distinction between 'facts' and 'values'. Now evaluative political realism holds at least this, that the fact–value distinction is not co-extensive with the is–ought distinction. The tendency to think of them as identical has played a large and undistinguished role in helping to justify a certain familiar conception of social science and its treatment of morals. Those who supported the Humean distinction between is and ought tended to assume that the fact–value distinction was simply a neo-Kantian formulation of

Hume's logical distinction. Moreover, the converse also seemed to hold, *viz.*, those who rejected the fact–value distinction tended to assume that its basis is the is–ought distinction, rejecting the latter as well. To understand why both parties to this hallowed dispute might (wrongly) think this, let us return briefly to the source of is–ought in Hume and then to fact–value as found in Max Weber. David Hume wrote:

> I cannot forbear adding to these reasonings an observation which may, perhaps, be found of some importance. In every system of morality, which I have hitherto met with, I have remarked, that the author proceeds for some time in the ordinary way of reasoning, and establishes the being of a God, or makes observations concerning human affairs; when of a sudden I am surprised to find, that instead of the usual copulations of propositions, *is* and *is not*, I meet with no proposition that is not connected with an *ought*, or an *ought-not*. This change is imperceptible, but is, however, of the last consequence. For as this ought, or ought not, expressed some new relation or affirmation, 'tis necessary that it should be observed, and explained; and at the same time that a reason should be given, for what seems altogether inconceivable, how this new relation can be a deduction from others, which are entirely different from it.[4]

And Max Weber wrote:

> What is really at issue, is the intrinsically simple demand that the investigator and teacher should keep unconditionally separate the establishment of empirical facts (including 'value-oriented' conduct of the empirical individual whom he is investigating) and his own practical evaluations, i.e. his evaluations of these facts as satisfactory or unsatisfactory (including among these facts evaluations made by empirical persons who are logically different) and to deal with them as though they were the same represents a confusion of entirely heterogeneous problems.[5]

Whereas Weber assumes that facts and values inhabit logically separate domains, that judgements in the value-domain are subjective and arbitrary, Hume's moral theory contains certain cognitive elements. For Hume, genuine moral judgements are not merely subjective responses or attitudes as they would have to be for Weber and those who follow him. Moral judgements can have cognitive truth-value if moral observers satisfy certain conditions. Observers must be disinterested parties to disputes; they must make genuine efforts to consider all the relevant facts; and they must avoid making disputes purely linguistic matters about the meanings of words.[6] If such conditions are satisfied, there seems no good reason why the moral judgements which meet these rational standards should not be considered a form of knowledge of some kind. To be sure, moral judgements could not, on Hume's view, be based entirely on reason; any account of moral judgement would need to add mention of something non-cognitive in origin such as desire, interest or, perhaps, feelings of sympathy since, for Hume, reason in itself is impotent to move human beings to moral action. Still, Hume's concession to the objectivity of moral judgements is important and not least of all because it marks a contrast between a partially cognitive view of morals and a Weberian perspective which requires wholly non-cognitive assumptions.

In Hume's moral theory there is still a gap, of course, between the is and the ought, although its import is different from what has usually been assumed in the social sciences. Hume is simply advancing the logical thesis that one cannot deduce by strict entailment an ought-proposition from is-propositions. The reason for this is that ought-propositions, in doing what they do, cannot be statements of fact concerning the natural universe. But from statements of fact, one cannot, quite obviously, deduce principles of action, choice and responsibility. This does not mean that there is any general logical interdict preventing legitimate inferences from our descriptions of events or people's actions to statements evaluating those events or actions. Rather, it means that ought-propositions are different because they do not reflect how the world is, but how it could be better. And if one permits, as one should do, bridging mechanisms between premises and conclusions other than deduction by strict entailment, then one would be able to draw evaluative conclusions from factual premises by adding a non-evaluative middle premise.[7]

Whereas Hume's point is a logical one and, as we shall see, heads us in the right direction, Weber's is a methodological-cum-philosophical point, implies 'subjectivism' and is mistaken. In Weber's thought about facts and values, subjectivism entails the thesis that rational individuals could agree about all the facts of the situation and yet disagree in their evaluation. On this view, it would be pointless to think that disagreements about values could be rationally resolved since they would have to be reflections of individual wills, subjective decisions or speakers' attitudes. These are, on Weber's view, quite unlike disagreements about facts which are based on objective processes of some kind. However that may (ultimately) be, Weber's contrast between factual thought which is derived from objective processes and moral thought which is derived from subjective will leads to a dilemma. Weber sees that any instruction that the will might be able to give us with respect to what we ought to do or ought not to do can only be made intelligible in terms of the ends or objectives we seek to attain by our actions. Yet, at the same time, Weber was imbued with the thought that the will and its deliverances of desire and purpose were thoroughly subjective and as such not at all of a sort to provide a universal, objective basis for duties and obligations. Weber clearly sought refuge in the second horn of this dilemma and committed himself to the self-defeating and paradoxical idea that reason had nothing whatsoever to tell us about which ends human beings should follow. Nor was Weber's view innocent of impact on international relations. His ideas created a context for accepting a similar distinction by Quincy Wright, a leading post-war positivist-empiricist in international relations.[8] In general, positivist-empiricism, as well as certain versions of political realism, have appealed to Weber's views to support a non-cognitivist ethics for international relations.

Positivist-empiricists (and others) who still accept the Weberian distinction between facts and value will now have to come to grips with counterarguments advanced by certain moral philosophers. Some philosophers have questioned the distinction between facts and values by drawing our attention to the indispensable idea that a good deal of moral thinking is neither purely factual nor purely moral. For example, Phillipa Foot invites us to consider such predicates as 'rude'.[9] On the one hand, this predicate seems to be evaluative since it expresses disapproval, annoyance and so on. But, on the other hand, the predicate would presumably only apply to a person if she met certain descriptive conditions concerning her behaviour, say, gratuitously insulting people on every available opportunity. If Foot's account of rudeness is correct, there is at least one kind of moral judgement which is inextricably bound up with a statement of fact. Accepting Foot's argument would be one way to problematise the fact–value distinction; but there are others.

Bernard Williams has provided us with a set of ethical concepts which also seem to fall between the purely factual and purely moral. He calls them 'thick ethical concepts' and gives, as examples, *treachery, promise, brutality* and *courage*. These concepts appear, Williams says, 'to express a union of fact and value'.[10] It seems right to say of someone who has just stepped between a gunman and an innocent person so that she and not the other is shot that she is morally courageous, that her act has moral worth. On the other hand, a bit of behaviour is courageous if it meets certain conditions of fact. Courage is a brave action; but it also appears correct to say that someone who enters a burning building to save a child should be described as courageous even apart from the obvious moral judgements which apply to that behaviour. And what is true of courage would apply to other thick moral concepts. Another philosopher, Judith J. Thomson, argues that there are necessary connections between facts and weak moral judgements, 'where weak moral judgements are judgements to the effect that there is something that is favourably relevant to the truth of a strong moral judgment to the effect that someone ought or ought not do a thing'.[11] In the face of such convincing counterexamples to the Weberian claim that facts and values can be strictly separated, the onus of proof appears to shift to fact–value separationists.

But although such arguments serve to refute certain popular forms of non-cognitivism, they will not be of much help in developing any positive form of moral objectivism. This requires different categories and distinctions. A good start in this task has been made by David Wiggins. In turning to one of his texts, we shall see more clearly how it is possible to preserve the logical distinction between *the is* and *the ought* while rejecting a non-cognitive ethical viewpoint which thrusts rational deliberation about human ends beyond the pale of truth and reason.

Wiggins' innovation

In *Truth, Invention and the Meaning of Life*, Wiggins makes a distinction between 'evaluations' and 'deliberations'.[12] Evaluations normally register some reported judgement of the form 'X is good', 'Y is bad', or 'Z is mediocre'. Deliberations, on the other hand, record some sort of judgement or guideline for action which one captures in such statements of moral and political agents as 'she should do X', 'he must do Y', or 'she ought to do Z'.[13] For Wiggins, evaluating some action (or character or state of affairs) implies believing of the action that it possesses a certain property or properties of which 'honesty','goodness', 'maliciousness', and 'baseness' are typical.

Evaluations, in this view, are cognitive insofar as they involve moral statements which describe 'how the world is'. An evaluative stance recoils from the prevailing disposition to regard evaluations as attitudes, decisions, rules, emotive expressions or, at any rate, something non-cognitive. By contrast, to take up a deliberative stance involves being disposed to perform some action, making some choice or assuming some responsibility. While evaluations are expressions of cognitive abilities, deliberative attitudes are practical in orientation. But perhaps the key difference between evaluations and deliberations is that the former, but not the latter, are amenable to assessment in terms of what Wiggins calls 'regular truth'. The most important characteristics of regular truth, for our purposes, are: that regular truth answers to evidence; that its truths are independent of our wills and our limited means of recognition; that it converges upon agreement; and that every regular truth is true in virtue of something.[14]

Judgements derived from the deliberative attitude – judgements introduced by such locutions as 'I ought', 'I should not', 'I have to', 'I must not', 'all things considered I should', etc. – are all inappropriate to the extension of regular truth, though some of these may be reformulated as assertions appropriate to evaluative, truth-bearing judgements. Still, in general, deliberative judgements are practical attitudes: they are not candidates for regular truth because their use lies not in characterising the world but in coming to grips with it through action. Deliberations, that is, have a special relation to action which we can express by saying that its deliverances are practical, action-guiding or prescriptive. Evaluations, on the other hand, make claims to satisfy standards of regular truth. For example, an evaluation of the statement: 'it is morally permissible to torture suspected terrorists for the fun of it' would be assessed as 'untrue' and in very much the same way as some ordinary untrue statement taken from the natural sciences or the everyday world in which we live and act. In this view, there is no good reason to deny that evaluative statements can satisfy rigorous standards of regular truth.

There are two important advantages that accrue to soft moral realism from accepting this distinction between evaluation and deliberation. First of all, it enables the kind of realist who sees politics and morality as inextricably bound up with one another to assimilate the acceptable face of the commonsense realist tradition. Morgenthau represented that face when he wrote: 'To know that nations are subject to the moral law is one thing, while to pretend to know with certainty what is good and evil in the relations among nations is quite another.'[15] Note that Morgenthau here says quite explicitly that one *knows* that nations are subject to 'the moral law', that this is something to which we have access in a cognitive way but, nonetheless, such knowledge would not in and of itself provide sufficient ground for saying what practical attitudes to take up 'in relations among nations'. Referring now to the distinction between evaluation and deliberation, Morganthau's claim may be reinterpreted to say that human beings can, and sometimes do, determine the truth about moral events in quite the same way as one can determine the truth about the natural world; but that knowing this would not automatically compel any statesperson to act in terms of that truth since the truthfulness of evaluations, however much it may inform practical deliberations, is not reducible to them. Adopting the distinction between evaluations and deliberations therefore helps realists avoid a false dichotomy: it is false to say that we cannot know what is morally right, but it is also a *suggestio falsi* that knowing what is right entitles one to force oneself, as well as other persons and other communities, to act in terms of that knowledge. Secondly, the evaluative/deliberative distinction helps to heal the split between neo-Aristotelian moral objectivism and forms of non-cognitivism. It does so not by overcoming or resolving the is–ought gap as such but by reconstructing it in terms of the somewhat different distinction between evaluations and deliberations. Although it would still be a logical mistake to 'move from' *the is* to *the ought* by strict deduction, this does not seriously constrain our capacity to use our evaluations as logical warrants for deliberations. Evaluative descriptions of situations as deceitful, courageous, cruel, honourable and so on are susceptible to assessment in terms of regular truth and will always count, in ways that it will be impossible or impractical to try to predict, as pertinent to one's deliberations about what to do about them. The very idea of morally deliberating on a particular case without taking into account the evaluations with which they are bound up would involve depriving the deliberator of just the sort of information she would need to pick out salient features of the case at hand. If, for example, it is a regular truth that Bosnian Serb military activities in Bosnia-Herzogovina are cruel and brutal, then this evaluation will be of central importance in any deliberations concerning what actions to take, if any, to curtail such activities. Whether one makes the right connections between truth-bearing evaluations and action-guiding deliberations will depend in large measure on whether political leaders have practical wisdom. To have the possibility of being *phronimos*, political leaders should be autonomous individuals, persons who carefully cultivate their rational abilities and who rationally consider how to engage in admirable actions by picking out salient evaluations from historically determined situations. A statesperson intelligently plans to act in ways that will enable such salient evaluations to be made in the light of new and necessarily unanticipated contingencies. She then must decide whether to engage in certain deliberative actions in response, on the one hand, to the demands of salient truth-bearing evaluations and, on the other, to the probable actions of her counterparts in other political communities. Soft moral realism claims that there is no basis for denying our capacity to make objective assessments of moral and/or political situations in terms of standards of regular truth. Nonetheless, accepting certain statements as regular truths does not force one to act, commit one to act, or motivate one to act. On the picture I am urging, there are ineliminable tensions between evaluations and deliberations.

Moral dilemmas

However, just as soft moral realism begins to see a way of bringing the two strands of political realism into closer contact, another problem appears on the horizon to threaten these bridge-building efforts, namely, a non-cognitivist and subjectivist interpretation of moral dilemmas which, if accepted, would re-open the gap between modern and classical versions of political realism. But let us see.

It is a commonplace that the older form of political realism underlines the role and significance of moral dilemmas for our understanding of international relations; it has been less clear how the logic of moral dilemmas is to be understood. As for the commonplace, it was Morgenthau who best identified the consequences of moral dilemmas for our understanding of the relation between morality and international politics:

> It is imagined that the tension between foreign policy and morality, given in immediate experience, could easily be made to disappear ... The truth is that there is no way out. The moral dilemma of foreign policy is but a special and ... a particularly flagrant case of the moral dilemma which faces man on all levels of social action.[16]

The idea that moral dilemmas are central to our understanding of morality and foreign policy may seem obvious, but it would, nevertheless, not be acceptable to adherents of a neo-Kantian rule-oriented conception of morality. On such a view, moral dilemmas are not real, they are apparent. Once we understand, unravel and develop the implications of the moral rules which lurk behind them, we shall, on this view, understand that all moral dilemmas are resolvable without remainder. Refusing to accept the reality of moral dilemmas, however, leads to counter-intuitive and unsatisfactory results.

Consider the problem of threatening to use nuclear weapons. For the soft moral realist, there would appear to be a dilemma between the threat to use nuclear weapons against unarmed civilians – a threat to commit 'mass murder' – on the one side and not threatening to use nuclear weapons which, in the hypothetical situation imagined here, constitutes 'surrender in advance' on the other. Those who would reject the thought that there is a real dilemma here might attempt to claim that once the moral issue is considered in sufficient depth, the moral dilemma disappears: there is always a situation which is morally preferred. For example, several nuclear strategists have effectively claimed that the morally preferred position for holders of nuclear weapons is to pursue a deterrence policy which implements the rule that it is morally right for a country to threaten the use of nuclear weapons to deter potential adversaries but that if deterrence fails, it would be morally wrong to retaliate because this would entail the murder of innocent civilians. Let's call this policy: The Rule of Basic Deterrence. According to the argument, The Rule of Basic Deterrence has at least two desirable features: it avoids the morally obnoxious feature of committing 'mass murder' by stipulating that the threat not be carried out and it circumvents the idea of surrendering in advance by allowing states to make nuclear threats against potential aggressors. The Rule of Basic Deterrence, thus conceived, has some rather patent logical difficulties but it is cited here nonetheless to illustrate the anti-dilemmatic claim that what first appears to be a dilemma can be resolved without remainder by thinking through the various moral options and devising morally efficacious rules.

But this is far too quick. For the supposition that a pre-commitment to The Rule of Basic Deterrence will always resolve nuclear dilemmas is a dangerous form of wishful thinking. As many nuclear strategists have observed, the Rule of Basic Deterrence lacks credibility; it is menaced with breakdown whenever some nuclear states have vastly superior forces and can threaten an adversary with pre-emptive nuclear strikes.[17] So it might turn out that in a crisis situation one state will be self-deterred by the recognition of its own inferiority in second-strike forces. And there is nothing in the Rule of Basic Deterrence which would enable nuclear states to make such a determination; one

Moral dillemma

has to look, not at the Rule, but at the world of nuclear states – their particular intentions and capabilities – to determine what would be the morally correct action to take. So the application of the Rule of Basic Deterrence is neither self-certifying nor automatic; its application is contingent upon the existence of certain empirical circumstances which may not in fact exist.

In general, those who reject the existence of moral dilemmas fail to see that it is logically possible for a political agent to deliberate about what she has otherwise ruled out as immoral. So although it might appear as if a particular moral dilemma has been satisfactorily resolved, the agent might still be considering options and this precisely because she is unwilling to rule out morally wrong positions! This is what occurs in cases involving practical necessity. The point of the concept of practical necessity is not just to rationalise actions which would otherwise give political agents a 'bad' historical press nor to find excuses retrospectively for morally repugnant actions. Rather, at least part of the point of using the concept lies in showing how a moral agent can truly say that a certain action may have been morally 'impossible' for her to do but she did it anyway and was fully conscious of what she was doing. She might explain this by saying that she had intentionally taken up a position of public responsibility and trust which required her to consider actions in consequentialist terms whose principles she would otherwise have rejected in her capacity as a private individual. There is a difference in levels of moral activity at work here. At the level of the individual, and acting in terms of moral character, the action, say, of using nuclear weapons, may appear to her to be morally repugnant; but at the public level of political agent, she might conclude that, all things considered, less harm would be done in retaliating against military targets with nuclear weapons than in not using them, even though the agent might consider such an action truly deplorable. She can conceive of herself as doing the repugnant action and still live with herself. The key point is that holding that an action is morally wrong need not constitute a prohibition on performing the action. This is especially so for political leaders in international politics who see themselves in situations of responsibility in which the special virtues of patriotism and loyalty may be at work.

If this is a description of a possible case, then one difficulty, in particular, with the moral-rule approach to moral dilemmas comes to light, namely that, in its urge to achieve consistency in its account, it reduces the different levels of moral activity to a single overall dimension. The moral-rule approach thus not only distorts moral reality, it also attempts to self-justify its failure to find a place for moral dilemmas – and the accompanying practical political dilemmas – which it has precluded so peremptorily. Moreover, the assumption in this approach to the effect that moral or political agents will always be able to find and apply the appropriate moral rule seems more the expression of vague hope than a genuine conviction. What is the basis for the belief that moral agents who choose rules to resolve their moral dilemmas will interpret them correctly? How will the moral agent be able to decide which of the many available rules to apply to a given moral dilemma? Will moral agents ever have available to them a sufficiently precise and complete codification of moral rules to mandate single courses of action? If not, then we may be justified in accepting Aristotle's dictum that even the most accurate and precise generalisations about moral matters hold 'only for the most part'.[18]

Still, it is no part of my purpose here to deny that morality can and should sometimes be directed by rules. Morality does have rule-guided elements, but there are other aspects of morality which the soft moral realist believes are far more salient to understanding the structure of morality in the realm of foreign affairs and which tend to be distorted by rule-oriented models. Insofar as the moral-rule approach has failed to show that moral dilemmas are eliminable, let us turn to consider their character and structure, keeping centre-stage our overall goal of avoiding an interpretation of such dilemmas which will effectively collapse into a non-cognitivist subjectivist conception of morality and ethics. Two sorts of conflict have now to be considered: two-party and one-party conflicts.

Two-party and one-party moral dilemmas

The paradigm case of two-party conflict is the conflict between Antigone and Creon in the classical Greek play *Antigone*. Antigone's personal and religious obligations to bury her dead brother's body conflicts with Creon's political obligations to keep the peace; these two obligations cannot both be fulfilled and so each must choose in recognising the tragic result of not being able to choose an alternative in which they both see great value. In any conflict of this sort, there is loss and regret at what one wanted to do and could do but did not do. Dilemmas of this sort cover a lot of ground in international relations as practised from time immemorial but since it does not pose the issue of subjectivism in the way required for our purposes, it will be largely ignored here and replaced by consideration of one-party conflicts. It is generally assumed, as Bernard Williams has insightfully put it, that, 'whatever may turn out to be the case with two-party conflicts, at any rate one-person conflict must be capable of being rationally resolved. At the very least, the theory of rational behaviour must make it an undisputed aim of the rational agent to reduce conflict in his personal set of values to the minimum.'[19]

Williams sets out to show that 'such an assumption is unreasonable' and, in handsomely succeeding, manages to throw considerable doubt on the rational choice theory of agency favoured by many positivist-empiricists. Williams points to cases, i.e. kinds of moral conflict, which are 'reasonable only with loss or remainder', a notion closely parallel to Isaiah Berlin's famous *aperçu* that there is no such thing as a world without loss.[20] One kind of dilemma involving loss or remainder is what Williams identifies as 'tragic' cases, i.e. cases in which 'an agent can justifiably think that whatever he does will be wrong: that there are conflicting moral requirements, and that neither of them succeeds in overriding or outweighing the other'.[21] In this view, moral and political agents will have reason to regret whichever course of action they eventually choose; but it nonetheless remains true that each course of action is morally required. In these tragic cases we do not necessarily blame the agent by saying that the victims of whichever course of action the agent finally chooses have a justifiable complaint. Tragic dilemmas arise in situations of ambiguity and uncertainty, when it is difficult to predict the consequences of one's actions, and when the general principles upon which one normally relies either offer no help or seem to contradict one another; and these, as well as conditions for two-party conflicts, are just the sort of situations that abound in international relations. Time and again, 'older' political realists have pointed to this element of tragedy in the morality of politics, even though its logic has not always been made perspicuous.

Let us consider an historical case, Thomas Jefferson's Louisiana Purchase. The summary description by Adrienne Koch and William Peden will draw out the essential raw materials of the case. The authors write:

> For years Jefferson had been the guardian of democratic rights for the individual, small local units and the states. He had taken his stand on the 'strict construction' interpretation of the Constitution. Now he was faced with a decision in which quick – and unauthorised –

executive action would guarantee doubling America's territory and increasing the chance of maintaining the self-government and independence for which American blood had been spilled. Was he to take Napoleon's offer and violate a cherished principle, or should he wait upon a constitutional amendment authorising such an act and possibly lose the very territory so vital to national existence and well-being? In *very great distress*, he wrote to his friends Thomas Paine, John Breckenridge, and Wilson Cary Nicholas soliciting their opinions. Eventually, of course, after *tremendous* moral strain, Jefferson authorised the purchase... Although *he was reluctant to do so*, he was fortified largely by the consideration that his dictatorial use of power was in this case the lesser evil.[22]

As the authors' account suggests, the dilemma for Jefferson was real; they give us to understand that he experienced tremendous emotional conflict concerning which alternative to choose. That dilemma was real, moreover, even if, as the authors claim, he may have decided that the reasons for authorising The Purchase outweighed the reasons for not authorising it, i.e. authorising The Purchase was the lesser evil. As long as there is an obligation to do X and a conflicting obligation to do Y where both obligations cannot be met, there is a moral dilemma which involves loss. Two philosophical points enter just here. First, the neo-Kantian claim that moral wrongs are absolutely forbidden is not sustained by this case. Since it is clearly possible to recommend an action which, though the lesser evil, is still evil, i.e. morally wrong, the claim that an action is morally wrong is not in itself an adequate guide as to whether it should be performed or not. Hence, the idea that moral rules always assist in guiding action appears to be problematic. Secondly, this case raises the question of how much sense we can give to the notion of someone's knowing that she still ought to have done Y even though she thinks it right to have chosen X.

If one accepts for this case, as positivist-empiricism would be inclined to do, the model of reasoning appropriate for the case of beliefs in which it would be irrational to regret giving up a false belief, it would be impossible to do justice to Jefferson's dilemma or to other related facts of moral and political conflict. The evaluative political realist, however, has an understanding of moral epistemology which leads her to resist the dismissal or radical reconstruction of agent-regret and kindred phenomena such as self-deception and weakness of will. For the soft moral realist, Thomas Jefferson's sense of regret is not a theory but a practice and would normally be explained by the existence of internal moral conflict and agent-regret. If Jefferson truly believed that he ought to have signed the Louisiana Purchase and that he ought not to have signed it and found, nonetheless, that the circumstances were such that he had to act against his beliefs in democratic rights for the individual and for states, we would have expected him to show the kind of distress and reluctance to commit himself ascribed to him by his biographers. According to the soft moral realist, Jefferson's reluctance to act and the subsequent reports of his very real distress in making the decision provide ample evidence for the belief that, in his view, he ought not to have done it, even though, paradoxically, he had to. There is evidence, that is, that Jefferson felt guilty about not having chosen the course of action consistent with his beliefs. In exhibiting guilt in such cases he was, in effect, acknowledging that a wrong had been committed because it was in his power to do otherwise. The wrong is not eradicated by the thought that he chose the lesser evil, even though his feelings of self-blame and responsibility might be diminished sufficiently to enable him to live with the moral burden.

Objections may be raised about the Jefferson case, as here interpreted, on both logical and ideological grounds. The former would perhaps be the basis of the positivist-empiricist's objection, given her commitment to the claim that the logic of moral conflict mirrors the logic of belief conflict. The positivist-empiricist would simply deny the existence of moral dilemmas and claim that reason requires an ordering of moral claims in just the way that one orders belief claims. However, *prima facie*, it seems very implausible to think that conflicting moral judgements are logically contradictory in the same way that beliefs about the world are logically contradictory. Such a view would seem to require that such well-known phenomena as agent-regret, self-deception and moral negligence should not be counted as central data in our moral reasoning. But what would justify such a conclusion? It seems to me that we have no intelligible conception of what would do so.

This is not the Marxist's difficulty. For the Marxist, the claim that certain conflicts are inherently unresolvable because they are rooted in intrinsic aspects of human beings and societal structures might smack of ideological mystification designed to keep human beings and social structures from being transformed and to prevent our moving to higher stages of human and social praxis. But the realist wonders where the future transformation of human beings is going to come from, and why reasonable people would believe in it. Appealing to historical materialism, in the face of continuing difficulties in the coherence of this idea, will not suffice. Moreover, in the moral context, Marxism raises the 'interesting metaphysical question: what would have to be true of the world and of an agent that it should be impossible for him to be in a situation where whatever he did was wrong?'[23] To help answer this question, let us consider a case in which the features ascribed to Jefferson's condition – 'genuine distress', 'tremendous moral strain', 'reluctance', etc. – are either not present at all, or are present only in a dramatically attenuated form.

Stalin's route to overcoming moral dilemmas

According to Winston Churchill, he and Joseph Stalin discussed the difficulties of Stalin's collective farm policy in August 1942.[24] To Churchill's question of whether World War II had been 'as bad to you personally' as carrying through the policy of the collective farms, Stalin allegedly replied:

> Oh, no, the collective farm policy was a terrible struggle.
>
> CHURCHILL: I thought you would have found it bad because you were not dealing with a few score thousands of Aristocrats or big landowners, but with millions of small men.
>
> STALIN: Ten million. It was fearful. Four years it lasted. It was absolutely necessary for Russia, if we were to avoid periodic famines to plough the land with tractors... It was very bad and difficult – but necessary.
>
> CHURCHILL: What happened?
>
> STALIN: Oh, well, many of them agreed to come in with us. Some of them were given land of their own to cultivate in the province of Tomsk or the province of Irkutsk or further north, but the great bulk were very unpopular and were wiped out by these la-bourers... Not only have we vastly increased the food supply but we have improved the quality of the grain beyond all measure.[25]

Now the contrast between Stalin's conception of moral conflict and Jefferson's is striking and revealing. In Jefferson's case, as presumably understood not only by his biographers but by Jefferson himself, no matter which option he chose, he would be committing a moral wrong. In Stalin's case, as he presumably viewed it, the action of 'allowing' so-called 'unpopular' peasants to be killed by 'labourers' was justified by its consequences – vastly increasing the quality and output of grain. All actions can be justified, we are led to believe, on the supposition that a society can be attained in which all genuinely valuable human char-acteristics have been equally and harmoniously ordered. In other words, from an instrumentally conceived consequentialist moral perspective, there is no genuine moral conflict here at all, no cause for agent-regret and no tragedy. If one faces a dilemma only as the result of an externally contingent, historical situation over which one has no control and with the supposed knowledge that the forces of history are bringing into being the Good of the Communist Society (or whatever), then that seems to lead quite directly to the view that someone who feels no moral conflict and no moral regret – as Stalin evidently did not – should not be held to have done anything morally wrong. For the evaluative political realist, any such view is a warrant to commit atrocities under the colour of political and economic progress. Against this, soft moral realism reiterates Williams' warning that we have no conception of moral choice without remainder, of a world, that is, without 'tragic cases'. Those who share Williams' view will no doubt also think that while international society can move to recognise and express new virtues and ideals, perhaps even a wider range of them, nevertheless there must be at the same time unrecoverable losses. The fact that Jefferson chose to act against his Rousseauistic values of democratic rights for the individual, etc. is an unrecoverable loss of human value. On this view, for every given choice at a given time one value has to be set against another and there is loss of genuine value over time. We can't avoid moral and political remainders and the tragic consequences which so often attend them in international relations.

Thus far we have examined only one kind of case: moral dilemmas. Still, the *genre* is of great importance. Suppose that the Jeffersonian case is a consistent, 'correct' description and suppose we find in our everyday world and in world politics very many similar instances of genuine moral dilemmas. Then it seems that we would have a refutation of positivist-empiricist and emancipatory conceptions of morality in international politics. For neither of these views allows morality to be cognitive, yet there seems good reason to interpret tragic moral dilemmas in at least partially cognitive terms. Admittedly, this claim goes against the grain of Williams' account of moral dilemmas upon which we have thus far generally relied. For, according to Williams, when we are in a moral dilemma, we are in a situation in which we are obliged to say that an agent 'ought to do X' and 'ought not to do X' and moral cognitivism cannot make any sense of the dilemmatic character of the situation, e.g. it is incoherent for both these conflicting statements to be true, yet this is precisely what the cognitivist must claim.[26] But is the cognitivist wrong? Williams' argument rests upon conceiving of the conflicting oughts as reducible to *logical* contradictions; but we see no good reason to treat the conflicting oughts in this way. For, as argued above, there is a gap between accepting the truth of an evaluative statement and the deliberative reasons for taking action on behalf of that truth. So evaluating ought statements as true doesn't imply that after deliberation the ought statements are still considered solely in terms of their truth-bearing character. Deliberative reasons concerning what to do become dominant. Of course, in making the final decision after deliberation only one of the ought statements can remain efficacious. In choosing the lesser evil, Jefferson was ridding himself of deliberative reasons for thinking that his conception of democratic rights necessarily prevented him from signing the Louisiana Purchase. But Jefferson was not, *ex hypothesi*, supposing that all the features which made up his understanding of democratic rights formed part of an option which was untrue. It is rather that after deliberation concerning what to do, the oughtness of one of the options diminished sufficiently so that the logical contradiction between oughts evaporated. Evaluating truths and deliberating about oughts are not identical to one another.

On the soft moral realist account, *both* 'options' can be *true* representations of the situation at hand. This is because evaluations only partially overlap with deliberations: evaluations, unlike deliberations, can be true. And tragic moral dilemmas require evaluation as well as deliberation. How else could the deliberator come to understand the depth of the moral conflict facing her? It would be absurd to say that although an evaluator found herself in a moral dilemma, one of her two options was false, for that would be to suppose that the moral dilemma did not in fact exist, that it was an illusion fostered by an agent's feelings or attitudes perhaps. But although this may turn out to be so in a particular case, we know that, in general, it cannot be correct since history, world literature and our own general experience suggest that moral dilemmas get their power because the options are regarded as true. General scepticism concerning this construal of moral dilemmas would be gratuitous. We have no basis for a general sceptical attitude which would deny that moral dilemmas are requirements of reason that capture what is there in the world. And the way in which we mark the objectivity of moral dilemmas is by saying of each option that it is true. However, this is not to say that moral dilemmas can be described in terms that would satisfy some strong version of moral realism.

According to the soft moral realist, moral dilemmas have inelimin-able internalist features. Unlike purely external phenomena, it is impossible to predict their occurrence, even in principle. Although moral dilemmas are demands of reason which are there in the world, the final determination of when a moral dilemma begins and ends will always be 'up to' the individual subject who is experiencing the tension of being pulled in opposite directions. Secondly, and connect-edly, residues of dilemmas are always *to* the subject who, say, in choosing X over Y where each option is equally valuable, will have to suffer the guilt and remorse of not having chosen Y when she could have done so but did not. Moreover, given the gap between evaluation and deliberation for action, there may well be cases, for example, in which a decision to choose X or not-X is impossible because they are, in effect, incommensurable. For example, Western foreign policy leaders may have nothing to say about the moral consequences of certain aspects of fundamentalist Islamic international relations because the whole framework of that form of life may be incommensurable with Western ideals. Where ways of life are genuinely incommensurable, the dilemmas may be irresolvable and not require any choice.[27]

If moral dilemmas have to be described as partly internal in character, then I think that we have to say that the maximum goal of an Aristotelian objective realism – hard moral realism – is unattainable. We can describe that goal as the elimination of disagreement con-cerning knowledge of The Good. It is a feature of such knowledge that if there are two rival claimants concerning what the good consists of, one of them must be contradicting himself. But if moral conflicts, as we have suggested, are unlike belief conflicts in that conflicting ought statements are not necessarily contradictory, then the existence of a moral conflict does not necessarily imply a contradiction at all. The logic and role of reason in moral conflict is just not the same as it is in belief conflict. But in asking the neo-Aristotelian moral objectivist to give up his maximal claim, is one really asking so much? Was not the expectation of a single, consistent description of The Good too much to ask for in the first place? Can one still remain realist and yet think that rival claims to The Good will be examined without rancour, prevarica-tion, equivocation, or personal interest entering into one's moral argument? On any understanding of realism, this seems very doubtful. However, to give this up does not force political realists to give up using the idiom of moral goodness or truth as these are construed in the moderate version of realist ethics we have been calling soft moral realism. We turn now to the third and final attribute of soft moral realism: moral pluralism.

Pluralism into relativism need not go

Soft moral realism endorses pluralism not relativism. Establishing a pluralism that avoids relativism is central to the intelligibility of the soft moral realist's project since if relativism is true, the very idea of being able to rationally assess ethical values different from one's own is senseless. My self-conceived task here is not, thankfully enough, to try to disprove relativism. Rather, I shall examine a brilliant effort by Susan Wolf to sustain moral relativism and suggest that, notwithstanding the attractiveness of her arguments, they do not succeed. I shall then make certain suggestions about how to avoid relativism without having to give up pluralism.

Wolf's starting point is 'pluralism', which she says 'offers an alternative to the relativist position that my views are right for me and your views are right for you, as well as to the absolutist position that only one of us can be right'.[28] This sounds like what any sensible, i.e. non-absolute moral cognitivist would want. On this view, pluralism in ethics is the idea that there is an irreducible plurality of morally significant values such that they cannot be subject to a complete rational ordering. Wolf does not argue for the truth of this form of pluralism. Rather, she argues that 'the possibility of pluralism allows two different responses: at one level, pluralism provides a way of acknowledging the legitimacy of some moral disagreement without any assumption of relativism. At another level, pluralism does encourage us to accept a kind of relativism, but it is a kind that does not support or lead the way to subjectivism.'[29] Wolf contends that pluralism conceived as diversity of ways of life does not lead automatically to relativism. For Wolf, there are two levels of pluralism which I shall denominate Pluralist-I and Pluralist-II. Only Pluralist-II leads to relativism, in Wolf's view, and it is not in any case a relativism that entails moral subjectivism. For Pluralist-I a possible response to moral disagreement in the face of a plurality of values is to expect a certain amount of indeterminacy in the realm of moral fact. As Wolf says: 'There will be cases in which there are good reasons for one position and good reasons for an incompatible position and no further overarching principle and perspective from which these can be put into any further objective balance.'[30] There is nothing in what Wolf says here about Pluralism-I which would push a position towards relativism. For example, the pluralistic moral cognitivist, an Aristotelian position, would presumably find little difficulty in accepting the thought that no act or practice can be assessed right or wrong, good or bad, etc. without a full specification of circumstances and context. Wolf's Pluralist-I position may be viewed as an undogmatic form of objectivism providing a coherent response to undeniable facts about ethical diversity.

Pluralism-I falls somewhere between the absolutist and the relativist positions. According to Wolf, the absolutist and the relativist give different answers to two questions: is there a true view of morality? and, when there are two conflicting views, isn't at least one of them wrong? To these leading questions, Wolf says, 'the absolutist answers "yes" – there is always a right answer, given by the single correct moral system. The pluralist can be expected to answer "sometimes" – for even if some situations will set irreducibly different values into oppositions that cannot rationally be resolved, there is no reason to expect that all, or most, moral issues will be of this sort.'[31]

What is the difference, though, between pluralism and relativism? Does pluralism simply amount to subjectivism and relativism rather than a view which, as Wolf says, takes away the motivation for those views? The difference lies in the status accorded to moral truth. For example, Terry Nardin regards relativism as offering a solution to diversity which gives one kind of status to moral truth, namely, that '[w]hat counts as true in a given context depends on the conventions of particular societies, traditions, scientific paradigms, or modes of discourse'.[32] In other words, moral truth is not, on this view, independent of the subject. But as Wolf says:

> The pluralist ... is in no way committed to that view, either in general or in the cases in which morality is indeterminate, for pluralism does not say that it is up to an individual subject to determine which moral views are indeterminate. Nor does it say that it is up to the individual to make one position right and the others wrong in the cases in which it is indeterminate. If the subjectivist can be understood as denying the existence of moral truth, the pluralist is better interpreted as believing that, though there may be a moral truth, the truth will be more complicated than one might have wished – complicated, specifically, in such a way as to make the answers to certain questions indeterminate.
>
> The considerations that show that pluralism does not collapse into subjectivism also show that pluralism does not collapse into or imply

213

> relativism. For unlike the relativist, who believes that what is right for
> you is different from what is right for me, the pluralist holds that, for
> each and every one of us, the question of what is right in some cases
> lacks a unique and determinate answer. Rightness, on this view, is not
> relative to anything, it is not a matter of perspective. It is just
> indeterminate.[33]

Pluralism so understood shows why absolute positions may be
attractive. For the pluralist will say that both Kantianism and utilitarianism have something of importance to offer. Kantianism's focus on
respect for autonomy and utilitarianism's on maximising pleasure
constitute plausible forms of moral commitment. They represent deep
human longings. When these are put into the framework of certain
conceptions of moral theory which validate simplicity, completeness
and, most of all, uniqueness we are moved, wrongly on Wolf's
Pluralist-I view, to accept one of these theories as the whole of moral
truth.

If, as pluralists like Stuart Hampshire and Thomas Nagel have
persistently urged upon us, there is an irreducible plurality of morally
significant values and no principle that orders them completely, then
at least some persistent moral disagreements are apt to be a consequence.[34] Different parties to the disagreement may be focusing on
different independently significant values, and since there is no decision procedure for balancing these values any attempt by one party to
claim priority over the other will simply beg the question. But it is
important to see that this does not imply that there are no wrong
answers. Pluralism does not commit one, as subjectivism does, to
'anything goes' in morality. But Wolf wants to go beyond Pluralism-I
to carve out a place for a kind of pluralism which is relativistic:
Pluralism-II. She argues that while there may be a form of pluralism
which does not collapse into relativism, there is 'a second level
pluralism' which does but this should worry no-one. She writes:
'Moral pluralism ... can be understood at either of two levels, and
either or both can be attractive.'[35] At the second level of Pluralism-II
one would be accepting a form of relativism which 'would neither
constitute nor provide any support for subjectivism'.[36]

In arguing the case for the coherence of Pluralism-II, Wolf draws
out the implications of a scene from the movie *Witness*, a 1985 film
directed by Peter Weir and starring Harrison Ford, in which a detective
named 'Book' is forced to live in an Amish community to avoid some
corrupt police who are trying to kill him. She tells us that there is a

scene in the movie in which one of the Amish men 'is insulted by a bully and just stands there, submitting to the bully's abuse... But the detective cannot just stand there allowing the thug to go on and hauls off and breaks the bully's nose.'[37]

Wolf first analyses the case from the point of view of Pluralism-I, the pluralism which can acknowledge that there is something to be said for the policy of fighting injustice with violence and something to be said for the policy of pacifism, but which does not deny that one can isolate plenty of wrong answers with respect to such questions. At this first level of pluralism such considerations would not lead one to be indifferent about which of two options is best all things considered. One is not pressed into relativism here. However, Wolf's main point is that a description at the first, non-relativist level would not constitute an adequate description either of the scene in the movie or of the conceptual space available to pluralists attracted to relativism. She writes that although

> this position [Pluralist-I] approves of, maybe even admires, the choices and actions of Amish men, however, it seems to me that it does not fully approve of the man's moral point of view, for although, according to the pluralist position, it was not wrong to refrain from violence in this instance, neither would it have been wrong to use violence here. From the Amish man's point of view, on the other hand, it *would* have been wrong for him to use violence, in that or any instance. That is precisely why he refrained.[38]

So for the moral pluralist committed to Pluralism-II the scene from *Witness* prompts the following response: for the detective Book it would not really have been morally wrong to hit the bully but for the Amish man it was. Relativism here comes naturally into the picture.

> If we take seriously the supposition that [the Amish man's] culture is no worse a culture than ours ... I am not sure we would want to say that his beliefs are false and his views are mistaken. For if, as I have supposed, a commitment to the principle of nonviolence is funda-mental to Amish culture, and if that culture, that way of life, is no worse, if also no better, than [the detective's] way of life, or mine, or yours, then [he] makes no mistake in accepting the commitment to nonviolence that is essential to that culture.[39]

We are thus asked to conclude that 'judging what is right for one person is not right for another, and that, furthermore, what is right for these people is relative to their respective cultures'.[40]

On the basis of this example we seem to have gathered up sufficient conceptual materials to distinguish Pluralism-I from Pluralism-II. Pluralism-I acknowledges the fact that there may be good reasons to support conflicting moral positions without there being a further principle or reason that can settle the choice between them. On the other hand, for Pluralism-II:

> an action may be morally required of someone not because it is a consequence of a universal principle in conjunction with nonevaluative facts, but because it follows from an acceptable component of a moral code that constitutes one good, or good enough, set of standards among others. Such a position does seem to me to capture much of the spirit of relativism, for it acknowledges that culture may contribute to the determination of a person's moral requirements and prohibitions in a much more thoroughgoing way than absolutism appears to allow.[41]

The conclusion Wolf reaches is:

> This case ... offers us an example of a situation in which we may be drawn to judging that what is right for one person is not right for another, and that, furthermore, what is right for these people is relative to their respective cultures... such a position would be explicitly, unequivocally relativist. For relativism just is the position that moral standards of right and wrong are relative to cultures.[42]

Wolf's argument, if correct, would give considerable support to a relativist position in international ethics. After all, it should not be difficult to find parallels with the scene in *Witness* in international politics in which a conflict between states is described as a conflict between morally incompatible cultures. For example, there is a case cited by James Wallace which would appear to *fit* Wolf's Pluralism-II category quite well.[43] Wallace recounts a situation described by historian William McNeill in which what is (allegedly) right for one nation-state seems to be wrong for another nation-state and in which rightness and wrongness are relative to the respective cultures of the different nation-states. In China, in 1839, McNeill says:

> a British sailor committed murder; and when the guilty individual could not be identified, the Chinese, in accordance with their practice of holding the community responsible for infractions of law and order, demanded that an Englishman – any Englishman – be turned over to them for punishment. No apter instance of conflict between European and Chinese outlooks could have offered itself; for both sides naturally felt themselves completely in the right.[44]

Wallace goes on to say that both sides were shocked and

indignant at the demands and refusals of the other. Western justice requires that individuals not be held legally responsible for offences committed by others: 'This is a fundamental requirement of justice, and our judicial system is built upon it.'[45] But for the Chinese, '[i]t is unlikely ... that this requirement could similarly be justified in terms of Chinese ways and values'.[46] The case seems similar in structure to Wolf's and would presumably warrant the conclusion that 'what is right for one person [or nation-state] is not right for another' and that 'what is right for these people [or nation-states] is relative to their respective cultures...'[47]

But although there seems to be a close parallel with Wolf, appearances are deceiving: we should not give in to the widespread tendency to construe situations as examples of relativism when they are not. For one thing, Wallace's analysis resonates with an unnecessary dichotomy: either we must appeal to an overarching, absolute principle to resolve cases of clashing values or we have to accept subjective relativism.[48] As we have seen, Wolf's project is different: she is trying to carve out a place for a relativist position which is neither subjectivist nor absolutist. For another thing, questions can be raised about the empirical facts in this case which would undercut the possibility of an analogy between the two situations. The case Wallace cites is a footnote in William McNeill's Book *The Rise of the West*. However, the incident has been described quite differently by Immanuel C. Y. Hsu in *The Rise of Modern China*. In this latter account, the Chinese did not demand that *any* Englishman be turned over to the Chinese but that the 'culprits' be turned over to the Chinese.[49] If the Chinese commissioner had demanded that *any* Englishman be turned over for punishment, he would have been making morally wrong demands. And it is worth pointing out that he would have been making morally wrong demands not just in terms of English culture but in terms of Chinese culture: such a demand would have violated Confucian moral codes. Despite differences of emphasis, there is sufficient overlap between Confucian moral codes and Western moral codes that under both it would be morally wrong to punish an individual for crimes he did not commit. So if the commissioner had demanded that *any* Englishman be turned over to the Chinese for punishment, his action would have been morally wrong.

However, let's put this particular historical dispute aside and return to Wolf's arguments. If they are substantially correct, they will immeasurably assist the relativist case in international relations and this for three reasons. First, many international relationists are both pluralists and relativists and consequently would find a case for relativism grounded in pluralism intuitively attractive. Secondly, this sort of pluralism sustains the sort of tolerance towards others which many international relationists regard as indispensable to achieving a peaceful world.[50] And third, the framework, if not the substance, of Wolf's relativism might be regarded as useful, when given an appropriate reconstrual, to those Marxists in international relations who hold that ethical norms are relative to social classes. Nonetheless, despite the attractiveness of Pluralism-II, I shall argue that Wolf has not presented us with a compelling argument for accepting it.

One problem concerns Wolf's treatment of culture. She seems to think that culture strongly determines commitment to values and principles: 'for if', she writes, 'a commitment to the principle of nonviolence is fundamental to Amish culture, and if that culture, that way of life, is no worse, if also no better, than Book's way of life, or mine or yours, then Daniel makes no mistake in accepting the commitment that is essential to that culture'. This notion of culture echoes Hegel's conception of *sittlich* communities: determinative, fully integrated, internally harmonious, hermetically sealed off from one another and internally determined. Wolf thus talks of '[t]he crystallisation of principles, values, and priorities that his [Daniel's] culture has come to embrace...'[51] Once principles become 'crystallised' to make up a moral system which is radically different from other moral systems, then we need only one additional idea to get a *sittlich* community: the community must be bound up with a person's identity. And we do get it for, as Wolf tells us, the code which Daniel follows 'is *his* code', and therefore 'it is right for him to comply. What is right (and wrong) for Daniel is relative to his moral code, and what is right (and wrong) for Book is relative to his.'[52] Wolf's cultures are thus comparable to ethical substances in the Hegelian sense despite the fact that all actual historical societies we have known fail to resemble Hegelian *sittlich* communities. Actual communities, except perhaps in movies, aren't like that.

First of all, no society is without differentiated sub-groups and sub-categories, minimally divided along age, sex and geographical lines. Second, even people in strongly homogeneous cultures develop concerns that arise from belonging to mixed groups with the potential for conflict of interest and values. Third, there are always alternative points of view within a society such that different narratives can be told about how they have mixed together (or have failed to mix together) during the society's history. And fourth, even within strongly homogeneous groups, there may well be varying understandings and weightings of moral claims. For us to understand such variation in appropriately detailed ways requires our conceiving culture to be far more varied and contingent than Wolf's self-sufficiency picture would permit. We are not pushed, as Wolf's argument implies, into taking the culture as a whole or rejecting it as a whole. What Bernard Williams, no enemy of relativism, says about society applies equally to cultures. Williams writes that 'it is implausible to suppose that ethical conceptions of right and wrong have a logically inherent relativity to a given society'.[53]

To be sure, Wolf's argument is persuasive on one point: moral theory does need to avoid evaluations of particular traditions which effectively constitute unacceptable external impositions on one culture by another. So Wolf is correct to point to indeterminacies and lack of uniqueness as part of the warp and woof of making moral judgements. Nonetheless, a proper conception of moral pluralism does not require us to give up our hold on non-local rightness or moral truth in the way that Wolf's argument for Pluralism-II requires. Our reluctance to criticise other cultures or societies may arise from the belief that external criticism is detached, remote and rationalistic. This means that such criticism may be insufficiently respectful of cultural traditions. To avoid such disrespect what is needed is a way of evaluating and criticising cultural traditions that would be sensitive to concerns about external imposition. Such a criticism would, first of all, carve out conceptual space for *internal* criticism in the sense of using the resources within the culture itself to criticise certain moral or ethical features of that culture.[54] Carving out a space for internal criticism would help to preserve commitment to Wolf's Pluralism-I where we recognise that there is something to be said for a certain culture's principle and something to be said against it. But it need not set limits in advance on the possibility of convergent answers which might overcome disagreement. And it would not lead to Pluralism-II since there is no motivation in it for either absolutising the relation between persons or moral systems or of relativising them to 'ethical substances' or moral codes of some kind.

One aspect of internal criticism that is relevant here is that, in accepting it, one is giving up claims to detachment. Instead of criticism of other cultures and moral systems being impersonal, it would be better to think of it as *immersed criticism* in the sense that the norm of objectivity would not involve detachment of the judging subject from the practices, the perceptions or the emotions of the culture itself. Now, it may be that a community is not going to be responsive at all to criticism either from inside or outside. But this would not entail relativism unless the difference between the criticisms and what the society believes are so utterly different that the disputants cannot even arrive at a point where they can comprehend that they disagree. Apart from this special case, relativism would not go through since surely a community which blankly refused to respond to any criticism whatsoever would be held to be morally blamable.

If one describes cultures on the model that Wolf uses to describe the Amish, one wonders whether one would be rendering their morality culturally irrelevant. This sounds paradoxical if not downright perverse. Isn't the whole idea behind Wolf's relativism to give the Amish's culture its moral due, so to speak? But moral seriousness is not the same as complete tolerance or a self-imposed refusal to make moral judgements. So although Wolf has highlighted the radical differences in liberal and Amish moral systems, thoroughgoing tolerance of these differences may actually reduce moral interest and concern. Suppose, after accepting relativism and the thoroughgoing tolerance bound up with it, Amish culture began to interact more with liberal culture. Suppose they interacted commercially and that people from Book's world became involved with the Amish in different initiatives of one kind or another. But the people in Book's culture, if Wolf's moral relativism became the accepted practice, would not be able to regard themselves as living in the same moral world as the Amish, that is, as constrained and guided by the same types of moral considerations. This would be one way in which Pluralism-II could discount the moral reality of others, i.e. fail to take them seriously. 'Oh', those in Book's moral system might say if they were deep believers in Wolf's Pluralism-II, 'what's true for them is not true for us. They're just doing their thing.' Relativism here might result in moral indifference.

But since we haven't yet adopted Wolf's brand of relativism, some reasonable people who live in Book's world might regard Daniel – who refused to 'fight back' when provoked – as the unfortunate victim of an absolute form of pacifism which, however well-meaning, is shallow and dogmatic. This assessment presupposes that ethical judgements make more powerful demands on human reason than Wolf supposes, that they should be regarded with deep seriousness, and that tolerance has limits. In refusing to jump to the conclusion that relativism comes automatically into play, we gather up reasons for continued reflection on the ethical questions at issue. In so doing we might come to challenge the rightness of any form of absolute pacifism, notwithstanding our respect for those cultures or groups which have adopted it. We might come to believe, as the pluralist recommends, that while there is something to be said for pacifism and something to be said for self-defensive action against aggressive bullies, there is not much to be said for absolute pacifism. Wolf's argument slides into an absolutism which Pluralism-I was able to circumvent.

For these reasons I think soft moral realists can dismiss the arguments that Wolf makes on behalf of Pluralism-II, while nonetheless accepting her appealing defense of Pluralism-I. If we do, we will have some useful materials for constructing a pluralist view of international ethics which will be neither absolutist nor relativist and which, more importantly, will stand up to critical scrutiny.

How to maintain Pluralism-I without being tempted by absolutism or relativism

In the case which Wolf describes there seemed to be no intrinsic reason why a philosopher attracted to Pluralism-I could not legitimately say that, while there is something to be said for the sort of life lived by Daniel and something to be said for the sort of life lived by Detective Book, in any particular case involving these individuals and their cultures there is the possibility of attaining moral truth.

If we hold, following John McDowell, that a virtue is a 'reliable sensitivity to a certain sort of requirement which situations impose on behaviour',[55] then we can avoid the cultural determinism which Wolf sees as the distinctive factor that yields Pluralism-II.[56] For, on this view, virtue is a single sensibility to requirements imposed by a situation. In the case of Daniel, Detective Book and the Bully we might plausibly hold that the ethically sensitive person would perceive Daniel's anguish and distress at not being able to respond because it is not the Amish way. The ethically insensitive person would perhaps regard the scene as curious, annoying or just amusing; he would be blind to Daniel's need for assistance. Understood this way we do not get relativism. For the relativist would repeat the phrase of the Amish elder who tries to restrain Book from interfering: 'it's not our way'. For the relativist, values depend on attitudes. The Amish elder, the non-relativist might say, is so deeply entrenched in the *sittlich* of his community that he lacks the moral resources for seeing that the situation calls for intervention. Unlike the moral nihilist, the relativist elder may see that Daniel is in need but he does not feel moved to help. His conception of self and other prevents him from detaching himself from his roles and responsibilities. Sometimes – as in the case of the Amish elder – the entrenchment in the *sittlich* of community is very deep and the person's conception of rationality and moral value is so bound up with that community that the more general conceptions of moral value are ignored. By contrast, Detective Book – though himself partially entrenched in the ways of liberal/democratic society – perceives not only Daniel's distress and the need that arises out of it but he is, unlike the Amish elder, moved to help. We may argue whether Book's action should be considered an act of courage or mere bravado, and there are good reasons for thinking that a decision to describe it one way rather than another is not entirely divorced from the culturally informed moral codes of those making the decision; but that still does not compel us to accept relativism. After evaluation, we might judge Book to be sufficiently sensitive to have perceived the situation in a morally correct way, that though his action may have been consistent with his liberal moral code, we may correctly describe it in a way which circumvents that touchstone, i.e. as morally coura-geous. If this is a bare possibility, then we can, it seems to me, avoid Pluralist-II type relativism. Without denying the moral equivalence of Amish and liberal moral codes, there may be – at least in a situation where we have sufficient facts – a morally right way for a virtuous person to act which is not reducible to culturally informed moral codes and which is sustained by evaluative scrutiny available from within a certain system of concepts.

But now what is the bearing of this for international relations? Well, it means that soft moral realism need not, in general, accept moral relativism. Consider some facts about the world in which we live. There is a great deal of deprivation in the Fourth World. Many people in the Fourth World suffer from severe poverty and malnutrition. Insofar as there are civil and political rights in the countries where they live, they are ineffective. They are often completely defenceless against violence and abuse by police, soldiers and bandits. Many lack access to even minimal health care, and even where it is available it tends to be drastically inadequate; the poor who people the Fourth World are liable to die early from trivial diseases. Many of the same people lack enough education to be able to read and write; and they do not know elementary mathematics. They are deeply entrenched in a situation from which they do not know how to escape or even what would count as 'escape'. The situation of such people is properly described as one of misery and extreme deprivation. And without assistance they are in no position to improve their situation. Such widespread misery provides the basis for moral reflection in international relations.

Now, it may turn out that in giving an account of these facts there could well be different initial moral judgements relative to different sensitivities; but this difference need not imply that it is senseless to urge that the matter be deliberated further. For surely reflective people can try to overcome that difference by any means that may come to hand. What is more, before such people continue argument on the level of reasons, they must sometimes interrogate one another and themselves about the aetiology of their beliefs. In the scene Wolf discusses in *Witness*, if Daniel and Book had understood better the provenance of their own beliefs, then, despite differences in their starting points, one or the other or both parties might still have arrived at an improved moral sensitivity that is continuous with the weaker sensitivity they began with. If so, why can they not arrive at an improved standard of correctness? An account of morality that begins by grounding the phenomenon in human sensitivity and in the contingency of particular desires that arise from practices at particular times and places can postulate an *initial* relativity to that sensitivity, and then make room for what is central to any given morality to surmount that condition.

The same reasoning may be used regarding moral reflections on poverty in the Fourth World. In general, there seems no reason why perseverance should not enable the different moral sensitivities behind different moral judgements to surmount the initial differences in the search for a unitary understanding. Part of that process would involve bringing into our discourse a number of other facts concerning impoverished conditions in the Fourth World. Although there are ongoing debates concerning which distributive principle is the appropriate one to use for such cases and a division between right and left, a strong case can be made, whatever one's political view or cultural code, for providing assistance to starving children on moral grounds. If so, then we may have a basis for saying that there are some moral judgements which, in taking into account what is to be said on one side

223

and the other, cannot be construed as open to relativist interpretation. My second point is that in concluding that rich nations 'ought to' assist children who are the victims of extreme deprivation, it could turn out, as some relativist positions suggest, that there are wide differences in the understanding of the question of what one ought to do, that is, of the reference and extension of the words 'ought to'. But I see no reason for saying that disputants would not be able to arrive at an *improved* understanding of what is at issue in such a case through further questioning. My third point is that this case illustrates why relativism is not an option for ethically sensitive people. To judge that the starvation of children is 'cruel' is so bound up with what it means to continue to be a person in the face of humiliating deprivation that reason recoils, quite rightly, from any suggestion that one has the option of saying: 'it may be true that it's cruel for you, but it isn't true for me'. In such circumstances relativism is out of place.

Conclusion

There are many varied ways in which self-conscious realists can defend their favoured conception of the role of ethics in international politics. Following Raymond Aron, they can insist that 'social reality contains a multiplicity of partial orders, but does not contain in any obvious manner an overall (*global*) order'.[57] Following Hans Morgenthau, they might say that the 'main signpost that helps political realism to find its way through the landscape of international politics is the concept of interest defined in terms of power'.[58] Following Herbert Butterfield, they might underline the extent to which competing interests and uncertainty require that one trust one's adversaries only to the extent that such trust is continually confirmed in action.[59] To follow any of these routes, however, would be nostalgic. It is more illuminating to see political realism as a capacious set of ideas exhibiting fundamental tensions between an Aristotelian objectivism struggling to achieve identity between right desire and right reason, on the one side, and a Hobbesian non-cognitivism which alleges that human values are a human creation grounded in the desire for power, riches, knowledge and honour, all of which, according to Hobbes, 'may be reduced to desire for power', on the other.[60] The non-cognitivist says that all values are a human creation, that people make them up as they go along and apply them to a brute reality. Cognitivism, on the other hand, advances strong claims to truth and objectivity and regards international political philosophy as laying claims to an objective understanding of world politics. My suggestion is that cognitivism, when conceived in the non-absolutist way urged here, has much to recommend it and that political realism should avoid any vigorous version of non-cognitivism. I call my weak version of cognitivism 'soft moral realism' and I have suggested three ways in which tensions between Aristotelian cognitivism and Hobbesian non-cognitivism may be alleviated in favour of cognitivism.

First, I have argued that we can distinguish evaluations, which are amenable to cognitive determinations in terms of truth and falsity, and deliberations, which are not. The notion of evaluations, so understood, enables soft moral realists to claim of their moral judgements that they can be assessed in terms of regular truth. Deliberations, though inextricably bound up with evaluations, are practical in the sense that they require us to ask what action is to be taken in particular, historically determined situations. Though deliberations are impossible without the evaluations which bring them forth, the deliverances of deliberations are not assessed in cognitive terms as true or false but in terms of such criteria as the consequences of action for other features of the situation which are valued and the impact of actions on the participant's well-being.

The distinction between evaluations and deliberations may initially appear to open a gap comparable to the fact–value or the is–ought gaps, but this is not the case. For the evaluation–deliberation distinction is meant to permit the possibility of a statesperson who is *phronimos*, of someone who knows how to evaluate moral truths and who, though not logically compelled to do so, acts in terms of that knowledge in her deliberations. So, in principle, the tension between evaluations and deliberations can be closed by the phronomatic person. Nonetheless, the soft moral realist, as realist, accepts the fact that there are many things which may prevent a statesperson from becoming *phronimos*. The statesperson may have faulty training, or he may be too egotistical, or too proud or irrational to get things right. And because such individual defects are very widespread, the phronomatic statesperson will probably be very rare in practice. Still, the idea of a phronomatic person is a valuable one insofar as it presents the conceptual possibility of building a cognitive conception of politics grounded in virtue ethics.

A second way of reducing the tension between Aristotelian cognitivism and Hobbesian non-cognitivism is to adopt an appropriate

conception of moral dilemmas. Although no interpretation will eliminate all subjectivity from this centrally important concept, nonetheless,
I have argued that in crucial respects moral dilemmas can, without
distortion, be placed in a cognitivist mould. There is no compelling
need to treat moral dilemmas as bereft altogether of objective elements.
The objects which give rise to moral dilemmas are in the world and we
have criteria, e.g. whether moral dilemmas have been rightfully
described and so on, which enable us to determine whether evaluative
statements in moral dilemmas are true or false. Once we become clear
that moral dilemmas are not radically non-cognitive, we can begin to
understand why it would be appropriate to say of certain judgements
that they are true, even though moral and political agents may not be
able to act in terms of those judgements.

A third way in which we have tried to ease the tension between
cognitivism and non-cognitivism is by making claims for a kind of
pluralism which does not collapse into relativism. Although the discussion focused on Wolf's ideas, a more extended treatment would profit
from drawing on some insights of Isaiah Berlin. In an article published
some years ago, Berlin said we have not been able to see that there are
alternative good ways of life, alternative fulfilling conceptions of the
good. Berlin wrote:

> Communities may resemble each other in many respects, but the
> Greeks differ from Lutheran Germans, the Chinese differ from both;
> what they strive after and what they fear or worship is scarcely ever
> similar.

On Berlin's diagnosis, however, this

> is not relativism. Members of one culture can by the force of the
> imaginative insight understand (what Vico called *entrare*) the values,
> the ideals, the forms of life of another culture or society, even those
> remote in time or space. They may find these values unacceptable, but
> if they open their minds sufficiently they can grasp how one might be
> a full human being, with whom one could communicate and at the
> same time live in the light of values widely different from one's own,
> but which nevertheless one can see to be values, ends of life, by the
> realisation of which men could be fulfilled. [61]

Is it possible to maintain this distinction between pluralism and
relativism? Soft moral realists hold, for reasons given above which we
need not rehearse here, that we can do so. Berlin's insight serves to
remind us that we should not make too much of the incompatibility of

values. For, as a matter of fact, there are many priorities on which we are in agreement, many issues to which most people can say, 'There is no justification for compromise on this.' This observation helps, the soft moral realist holds, to support the argument in the previous section to the effect that pluralism is distinguishable from relativism and that in accepting the former there is no compelling urge to accept the latter.

The evaluative political realist, in her guise as soft moral realist, sees moral activity (of which political activity is an inextricable part) as a struggle to get people to see the world and situations like the Vietnam War, intervention in Third World countries, food aid, human rights and so on in a certain way, namely, that some actions are right and others are wrong. To do so the evaluative political realist will appeal to evaluations and their regular truths. When the evaluative political realist succeeds in getting people to admit the force of perceptions of right and wrong, she does not appear to be getting people to see value properties in any way analogous to the way people see chairs, flowers, trees and computers. There is an irrepressible social component to our capacity to discriminate moral activity. On the other hand, the fact that so many human beings from so many different nation-states, representing such wide differences of culture and experience, are able to talk to one another and to pick out the same moral predicates for determination in terms of their truth and falsity suggests that there may be something after all in the cognitivist's key idea of a form of moral objectivity which is not just human agreement.

If the moral objectivity which the evaluative political realist claims to find in the world is challenged, however, it might be useful for her to press an analogy with a Wittgensteinian understanding of objectivity. She might say, for example, that mathematical statements are true by virtue of their applicability to the world ('their realism') and so if, in a particular instance, a pupil continues an N + 2 series with 1000, 1004, 1008 and refuses to admit a mistake by claiming to understand the order to add 2 as 'add 2 up to 1000, 4 up to 2000, 6 up to 3000', we are not tempted to challenge the objectivity of mathematics.[62] By the same token, if the prime minister of country X were to say 'it is not cruel to send innocent people out to sea in unseaworthy boats to their almost certain death by drowning', this would hardly give us a reason for throwing doubt on the objectivity of ethics. And if, after many attempts by an evaluative political realist to explain why such statements are false, the prime minister should say 'It may be wrong for you as a

Westerner but not wrong for me as an Easterner', this should no more be taken as testimony to the radical subjectivity of ethics than the failure of the pupil to learn a mathematical series or admit he is wrong. In the end, however, the evaluative political realist might, realistically speaking, have to appeal to another Wittgensteinian aphorism, to wit: 'If I have exhausted the justifications I have reached bedrock, and my spade is turned. Then I am inclined to say: "This is simply what I do."'[63] But here again there would be no difference in principle between the objectivity of justifications in mathematics and those to be found in the ethics of international politics.

To be sure, for this sort of realist the objectivity of our evaluations does not in itself morally determine what statespersons must do: evaluation as theory is only partially bound up with deliberations as practice. As a thinker, the evaluative political realist will distinguish between evaluation and what she believes she must do after deliberation; and recognise the possibility of conflict between them. The orientation of her thought is towards truth and her concern is to bring her deliberations into line with truth; only thus can she judge other beliefs she held or might hold to be wrong. The statesperson also distinguishes between the excellences and what she happens to desire: the orientation of her thought, if she is guided by practical wisdom, is always towards the various virtues to which she aspires with a realistic sense of what can be achieved within certain recognisable limits. The circumstances of a statesperson, however, differ from the citizen's search for true and virtuous action. For the statesperson not only represents the interests of the people of her own community, she is a member of several other moral communities as well. She cannot assume that goodness lies in the most extended community available since the values which she believes give content and meaning to the excellences may be located in one or a few communities, not necessarily including her own.

For the evaluative political realist, people are now, and are likely to remain, members of different political communities whose values conflict with one another because they are rooted in different conceptions of self and community and therefore different moral/political points of view. The evaluative political realist will say that there is a sense in which ethics is universal, namely, that human beings have the capacity to make true evaluations of how things are in the world. But, at the same time, the evaluative political realist will recognise that the thought that evaluations are of unconditional worth is an illusion fostered by failing to take deliberative attitudes into account. Within my own community, *political friendship* – what Aristotle calls *homonoia* – may develop to permit the sort of psychological identification required to treat everyone as equal and to pursue the common good. However, with respect to communities expressing widely different values, the possibility of political friendship, of being of like mind, may not exist, thus setting up psychological resistance to treating all people as I would my neighbours or myself. If the political community is founded for the sake of the common advantage derived from it by members who can experience political friendship, there will be, *vis-à-vis* people outside my community, clashes of interest and value. Political friendship exists, as Aristotle remarks, 'among good men. They are of the same mind each with himself and all with one another.'[64]

But if harmony requires good women and men who are at one with one another in a way which has never before been even remotely attainable on a worldwide basis, we can understand more clearly perhaps why moral universalism in practice has been so rebarbative to political realists. Given the fragmentation of interest and desire we find even in very small communities, the prospect of finding the requisite self-knowledge, likemindedness and goodness at the global level succumbs to the tyranny of conceptual opacity and distance. Human beings would have to differ too greatly from men and women as they have always been; and it is surely idle to discuss the prospects of beings who can never be on earth. Such talk is besides the point and only breeds dreams and fatal delusions. Statecraft is concerned with actions and events within the limits of human possibility and not with impossible dreams.

9   Conclusion

The Imperfect is our paradise.
                    Wallace Stevens

The argument of this study may be usefully construed as dialectical if one can avoid, as one should, putting too much epistemological pressure on the word 'dialectical'. Starting with certain assumptions and presuppositions derived from alternative conceptions of the subject, I have tried to show how, out of a process of asserting, denying and reasserting, a new kind of political realism – evaluative political realism – emerges to become a viable, coherent and incisive challenge to opposing conceptions of the subject.

The defence of evaluative political realism began with criticisms of two challenging alternative conceptions of the subject, positivist-empiricism and emancipatory international relations. Using the relation of theory and practice as *leitmotiv*, I have argued that these conceptions generated difficulties with which they were unable to cope satisfactorily. In conceiving *theory* as speech requiring reconstruction in a formal language and *practice* as behavioural movement requiring linguistic reformulation as event-data (or in some comparable way), positivist-empiricism creates a yawning gap between two languages ultimately resulting in a stultifying scepticism it lacks the internal resources to resolve. Emancipatory international relations, on the other hand, sees itself as developing a conception of the world which, in claiming to unite theory and practice, is supposed to show, incontestably and irrevocably, just where international relations (and the social practices with which it is bound up) has gone wrong and how it can only be radically improved by planning for its own self-destruction. The principal problematic of emancipatory international relations lies in the difficulty of formulating projects pursued in its name in reasonable, non-utopian and ethically viable ways.

Criticisms of the alternative conceptions are only meant to be suggestive of what someone might say if she were committed to a revisionary version of political realism. There is no implication in these criticisms that the conceptions have been refuted, invalidated or defeated. Conceptions are not, in any case, like hypotheses in terms of which the mounting of arguments for or against determines the extent of their acceptance. No crucial experiment or test can establish or refute a conception and any evidence of the sort we might produce for or against is bound to be inconclusive and variously interpretable. The main point of arguing against them in Part 1 was to prepare the ground for a new version of political realism by suggesting that these leading alternatives may be more problematic than its proponents, and even some of its detractors, allow. In general, Part 1 may be seen as a step in a 'softening up' process: intimations of difficulties with two rival contenders is followed by offering a better alternative in Part 2.

The more direct defence of evaluative political realism began with a claim advanced in Thesis One that *state* and *state-system* are sortal concepts used to pick out and place in high relief from the background jumble of other groups and organisations the entities which define what the science of international relations is a science of. The justification for this procedure lies in an Aristotelian understanding of science in terms of which we must first determine dialectically what the entities of a science are before we can determine its nature, its character or methods. Of the two entities, state and state-systems, it is state which is the more significant since only it has an essence and is able to answer the Aristotelian question *what is it?* The answer which the evaluative political realist gives is that the state is: essentially, externally sovereign. State-system too is anchored, but only indirectly, in the state's being essentially externally sovereign since without this property there could be no system of states. Only when we identify states as being externally sovereign would it make sense to speak of them as mutually adapting their activities to one another, i.e. as being part of a system. Unlike the empiricist's understanding of 'system', the historical state system view holds that to have a system in the requisite sense we must have sortal concepts which pick out something concrete. In accepting an historical state-system view, evaluative political realism is effectively admitting that the *scientific* claims of international relations will be realistically modest and mainly grounded in what can be delivered by historical methodology. But this need not create epistemological panic since there are hidden riches in this sort of modesty.

We then moved on to consider the second thesis for a revised realism. The historical state-system view of state and state-system links up with Thesis Two in that the entities with which they deal – states and state-systems – are conceived to be entities naturally formed by human beings who exhibit the two related components of biological animal and non-biological person. In contrast to frameworks derived, say, from positivist-empiricism within which human beings progressively lose their natural status, Thesis Two insists that human beings are, in certain ineliminable senses, animals and, as such, part of the living environment within which international relations takes place. Accepting Thesis Two involves (in part) accepting the consequences of an understanding of natural selection according to which human beings are naturally procreative animals. Since human resources are finite and each individual naturally inclined to provide for as many descendants as possible, competition, at least of the 'softer' cooperative kind identified in Chapter 6, is quite probably an inevitable genetic-cum-cultural property of human beings. On this view, individuals will use their positions of strength for their own advantage to gain wealth, power, prestige and to produce more progeny. If one regards this idea, as I do, with some revulsion, there seem to be two reasonable responses: either human beings are somehow exempt altogether from the constraints of natural selection or natural selection does not act on the individual level. Since neither of these alternatives seems warranted, a neo-Darwinian conclusion, however unpalatable, would appear to go through. The neo-Darwinian view, however aesthetically and ethically distasteful, generates insights which might help to explain why certain emancipatory projects have not been successful in the past and may not succeed in the future. Once again, theorists, whatever their views, should bear in mind that moral repugnance alone constitutes an inadequate basis for accepting or rejecting claims about human nature.

Despite the insights that realists can derive from evolutionary biology and cognate disciplines, however, there can be no question of *reducing* international relations to such disciplines. To assist in preventing reductionism, we have relied upon an *a priori* concept of personhood which, given the materials out of which it is constructed, is not susceptible to the usual strategies of reduction. Persons, unlike states and state-systems, have no real essence; their essence is nominal and determined by philosophical reflection. Moreover, although the concept of person is supervenient on animal as a natural kind, the supervenient relationship, being a logical one, puts reductionism out of harm's way. Understanding the relation of person and animal in this way has important methodological implications because it suggests that in attempting to understand human nature in international relations theorists cannot bypass the self-understandings which eva-luative political realists deploy in commonsense schemes of explana-tion. Such schemes suppose that human beings typically act so as to enhance their chances of getting the things they perceive as conducive to their wants, desires and interests and, if they are political leaders, to the interests of themselves and the states they represent. Since com-monsense explanations focus on actions and since actions are not physical events, they are not in direct competition with biology. Evolutionary biology provides explanations of the underlying mechan-isms at work but insofar as these are mediated by commonsense, there can be no question of reducing explanations in international relations to biological explanations. Once the relations between person and animal components are rightly ordered, fear of replacing commonsense explanations of the sort that abound in international relations with those derived from evolutionary biology should evaporate. The role of evolutionary biology lies elsewhere and is twofold: first, it hinders socially engineered projects for world government which take no account of what it is for human beings to have a complex and full subjectivity and second, it deepens our commonsense explanations of international activity by charting the evolutionary history that under-lies the proximate mechanisms which constitute the 'core' of any realist conception of international relations. Needless to say these are no mean accomplishments, not least of all because they anticipate Thesis Three, the evaluative political realist's conception of history as prac-tical, actional and partly objective.

When we move in Thesis Three to historical methodology, we need to mark the fact that although we are still talking about actions and states of affairs that evolve in time, we are referring to things that are not explicable in the same terms as those employed by sociobiologists or evolutionary biologists. At least this is clear to evaluative political realists who support Thesis Three. To be sure, it may not be clear to scientific empiricists who have developed an account of history – the deductive-nomological account – which is homomorphic to explanations provided in the natural sciences. According to the deductive-nomological view, explaining an historical event amounts to showing how the statement describing it could be deduced from some true general law or laws together with some statement of initial conditions. Such an account supposes three things, namely, that we can distinguish sharply between the data of experience and theoretical explanation; that understanding has no epistemological role to play in history; and that we can make a clear distinction between facts and meanings. None of these three assumptions, according to certain recent investigations in the philosophy of science, is self-evidently true; nor is the deductive-nomological model which requires them. What makes the deductive-nomological model of explanation attractive to positivist-empiricists is that it holds out the possibility of retrodicting, and therefore explaining, the past and, by virtue of the alleged symmetry between explanation and prediction, of eventually being able to predict future states of affairs in international relations. What worries evaluative political realists is that such a model takes up an absolute position on persons and ethics, distorts human practices, and depreciates the contribution of narrative to understanding international relations.

In the last analysis, positivist-empiricism conceives historical explanation as something engendered by some great machine – as imagined by Sir Isaiah Berlin – 'from which historians could deduce (together with knowledge of the initial conditions) either what would happen next, or what had happened in the past'. The great advantage of such a machine is that it would 'rescue historians from the tedious labours of adding fact to fact and attempting to construct a coherent account ...'[1] But there is no such machine and so what historians of international relations have to rely upon, according to historical realism, are all-too-fallible human beings using their modest powers to make judgements as best they can about the causes of past actions, the truth of historical events and the lessons to be drawn from these for the future conduct of international relations.

Historical realism, as understood by evaluative political realists, yields a conception of history which is both modest and libertarian. It is modest in the sense that it eschews attributing an overall meaning to history and it is libertarian insofar as it opposes determinism. It offers a basis for saying that action in history is the result of a process in which reasoned examination and alternative choices play important roles. It allows space, therefore, for *reason-explanation*, the idea that the characteristic mode of explaining what is going on in history is through identifying activities as having been brought about by agents for reasons which make intelligible the behaviour in which they and others have been involved. That is, we explain the actions of an agent by citing the reasons in terms of which what the agent was doing counts as reasonable in the particular context in which he or she acted. To be an agent's reason for doing something, the reason or reasons must have been efficacious in bringing about the action. One hastens to add that the evaluative political realist does not deny that when the reasons offered by political agents are 'bad' reasons, explanation by causes alone would be more appropriate; but when the reasons are good reasons, they alone suffice to explain the action in question.

Now, in defending the idea that human actions are the primary content of history, historical realists are not only defending a somewhat different form of individualism, but also a narrative account of history. With the demise of the positivist idea that any theory of knowledge should be an idealised version of how natural scientists obtain knowledge of the natural world, philosophers of history have turned their attention to what historians write and therefore to historical narration. I have tried to show above that we can have a conception of history that is realist – in the sense of countenancing verification-transcendent entities – and still make narrative a central focus for acquiring truths about the past.

In general, the evaluative political realist wants to defend the idea that when we attend to the history of disarmament conferences, of war, and of diplomacy between states, it is evident that we are dealing with events that differ from those that comprise the subject matter of natural history. The short-hand way of describing the difference is by saying that disarmament conferences, wars and diplomacy between states are mainly the products of human doings whereas the products of natural history are not. Disarmament conferences, wars and diplomatic activity between states do not in themselves have a history. We identify and explain them by reference to the doings of persons and by calling them actions. This realist view of history seems to cohere with the idea of persons as psychological and moral beings carved out in Thesis Two; but it also anticipates Thesis Four, which depicts persons as beings frequently caught in moral and political dilemmas as a result of the value properties they see in alternative actions.

Another important feature of Thesis Three is that our understanding of historical subjects in international relations will always remain partial or incomplete. The reason for this is that any view of history cannot take account of that portion of ourselves which is recording the activities as they occur and which moments later will become a part of the past. This idea – The Incomplete View of Reality – has two important implications. First, it will mean that even the most objective view of history – 'the view from nowhere' – will be incomplete: every view, in as much as it cannot include the viewer himself as object, cannot, even in principle, comprehend everything. And second, it will mean that the absolute perspective adopted by the natural sciences will not be the appropriate perspective for the historian to take up. If historians cannot, even in principle, include everything in their accounts of historical reality, perhaps they should make a virtue of necessity and make explicit their inclusion of subject-related properties in their accounts. In admitting that historical accounts should consider how things feel, seem and appear to subjects, one is effectively giving up a naturalistic account of historical methodology. In so doing one is giving up an implausible 'scientistic' project and replacing it with one which, in admitting subject-dependent properties, is paradigmatically realistic.

Consistent with the idea that history can be only partially objective, Thesis Four concedes to 'the subjective' the idea that some non-cognitivist desire or interest has to be present in any moral/political action; but, nonetheless, it retains the key idea in the cognitivist perspective that evaluative statements can be objectively determined on the grounds of truth and falsity. For the evaluative political realist, there is always a gap, not between 'facts' and 'values', but between evaluative and deliberative attitudes. On the basis of this distinction, the evaluative political realist can defend the objectivity of morals on the one side, while conceding the inclusion of 'subjective' elements in political/moral action on the other. To be sure, values have some kind of 'claim' on us; but this claim is not necessarily that we must do something, to make some observable change in the world. In deliberations concerning whether we should act, we need to consider the consequences of our actions on other values we esteem, attempting in the process to effect some sort of balance between them. In contrast to the neo-Kantian approach, we have no basis for assuming that moral values override non-moral values. Moral/political agents must always consider the values at stake in the case at hand. So, on this view, political leaders are neither self-compelled to 'maximise power' or to act in terms of 'the moral point of view'. To consider only power would be to strip the world of all value and to accept nihilism. To consider the moral point of view alone, oblivious to the demands of power, would be to indulge in self-defeating moralism and moral priggishness. What is needed is to balance, through the self-conscious exercise of *phronesis*, the moral and non-moral values at stake in the particular case at hand.

Also, from the perspective of evaluative political realism, it does not appear to be plausible to suggest that all moral values are intrinsically connected with universal values in the form of categorical imperatives; rather, we should look closely at the case before us. For example, deliberate and premeditated self-sacrifice surely possesses (in some circumstances) extremely high moral value. A woman who gives her life to save others is rightly regarded as a heroine after her death; but it would surely be absurd to claim that any categorical imperative of a practical kind followed from it. The main problem here lies in Kant's account of judgement which proceeds from the dubious assumption that the rules definitive of any concept suffice by themselves to determine whether something falls under that concept; judgement, on this account, is merely our capacity actually to apply such rules, to see something as the sort of thing those rules pick out. Is it always true, however, that the rules have enough content to settle by themselves whether something falls under the concept? Is it always true that judgement has no other task than simply to see that such rules suffice to identify the things of which the concept may be predicated? This does not appear to be so either in the moral/political domain or elsewhere. There are many moral duties whose rules cannot sufficiently determine whether in particular circumstances those duties have a claim on what we should do and what actions would satisfy them. In our discussion in Chapter 8, we have pointed to a whole class of cases – moral dilemmas – in which one gets no real assistance in judging the issue by appealing to rules. Consider Herman Melville's *Billy Budd*. Captain Vere and his officers are confronted with two incompatible demands of justice, requiring them both to acquit Billy, since they are confident that he is not legally or morally guilty of anything, and to condemn him, since, under the circumstances, the avoidance of mutiny requires his immediate execution. The application of moral rules offers little help with this and many other dilemmas that characters in world literature and political leaders in international relations face daily.

What needs to be stressed here is that the claim that objective values exist cannot simply be a claim that certain categorical imperatives are objectively valid. What does it mean to say, then, that values are cognitive? It means that the world – the human world – is not empty of value; it is already charged with value even though the content of that value may be understood differently in different historical communities. By virtue of their actions, human beings bring valuable things into existence; but they cannot create or destroy the value a thing possesses without changing the thing itself or destroying it. Values, on this view, are features or qualities of objects. Within particular communities, the content of such values is not something that is decreed by rules: it is something that is already there in an ongoing system of life consisting, as it does, of a continuing set of adjustments and claims and concessions made by real people already living together with settled interests and different degrees of influence and bargaining strengths. On this understanding we can intelligibly hold on to both a cognitive conception of values and the inescapable idea of a plurality in the way we articulate them.

The second point that we need to mark here is this, that taking the existence of objective values and disvalues as the starting point for an ethical understanding of international relations will be opposed to any beginning that passes straight to a theory of reasons for actions; as such, it will make possible a revival of the Greek idea of a receptive attitude to the world. We are too apt to interpret human rationality in either purely theoretical or purely practical terms. A view of theory which stresses the inappropriateness of a detached and impersonal response to the way things are points up the fact that the non-theoretical side of life is not just activity or an event but a form of life. An engaged view of the way things are will help us to register the fact that people are members of different communities whose moral principles often differ and whose interests frequently conflict. On this understanding of rationality one does not automatically assume that universal morality is clearly superior to local morality. We have to somehow come to grips with the fact that the world is now (as in the past) divided into different communities, each with its own history, traditions and institutions and each disposing of its own machinery of organised violence without whose support no moral system can be upheld.

Thesis Four also distinguishes pluralism and relativism. In the discussion in the text, I suggested that Susan Wolf's attempt to defend both pluralism and relativism amounted to a half-truth: her defence of pluralism succeeded but not her defence of relativism. I then suggested that if we adopt, on behalf of soft moral realism, the idea that statespersons can be morally sensitive beings practising practical wisdom, we shall be able to comprehend why initial impressions of relativism's necessity may realistically be turned into thoughts of possible moral/political consensus. Indeed, I argued that just such a consensus should be possible with our evaluations of certain statements concerning starving children. The line of argument shows, I believe, that pluralism is distinguishable from relativism and that is all we need to show. We do not have to show – what we cannot in any case show – that relativism is defeated only when we take up an absolute perspective on the world.[2] Pluralism enables us to give weight to the fact that the world's people live, and often seem to want to continue to live, in political communities (countries) which articulate local values derived from internal history, tradition, custom, language and so on without denying the existence of universal values derived from human nature and self. It provides scope for the idea that there are ties that bind us to our countries and that it is good that we avoid doing those things which might threaten the very existence of those ties. But, in contrast to any Kantian approach, pluralism says nothing about the so-called moral obligations we have to our country. For, on the pluralist view, we have no such moral obligations; we have only those myriad of interpersonal ties with others which derive their force from the customs, traditions, history and political friendships which naturally arise in any political community. So, on the one hand, in saying that these ties are good we are claiming that there are many incommensurable goods whose realisation is regarded as essential by people living in different countries. On the other hand, pluralism rejects relativism for its inherent incapacity to make ethical and moral comparisons between country A and country B because it refuses to countenance country-independent bases for making such comparisons. Are we really unable to say that Russia is better off today than it was under Stalin? that Germany since Hitler's demise no longer participates in evil? and that the vast inequalities in incomes and life conditions between the First and Third worlds is unjust? The evaluative political realist thinks we are able to say such things and that the grounds for doing so may be found in the pluralistic moral cognitivism adumbrated in Chapter 8. On this understanding comparative moral judgements are possible and necessary; they would involve, in the ideal case, making contact with what morally sensitive people perceive to be admirable and deplorable in given situations. The nihilistic understanding bound up with neo-realism is no part of evaluative political realism which, in this respect, attempts to recover the traditional realist understanding of moral reflection as the search for a balance between the moral and the non-moral, between principle and practical necessity, between theory and practice. If this sounds suspiciously like commonsense, evaluative political realism at least refuses to deny the need to underline the great value of just such a conception of ethics and morality for rediscovering the content of a genuinely realist conception of international relations.

On the basis of these arguments (and arguments neither made nor unmade) it would appear that evaluative political realism is coherent, that is, that the four theses hang together and cover the main areas that need to be considered if any conception of international relations is going to make a legitimate claim to be about international relations. The four theses of evaluative political realism are not presented as self-evidently true nor are they held to be true because each one individually matches the world. Rather, they are to be regarded as truths in the sense of being rationally acceptable for the context of the way things are, and the way things are likely to remain, in any future international relations we are likely to care about. To put this in a somewhat different idiom, what I am saying is that evaluative political realism, understood in terms of the four theses, constitutes a coherent conception of international politics which, however much we may be unable to establish its truth in every possible world, *seems* to be true in every *non-utopian* international world which is a possible international world for *us*, for human beings with our natures, our histories and our values. Evaluative political realism, then, would be true in every possible international world which is sufficiently like the actual world that all-too-fallible human beings could have a chance of realising it. They are in this sense rationally acceptable. But the fact that they are rationally acceptable does not mean that I could not possibly be mistaken about them. I am quite willing to admit that I could be mistaken about the truth of these four theses or, for that matter, about anything else. Any one of my beliefs is subject to revision in the light of experience. Evaluative political realism wants no truck with dogmatism.

Nonetheless, in defending these four theses, sufficient ground has been won to make plausible the claim that evaluative political realism is a defendable conception of international relations with many advantages over its main rivals. Suppose this is so. Students of international relations might still feel the urge to press evaluative political realism to say, more concretely, what the study of international relations consists of. But evaluative political realists need not feel tempted to accede to such requests. For the point of using the term 'conceiving' and its cognates (as opposed to 'theorising') to describe the point of view which has animated this study is both to circumvent the instrumentalistic insistence that unless something has utility, in the sense of telling us what we ought to do, it lacks utility altogether. In effect, evaluative political realism is urging us to see that the way in which we conceive theory, practice and their relation is vitally important to the way in which we represent to ourselves and to others what we actually think and do. To conceive of the different ways in which theory, practice and their relations have been organised is not just to theorise but also to *picture* the relations which have played significant roles in shaping our view of what international relations consists of. Pictures, as understood here, are not fully developed philosophical views; they consist of all those assumptions and presuppositions, explicit and tacit, that shape our engagement and interest in a subject but which, like ambitious extras waiting in the wings, are only called upon in a crisis. For the evaluative political realist, the crisis is now; it manifests itself in the increasingly strident discourse concerning all those epistemological, ontological and ethical issues or concerns which positivism and postpositivism conceal from view. In negotiating its way through some of these assumptions and presuppositions, this study has struggled towards a somewhat different picture of what might be required to attenuate the crisis. Evaluative political realism holds that there are two controversial claims we want to accept if we are to have an adequate understanding of international relations: a commonsense framework of explanation and a cognitivist view of ethics. These are, one could say, essential to our thoughts, to how we live and how we act; giving them up is not a realistic option for us.

The commonsense framework we use to explain human action in life and history rests upon our knowledge of human character, our general capacity to understand what people are like, and how they are likely to act in certain circumstances. Only an extraordinary theory of international relations would enable us to obviate essential reliance on commonsense. No such theory has yet been developed nor do we have any clear idea of what it would consist of. Being realistic about theory in international relations, then, means accepting the quasi-theoretical commonsense framework of explanation which we have good reason to think is ineliminable. At the same time, evaluative political realism defends a conception of practice which, though it stays close to 'the world of appearances', does not collapse into it. Being realistic in the realm of practice requires making a capacious place for ethics as a form of knowledge, an idea which gives practice a substantive seriousness that reflective commonsense thinking would also endorse. Ethical and political practices are, of course, shaped by what different cultures count as virtuous and this varies widely in time and space. But for the evaluative political realist what the virtues are and how they relate to genuine human interests and needs are not solely matters that are variable and plastic. While different circumstances and times make different sorts of demands on people, there is yet a coherent conception of what the virtues are and what sort of understanding and dispositions they involve that is not undone or made obsolete or irrelevant by those differences. However, notwithstanding the fact that quasi-theoretical accounts of both how things are and how to live well are possible, evaluative political realism remains ever mindful of the fact that there is a complex tension between theory and practice which, in the spirit of realism, we have every reason to think will remain a characteristic feature of international relations. The world which our quasi-theoretical commonsense framework describes and our quotidian practices reinforce contains cultural and national communities whose values are so diverse that no conception of world politics claiming to bring theory into unity with practice would be acceptable to them all.

The picture of international relations which the evaluative political realist presents resonates with a spirit of realism which is either absent from positivist-empiricism and emancipatory international relations altogether or is present only in a radically undeveloped state. The spirit of realism rises from reflection on the junkheap of the discarded theory-offerings which have proliferated in the discipline since its academic founding. The hypertrophy of theory has pulled us away from the details and particularity of international relations and towards a fragmenting array of theoretical constructions which, as critical reflection has persistently shown, turn out to be myths, fantasies or superstitions. A large part of this study involves dealing with these myths, fantasies and superstitions. These include: the myth that a naturalistic (reductivist) understanding of international relations is intrinsically superior to a non-naturalistic science of international relations; the fantasy that there is a genuine prospect of living in a world state; and the essentially superstitious notion that pluralism is somehow equivalent to relativism. And so on and so forth. The fact that for the evaluative political realist there are many such myths, fantasies and superstitions gives evaluative political realism an unavoidably negative cast. But there is no need to apologise for this negativity since there is, given the excesses of hypertrophic theory, a good deal to be negative about.

It will not be to the point to argue against this conclusion that the international order which evaluative political realism pictures is *too* similar to the status quo, i.e. a world in which sovereign states continue to pursue their goals partly in cooperation and partly in conflict with one another. There are at least two good reasons why this criticism may be put aside: first, that, historically, projects for so-called radical change in international politics have been eternal returns of the same, instant replays of dead or deadening ideologies and second, that it is not true. Evaluative political realism proposes radical changes in the way in which we understand ethics and human nature. In effect, evaluative political realism is on all fours with these words of Vaclav Havel, Eastern Europe's justly renowned statesman/poet:

> We are looking for new scientific recipes, new ideologies, new control systems, new institutions, new instruments to eliminate the dreadful consequences of our previous recipes, ideologies, control systems, institutions, and instruments. We treat the fatal consequences of technology as though they were a technical defect that could be remedied by technology alone. We are looking for an objective way out of a crisis of objectivism. What is needed is something different, something larger. Man's attitude to the world must be radically changed. We have to abandon the arrogant belief that the world is merely a puzzle to be solved, a machine with instructions for use waiting to be discovered, a body of information to be fed into a computer in the hope that, sooner or later, it will spit out the solution.[3]

To accept the idea that something different and larger is needed in the context of a conception of thinking about international politics which holds that we cannot start all over again is what evaluative political realism is all about.

This study opened with an aphorism from Wittgenstein concerning how we can tell we have a philosophical problem. In the course of this study, I have tried to show the extent to which our understanding of international relations is bound up with all manner of philosophical problems most of which we do not know how to solve or even what would count as a solution. Where this does not lead to a massive attack of vertigo, it would seem to warrant a large dose of scepticism concerning the value of philosophising in international relations. And so it may do. But if we are able to get ourselves to see that philosophising in international relations need not reverberate between dogmatic scientism and transcendental utopianism, we might begin to think more positively about the possibility of an approach to the subject which recognises at the outset the uncertainties, the contentiousness, the waverings that constitute its core. We might then go on to think that the asking of philosophical questions of the sort we have discussed in this study is redolent with a kind of necessity, even though that we cannot answer them by empirical means. We might even get ourselves into a realistic modality in terms of which we actually prize the chronic debates in the discipline because they deflate the dogmatic pretensions of those who claim to know rather than just believe. In taking this unmarked and hazardous route we could perhaps come to appreciate philosophical activity in the realistic spirit: of thinking through the alternatives, of evaluating their implications and their relative plausibility and, above all, of seeing the connection between such activity and what we are as human beings. It is at this point that we might also be able to say, *pace* Wittgenstein, 'Now you know what is in question.'[4] What? 'I have already said *what*.'[5]

Notes

1 Theory and practice in international relations

1   See Yosef Lapid, 'Quo Vadis International Relations? Further Reflections on the "Next Stage" of International Theory', *Millennium: Journal of International Studies* 18 (1989): 77–88; 'The Third Debate: On the Prospects of International Theory in a Post-Positivist Era', *International Studies Quarterly* 35 (1989): 235–54; Mark Neufield, 'Reflexivity and International Relations Theory', *Millennium* 22 (1993): 53–76; James N. Rosenau (ed.), *Global Voices: Dialogues in International Relations* (Boulder, CO: Westview Press, 1993); and Andrew Linklater, 'Dialogue, Dialectic and Emancipation in International Relations at the End of the Post-War Age', *Millennium* 23 (1994): 119–31.

2   Cf. Linklater, 'Dialogue, Dialectic and Emancipation', p. 119.

3   Hayward R. Alker, Jr and Thomas J. Biersteker, 'The Dialectics of World Order: Notes for a Future Archaeologist of International *Savoir Faire*', *International Studies Quarterly* 28 (1984): 121–42.

4   K. J. Holsti, *The Dividing Discipline* (Boston: Allen Unwin, 1985).

5   Michael Banks, 'The Inter-Paradigm Debate', in *International Relations: A Handbook of Current Theory*, ed. Margot Light and A. J. R. Groom (Boulder, CO: Lynne Rienner, 1985), 9.

6   Robert O. Keohane, 'International Institutions: Two Approaches', in *International Institutions and State Power: Essays in International Relations Theory* (Boulder, CO: Westview Press, 1989), 158.

7   Charles Taylor, *Human Agency and Language, Philosophical Papers*, 2 vols. (Cambridge University Press, 1985), I especially chs. 1 and 4.

8   Fred Halliday, 'Vigilantism in International Relations: Kubalkova, Cruickshank and Marxist Theory', *Review of International Relations* 13 (1987), 164.

9   Jürgen Habermas, 'Foucault's Lecture on Kant', *Thesis Eleven*, no. 14 (1986), 6.

10   For a good example of 'deconstructive' conceptions of international relations which bear the heavy imprint of Foucault and Derrida, see *International/Intertextual Relations*, ed. James Der Derian and Michael J. Shapiro (Lexington, MA: Lexington Books, 1989).

11 See my 'Richard Ashley's Discourse for International Relations', *Millennium* 21 (1992): 147–82.
12 Robert Keohane, 'International Relations Theory: Contributions of a Feminist Standpoint', *Millennium* 18 (1989): 245–54. Christine Sylvester also uses the distinction, with certain modifications, in *Feminist Theory and International Relations in a Postmodern Era* (Cambridge University Press, 1994). The distinction seems to be due to Sandra Harding, *The Science Question in Feminism* (Ithaca: Cornell University, 1986).
13 N. Hartsock, 'The Feminist Standpoint: Developing the Ground for a Specifically Feminist Historical Materialism', in *Discovering Reality*, ed. Sandra Harding and Merrill Hintikka (London: D. Reidl, 1983).
14 Ibid., p. 304.
15 Sylvester, *Feminist Theory*, p. 59.
16 Christine Sylvester, 'Riding the Hyphens of Feminism, Peace, and Place in Four-(or more) Part Cacophony', *Alternatives* 28 (1993): 109–18.
17 Sylvester, *Feminist Theory*, p. 213.
18 Ibid.
19 Ibid.
20 Ibid., p. 14.
21 Ibid., p. 216.
22 Ibid.
23 Robert Gilpin, *War and Change in World Politics* (New York: Cambridge University Press, 1981) and 'The Richness of the Tradition of Political Realism', in Robert Keohane ed., *Neorealism and Its Critics* (New York: Columbia University Press, 1986).
24 Stephen Krasner, *Structural Conflict: The Third World Against Global Liberalism* (Berkeley: University of California Press, 1985).
25 Joseph Grieco, *Cooperation Among Nations: Europe, America and Non-Tariff Barriers to Trade* (Ithaca: Cornell University Press, 1990).
26 Kenneth Waltz, *Theory of International Politics* (Reading, MA: Addison-Wesley, 1979) and 'Realist Thought and Neorealist Thought' in Robert Rothstein, ed., *The Evolution of Theory in International Relations* (Columbia, SC: University of South Carolina Press, 1991), 21–38.
27 Waltz, 'Realist Thought', p. 22.
28 Ibid., p. 26.
29 Waltz, *Theory of International Politics*, p. 8.
30 Ibid.
31 Ibid.
32 Ibid., p. 6.
33 Waltz, 'Realist Thought', p. 31. My emphasis.
34 Waltz, *Theory of International Politics*, p. 6.
35 Ibid., pp. 8–9.
36 Ibid., p. 9.
37 Hilary Putnam, *Representation and Reality* (Cambridge, MA: MIT Press, 1988), ch. 2.

38 Ibid., p. 22.
39 Recently, efforts have been undertaken to eliminate this ignorance. See, for example, Howard Williams, *International Relations in Political Theory* (Milton Keynes: Open University Press, 1992). Nonetheless, without denying the value of Williams' book much remains to be accomplished if we are to come to grips with the history of thought in international relations.

2 Positivist-empiricism and international relations

1 See the interesting article on the priority which Descartes gave to reason over the senses. Louis E. Loeb, 'The Priority of Reason in Descartes', *The Philosophical Review* 99 (1990): 3–43.
2 Charles Taylor, 'Understanding and the Human Sciences', *Review of Metaphysics* 34 (1980): 30–7.
3 Ernst Haas, 'Reason and Change in International Life; A Justifying Hypothesis', *Journal of International Affairs* 44 (1990): 232.
4 Charles Taylor, 'Understanding in Human Science', pp. 30–7.
5 Haas, 'Reason and Change', p. 240.
6 The felicitous phrase 'the age of the world picture' is taken from the title of Heidegger's essay in *The Question Concerning Technology and Other Essays*, trans. William Lovitt (New York: Harper & Row, 1977). The phrase is here meant to apply to thinking driven by technology and instrumental concerns such as, e.g. positivist-empiricism.
7 *The Philosophical Works of Descartes*, trans., E. S. Haldane and G.R.T. Ross. 2 vols. (New York: Cambridge, 1968), I, p. 119.
8 Ibid., vol. 1, 119–120
9 Ibid., vol, 1, 211.
10 Ibid., vol. 1, 89.
11 On this point, see Hiram Caton, *The Origin of Subjectivity* (New Haven: Yale University Press, 1973), 4.
12 On this point, see Richard Kennington, 'The "Teaching of Nature" in Descartes' Soul Doctrine', *Review of Metaphysics* 26 (1972–3), 98–9.
13 Oran Young, 'The Perils of Odysseus: On Constructing Theories of International Relations', in Raymond Tanter and Richard H. Ullman *Theory and Policy in International Relations* (Princeton University Press, 1972), 183; emphasis added.
14 Waltz, *Theory of International Politics*, 6.
15 Deutsch, *The Nerves of Government* (New York: Free Press, 1966), 14; emphasis in text.
16 E. Haas, 'Why Collaborate? Issue Linkage and International Regimes', *World Politics* 32 (1980), 367–8; emphasis in text.
17 Nazli Choucri, 'Key Issues in International Relations Forecasting', in Choucri and Thomas W. Robinson, eds., *Forecasting in International Relations* (San Francisco: W.H. Freeman, 1978), 5; emphasis in text.
18 R. J. Rummel, 'The Roots of Faith', in James N. Rosenau, ed., *In Search of Global Patterns* (New York: Free Press, 1976), 11.

19 Patrick J. McGowan and Howard B. Shapiro, *The Comparative Study of Foreign Policy: A Survey of Scientific Findings* (Beverly Hills, CA: Sage, 1973), 223; emphasis added.

20 R. Rosecrance, *International Relations: Peace or War?* (New York: McGraw Hill, 1973), 13.

21 R. Keohane, *International Institutions and State Power* (Boulder, CO: Westview Press, 1989), 167.

22 Steve Chan, *International Relations in Perspective* (New York: Macmillan, 1984), 17.

23 For an expression of this view see John Gillepsie, 'Why Mathematical Models?', in Dina Zinnes and John Gillepsie, eds., *Mathematical Models in International Relations* (New York: Praeger, 1976).

24 R. Keohane, 'Neoliberal Institutionalism', in *International Institutions and State Power* (Boulder, CO: Westview Press, 1989), 1–20.

25 The concept of a thin, unencumbered self has been brilliantly explored by Michael Sandel, *Liberalism and the Limits of Justice* (Cambridge University Press, 1982) and 'The Procedural Republic and the Unencumbered Self', *Political Theory* 12 (1984): 81.

26 Sandel, *Liberalism and the Limits of Justice, passim.*

27 Ibid., p. 59.

28 The distinction between thin and thick *selves* was suggested by, and partially incorporates, Williams' distinction between thin and thick *concepts* See Bernard Williams, *Ethics and the Limits of Philosophy* (London: Fontana Press, 1985), especially 143–5.

29 On this, see the interesting essay by John Gray, 'Mill's and Other Liberalisms' in Knud Haakonssen, ed., *Traditions of Liberalism* (No place: Centre For Independent Studies, 1988), 119–39.

30 For the concept of weak evaluation, and its contrasting alternative strong evaluation, see Charles Taylor, 'What is Human Agency?' in *Human Agency and Language, Philosophical Papers*, 2 vols. (Cambridge University Press, 1985), I, 15–44.

31 Robert O. Keohane, 'Reciprocity in International Relations', *International Organisation* 40 (1986): 1–27.

32 Taylor, 'Self-interpreting Animals', in *Human Agency and Language*, 45–76.

33 Arnold Wolfers, 'The Actors in International Politics', in William T.R. Fox, ed., *Theoretical Aspects of International Relations* (University of Notre Dame Press, 1959), 93–106 at p. 83.

34 Ibid., p. 83.

35 Martin Hollis, *Models of Man: Philosophical Thoughts on Social Action* (Cambridge University Press, 1977), 5.

36 Young, 'The Perils of Odysseus', *passim.*

37 Talco H. Parsons, *The Structure of Social Action* (New York: Free Press, 1968), *passim.*

38 John Steinbrunner, *The Cybernetic Theory of Decision* (Princeton University Press, 1974), *passim.*

39 Deutsch, *The Nerves of Government*, pp. 82–3.

40 George Modelski, *Principles of World Politics* (New York: Free Press, 1972), 16.

41 Herbert A. Simon, *Models of Discovery* (Dordrecht: Reidel, 1977), *passim*.

42 Greg Cashman, *What Causes War? An Introduction to Theories of International Conflict* (New York: Lexington, 1993), especially chs. 1–3.

43 For a contrary view, see Richard Rorty, 'Freud and Moral Reflection', in *Essays on Heidegger and Others, Philosophical Papers*, 2 vols. (Cambridge University Press, 1991), I.

44 Modelski, *Principles of World Politics*, 15.

45 Ibid., 16.

46 See below ch. 4.

47 For an example of radical historicism, see, in particular, R.B.J. Walker, 'Realism, Change, and International Relations Theory', *International Studies Quarterly* 31 (1987): 65–86 and ' "The Prince" and "The Pauper": Tradition, Modernity, and Practice in the Theory of International Relations', in Der Derian and Shapiro, *International/Intertextual Relations*, pp. 25–48. For radical feminism, see the collection of articles in V. Spike Peterson, ed., *Gendered States: Feminist (Re) Visions of International Relations Theory* (Boulder, CO: Lynne Rienner 1992) and Christine Sylvester, 'Riding the Hyphens of Feminism, Peace, and Place in Four- (or more) Part Cacophony', *Alternatives* 18 (1993): 109–18.

48 For a recent expression of this pessimism, see Yale H. Ferguson and Richard W. Mansbach, *The Elusive Quest* (Columbia, SC: University of South Carolina Press, 1988), especially ch. 9.

49 Charles A. McClelland, *Theory and the International System* (New York: Macmillan, 1966), 16; emphasis added.

50 Bruce Russett and Harvey Starr, *World Politics: Menu For Choice*, 2nd edn (New York: W.H. Freeman, 1985), especially ch. 2.

51 Ibid., p. 33.

52 Ibid., emphasis added.

53 Ludwig Wittgenstein, *Remarks on the Philosophy of Psychology*, I, ed. G.E.M. Anscombe and G.H. von Wright, trans. G.E.M. Anscombe (Oxford: Basil Blackwell, 1980), 397.

54 It has frequently been assumed that rationalism and empiricism are contraries and that the inductivism is a feature of the latter. In my view this assumption deprives us in advance of seeing that empiricism and rationalism are parts of a whole piece of cloth located in Cartesian metaphysics. Although Bacon had ideas quite different from Descartes' about how to overcome doubt, he agreed with Descartes on the necessity of grounding theory or reason in something external and non-historical. Descartes himself attempted to ground reason in the belief that God gave us mathematics and deductive logic and God was no deceiver. Although Sir Francis Bacon was opposed to Descartes' deductive method, replacing it with induction, he too appealed to reason and 'the word of God' to

justify our knowledge from the scourge of Pyrrhonianism. Deductivism and inductivism are best seen as part of the same rationalist project of finding foundations for knowledge in order to overcome scepticism.

55 J. David Singer, 'The Behavioural Science Approach to International Relations', *SAIS* 10 (Summer 1966), 13.

56 J. David Singer and Susan D. Jones, *Beyond Conjecture in International Politics* (Itasca, IL: Peacock, 1972), 3.

57 Ibid., p. 3.

58 Ibid., p. 4.

59 John Vasquez, *The Power of Power Politics: A critique* (London: Francis Pinter, 1983). One reason for focusing on Vasquez is that his work has been the source of extravagant praise from within the positivist-empiricist conception of international relations. For example, Michael Banks calls it 'the single most important work to have emerged from the behavioural movement in international relations'. Michael Banks, 'Where We Are Now', *Review of International Studies* 11 (1985), 220. Whether such acclaim is justified is best left to Vasquez' readers.

60 *The Philosophical Works of Descartes*, I, p. 7.

61 Ibid., I, p. 28.

62 Donald J. Puchala, 'Woe To the Orphans of the Scientific Revolution', *Journal of International Affairs* 44 (1990): 59–80.

63 Ibid., p. 64.

64 Ibid.

65 Ibid., p. 70.

66 Ibid.

67 Ibid.

68 Ibid.

69 Robert O. Keohane, 'Theory of World Politics', in Keohane, ed., *Neorealism and Its Critics* (New York: Columbia University Press, 1986), 160.

70 Ibid., p. 160.

71 Ibid.

72 Ibid., pp. 160–1.

73 Imre Lakatos, *The Methodology of Scientific Research Programs, Philosophical Papers*, ed., John Worrall and Gregory Currie (Cambridge University Press, 1978), I, p. 113.

74 Ibid., p. 5.

75 Vasquez, *The Power of Power Politics*, ch. 1.

76 Ibid., p. 177.

77 Ibid., pp. 158, 177–81.

78 Ibid., p. 9.

79 Ibid., p. 5.

80 Ibid., p. 10.

81 Ibid., p. 12.

82 Ibid., p. 12.

83 Stephen D. Krasner, 'Toward Understanding in International Relations', *International Studies Quarterly* 29 (1985): 138.
84 Ibid., p. 139.
85 Thomas Kuhn, *The Structure of Scientific Revolutions*, 2nd edn (University of Chicago Press, 1970), 206.
86 Hilary Putnam, *Reason, Truth and History* (Cambridge University Press: 1981), 56–69, 72–4.
87 Richard Rorty, 'Science as Solidarity', in *Objectivity, Relativism, and Truth, Philosophical Papers*, 2 vols. (Cambridge University Press, 1991), I, p. 39.
88 Michael Donelan, *Elements of International Political Theory* (Oxford: Clarendon Press, 1990), 56.
89 Ferguson and Mansbach, *The Elusive Quest*, p. 23.
90 Sir Isaiah Berlin, *Four Essays on Liberty* (Oxford University Press, 1969), lv–lvi.

3 Emancipatory international relations: a first cut

1 Andrew Linklater, *Men and Citizens in the Theory of International Relations* (London: Macmillan, 1982) and *Beyond Realism and Marxism* (New York: St Martin's Press, 1989).
2 Linklater, *Men and Citizens*, p. 160.
3 Andrew Linklater, 'Realism, Marxism and Critical International Theory', *Review of International Studies* 12 (1986): 301–12 at p. 303.
4 Ibid., p. 303.
5 Robert W. Cox, 'Social Forces' States and World Orders: Beyond International Relations Theory', *Millennium* 10 (1981): 126–54 at p. 129.
6 Ibid., p. 129.
7 Ibid., p. 130; emphases added.
8 Ibid.
9 Ibid., p. 127.
10 Ibid.
11 Ibid., p. 129.
12 Ibid.
13 Stephen Gill, 'Historical Materialism, Gramsci, and International Political Economy', in Craig N. Murphy and Roger Tooze, eds., *The New International Political Economy* (Boulder: Lynne Rienner, 1991), 57.
14 G.A. Cohen, *Karl Marx's Theory of History: A Defence* (Oxford: Clarendon Press, 1978). See also his *History, Labour, and Freedom* (Oxford: Clarendon Press, 1988), especially pp. 14–20.
15 For an example of this view, see Jonathan Rée, *Radical Philosophy* 60 (Spring 1992): 3–11. For a balanced response, see Ross Poole, *Racial Philosophy* 62 (Autumn 1992): 14–19.
16 R.B.J. Walker, *One World, Many Worlds: Struggles for a Just World Peace* (Boulder, CO: Lynne Rienner, 1988), 145–6.

17 See Thomas Pogge, 'Rawls and Social Justice', *Canadian Journal of Philosophy*, 18 (1988): 227–56 and Janna Thompson, *Justice and World Order: A Philosophical Inquiry* (London: Routledge, 1992).

18 See Jürgen Habermas, *Knowledge and Human Interests*, trans., Jeremy J. Shapiro (London: Heinemann 1972) and Ernesto Laclau and Chantal Mouffe, *Hegemony and Socialist Strategy: Towards a Democratic Politics* (London: Verso, 1985).

19 See Ken Booth, 'Security and Emancipation', *Review of International Studies* 17 (1991): 313–26.

20 V. Spike Peterson, 'Transgressing Boundaries: Theories of Knowledge, Gender and International Relations', *Millennium* 21 (Summer 1992): 183–206 at pp. 203–4.

21 James N. Rosenau (ed.), *Global Voices: Dialogues in International Relations* (Boulder, CO: Westview Press, 1993).

22 Karl Marx, 'On the Jewish Question', in *Collected Works* (London: Lawrence and Wishart, 1975), III, p. 168.

23 Ibid., p. 68.

24 Karl Marx, 'The Critique of Hegel's Philosophy of Right', in *Early Writings*, ed. T.B. Bottomore (London: McGraw Hill 1963), 52. Marx goes on to say on the same page that 'criticism of the speculative philosophy of right does not remain within its own sphere, but leads on to *tasks* which can only be solved by *means of practical activity*'. Emphasis in text.

25 On this point, see Cohen, *Karl Marx's Theory of History*, p. 27.

26 Linklater, *Men and Citizens*, p. 166.

27 Ibid., p. 199.

28 Ibid., p. 140.

29 Ibid., p. 147.

30 Ibid.

31 Ibid.

32 Linklater, *Beyond Realism and Marxism*, pp. 16–17.

33 Linklater, *Men and Citizens*, p. 199.

34 Ibid., p. 198.

35 Ibid., p. 203.

36 To be sure, Linklater requires a Kantian formalism to extend moral and legal obligations to the entire globe, but he does not address the obvious problem that as one stretches legal and moral obligations – embodying 'thin' ethics in the best of circumstances – across many cultures and communities, their hold on people's consciousness will diminish. It is of some interest to note that even a strong materialist defender of Marx's conception of historical materialism such as G.A. Cohen now concedes that Marx should be criticised for not leaving any scope for 'human groupings whose lines of demarcation are not economic, such as religious communities, and nations. ... Such groups are as strong and durable as they evidently are partly because they offer satisfaction to the individual's need for self identification. In adhering to traditionally defined collectiv-

ities people retain a sense of who they are.' Cohen, *History, Labour and Freedom*, p. 138.

37 Linklater, *Beyond Marxism and Realism*,p. 8; emphasis added.
38 Linklater, *Men and Citizens*, p. 200.
39 On this point, see Iris Marion Young, *Justice and the Politics of Difference* (Princeton University Press, 1990), 15–38.
40 Linklater, *Men and Citizens*, p. 200.
41 N. Scott Arnold, *Marx's Radical Critique of Capitalist Society* (New York: Oxford University Press, 1990), 225.
42 Linklater, *Men and Citizens*, p. 160.
43 Robert W. Cox, *Production, Power, and World Order* (New York: Columbia University Press, 1987), ix.
44 Ibid., p. ix.
45 On this point, see Nicholas Rescher, *The Philosophy of Leibniz* (Englewood Cliffs, NJ: Prentice-Hall, 1967), 59–60.
46 Cox, *Production*, p. 393.
47 Ibid., p. 394.
48 Ibid.
49 Ibid., p. 396.
50 Ibid., p. 403.
51 Remember Oscar Wilde's witticism: 'How many free nights does one have to give up to be a good socialist?' To show that this claim does not only arise from outside the Marxian legacy, see G.A. Cohen, *History, Labour, and Freedom*, ch. 8 and Jon Elster, *Making Sense of Marx* (Cambridge University Press, 1985), ch. 9.
52 Cox, *Production*, p. 403.
53 Ibid.
54 On this point, see Perry Anderson, *In the Tracks of Historical Materialism* (London: Verso, 1983), 9–14.
55 Cox, *Production*, p. 403.
56 Jean-François Lyotard, *The Postmodern Condition – A Report on Knowledge* (Manchester University Press, 1986), 60.
57 Jean-François Lyotard, *The Postmodern Explained to Children: Correspondence 1982–1985* (Sydney: Power, 1992), 110–11.
58 Ibid., p. 45.
59 Ibid., p. 46.
60 Jean-François Lyotard and Jean-Loup Thébaud, *Just Gaming*, trans., Wlad Godzich (Minneapolis: University of Minnesota Press, 1985), 23.
61 Ibid., pp. 71–2.
62 For an excellent discussion of the sources of pluralism, see Isaiah Berlin, 'The Originality of Machiavelli', in *Against the Current* (Oxford University Press, 1981), 25–79.
63 For a powerful argument which shows that pluralism, at least in certain cases, need not collapse into relativism, see Susan Wolf, 'Two Levels of Pluralism', *Ethics* 102 (1992): 785–98.

64 Jean-François Lyotard, *The Differend* (Manchester University Press, 1988), 14.
65 Lyotard, *The Postmodern Explained to Children*, p. 54.
66 Lyotard, *The Differend*, p. 129.
67 Ibid., p. 130.
68 Ibid., p. 135.
69 Lyotard, *The Postmodern Condition*, p. 60.
70 Lyotard and Thébaud, *Just Gaming*, p. 25.
71 Ibid.
72 Ibid., p. 26.
73 Ibid.
74 On this point, see Elster, *Making Sense of Marx*, p. 515.
75 Lyotard, *The Postmodern Explained to Children*, p. 61.
76 Ibid.
77 Ibid.
78 These are, I take it, the projects of Linklater and Robert W. Cox respectively. For the former, see *Men and Citizens*, and, somewhat differently, *Beyond Realism and Marxism*. For the latter, see *Production, Power and World Order*.
79 Lyotard, *The Postmodern Explained to Children*, p. 65.
80 Lyotard, *The Differend*, p. 157.
81 Lyotard, *The Postmodern Explained to Children*, p. 44.

4 Evaluative political realism: a beginning

1 Justin Rosenberg, 'What's the Matter with Realism?', *Review of International Studies* 16 (1990): 285–303 at p. 285.
2 Richard Ashley, 'The Geopolitics of Geopolitical Space: Toward a Critical Social Theory of International Politics', *Alternatives* 12, 4 (1987): 403–34 at p. 422.
3 Ludwig Wittgenstein, *On Certainty* (Oxford: Basil Blackwell, 1971), no. 139.
4 Martin Wight, *Power Politics* (Harmondsworth: Penguin, 1979), 132.
5 Hans J. Morgenthau, *Politics Among Nations*, 5th edn (New York: Knopf, 1973), ch. 1.
6 See Brian Porter, 'Patterns of Thought and Practice: Martin Wight's International Theory', in M. Donelan, ed., *The Reason of States* (London, George Allen & Unwin, 1978), 64–74.
7 See Kenneth N. Waltz, *Theory of International Politics* (Reading MA: Addison-Wesley, 1979), especially at p. 91; Robert Gilpin, *War and Change in World Politics* (New York: Cambridge University Press, 1981), especially at p. xiii; Joseph Grieco, *Cooperation Among Nations: Europe, America and Non-Tariff Barriers to Trade* (Ithaca: Cornell University Press, 1990), especially ch. 2. For a criticism of the deeper assumptions deployed by Waltz, Gilpin, Grieco and others who effectively locate their thought in the

framework of nineteenth-century physical mechanics, see Phillip Mir-owski, *More Heat Than Light* (Cambridge University Press, 1989), especially chs. 5 and 6.

8   Imre Lakatos, 'Falsification and the Methodology of Scientific Research Programmes', in I. Lakatos and Alan E. Musgrave, eds., *Criticism and the Growth of Scientific Knowledge* (Cambridge University Press, 1970), 171.

9   Arthur Fine, 'Unnatural Attitudes: Realist and Instrumentalist Attachments to Science', *Mind* 95 (1986): 149–79 at p. 174.

10 Arthur Fine, 'The Natural Ontological Attitude', in *Scientific Realism*, ed. Jarrett Leplin (Berkeley: University of California Press, 1984), 83–107.

11 Ibid., p. 98.

12 Arthur Fine, *The Shaky Game: Einstein, Realism and Quantum Theory* (University of Chicago Press, 1986), 147–48.

13 Fine, 'The Natural Ontological Attitude', p. 101.

14 Morgenthau, *Politics Among Nations*, pp. ix–x.

15 William James, *Pragmatism and The Meaning of Truth* (Cambridge, MA: Harvard University Press, 1978), 32.

16 John Dewey, *Later Works, 1925–1953*, 17 vols. (Carbondale, IL: Southern Illinois University Press, 1990), VI, p. 5.

17 Hans J. Morgenthau, *The Decline of Democratic Politics, Politics in the Twentieth Century*, 3 vols. (University of Chicago Press, 1962), I, 72.

18 Morgenthau, *Decline*, p. 73.

19 Hans J. Morgenthau, *Scientific Man vs. Power Politics* (University of Chicago Press, 1962), 145.

20 Ibid.

21 Martin Heidegger, *Being and Time*, tr. John Macquarrie and Edward Robinson (New York: Harper & Row, 1962), section 1.

22 This beautifully evocative metaphor is due to Thomas Nagel, *The View From Nowhere* (Oxford University Press, 1986), 15.

23 Aristotle, *Nicomachean Ethics*, trans. David Ross (Oxford University Press), 1144b, 30–33.

24 Hans-Georg Gadamer, 'Hermeneutics and Social Science', *Cultural Hermeneutics* 2 (1975): 312.

25 Hans-Georg Gadamer, *Kleine Schriften*, 3 vols. (Tubingen: J. C. B. Mohr, 1967–72), I, p. 58.

5 State and state-systems in evaluative political realism

1   Kenneth N. Waltz, *Man the State and War* (New York: Columbia University Press, 1959), 160.

2   R.J. Barry Jones, 'Concepts and Models of Change in International Relations' in Barry Buzan and R.J. Barry, eds., *Change and the Study of International Relations*, (London: Frances Pinter, 1981), p.13.

3   Dina A. Zinnes, 'Prerequisites in the Study of System Transformation', in

Ole R. Holsti, Randolph M. Siverson and Alexander L. George, eds., *Change in the International System* (Boulder, CO: Westview Press, 1980), 7.
4   Ibid., p. 4.
5   Alfred North Whitehead, *Adventures of Ideas* (New York: Macmillan, 1954), 262.
6   Ibid., p. 271.
7   Martin Wight, *Systems of States*, ed., Hedley Bull (Leicester University Press, 1977); R.S. Northedge, *International Political System* (London: Faber and Faber, 1976); Hedley Bull, *The Anarchical Society: A Study of Order in World Politics* (London: Macmillan, 1977); Adam Watson, 'Systems of States', *Review of International Studies* 16 (1990): 99–109; Robert G. Wesson, *State Systems, International Pluralism, Politics and Culture* (New York: Free Press, 1978).
8   David Wiggins, *Sameness and Substance* (Oxford: Basil Blackwell, 1980), ch. 1.
9   I am using the expression 'new realist theory of reference' as equivalent to 'new theorist of reference' as used by Howard Wettstein, 'Has Semantics Rested on a Mistake?' *Journal of Philosophy* 83 (April 1986): 185–209.
10 Kenneth N. Waltz, *Theory of International Politics* (Reading, MA.: Addison-Wesley, 1979), 93.
11 Ibid., p. 96.
12 See Wiggins, *Sameness and Substance*, ch. 1.
13 John A. Vasquez, *The Power of Power Politics: A Critique* (London: Frances Pinter, 1983), 119. I am not suggesting that Vasquez endorses this view.
14 Richard K. Ashley, 'Untying the Sovereign State. A Double Reading of the Anarchy Problematique', *Millennium* 17, 2 (1988): 230.
15 R.B.J. Walker, 'The Territorial State and the "Theme of Gulliver"', *International Journal* 39 (Summer 1984): 529–52.
16 For an expression of this attitude, see H.V. Hodson, 'Sovereignty Demoted', *The Round Table* 290 (1984): 130–8.
17 Ken Booth, 'Security in Anarchy: Utopian Realism in Theory and Practice', *International Affairs* 67 (1991): 527–45 at pp. 541 and 542. The term 'utopian realism' has also been used by Anthony Giddens, 'Modernity and Utopia', *New Statesman and Society*, 2 November 1990. Although it is too facile to claim that this term is a *contradiction ad adjecto*, given the long-term association of realism with anti-utopian projects, its deployers certainly owe us an *extended* explanation.
18 Bull, *The Anarchical Society*, p. 8.
19 J.D.B. Miller, 'Sovereignty as a Source of Vitality for the State', *Review of International Studies* 12 (1986): 79–89.
20 Bull, *The Anarchical Society*, p. 8.
21 Hilary Putnam, 'The Meaning of Meaning', in *Mind, Language and Reality* (Cambridge University Press, 1975), 215–71 at p. 223.
22 Saul Kripke, *Naming and Necessity* (Oxford University Press, 1980), 135.
23 Northedge, *The International Political System*, 64.

24 Saul Kripke, 'Identity and Necessity', in *Naming, Necessity and Natural Kinds*, ed., Stephen P. Schwartz (Ithaca: Cornell University Press, 1977), 66–101.

25 Alan James, *Sovereign Statehood: The Basis of International Society* (London: Allen & Unwin, 1986), 54.

26 Michael Oakeshott, *On Human Conduct* (Oxford: Clarendon, 1975), 243 ff.

27 Robert Nozick, *Anarchy, State and Utopia* (Oxford: Basil Blackwell, 1974), 310–11.

28 Waltz, *Theory*, ch. 2.

29 Sir Herbert Butterfield, *International Conflict in the Twentieth Century* (London: Routledge, 1960), 15.

30 Graham Macdonald and Philip Pettit, *Semantics and Social Sciences* (London: Routledge and Kegan Paul, 1981).

31 Ibid., p. 117.

32 Ibid., p. 115.

33 Ibid., p. 123.

34 Ibid., p. 131.

35 Sir Herbert Butterfield, *The Whig Interpretation of History* (London: Bell, 1931), 72.

36 Michael Oakeshott, *Experience and Its Modes* (Cambridge University Press, 1933), 143.

37 G.R. Elton, *The Practice of History* (London: Routledge, 1967), 11.

38 Morton Kaplan, *On Historical and Political Knowing* (University of Chicago Press, 1971), ch. 1.

6 Evaluative political realism and human nature

1 Henry Fielding, *The History of Tom Jones*, ed. Fredson Bowers (Oxford: Clarendon Press, 1974), I, 126.

2 Kenneth W. Thompson, 'Idealism and Realism: Beyond the Great Debate', *British Journal of International Studies* 3 (1977): 199–209.

3 Hans J. Morgenthau, *Politics Among Nations*, 5th edn (New York: Alfred Knopf, 1973), 4.

4 Reinhold Niebuhr, *Moral Man and Immoral Society* (New York: Charles Scribner's, 1932), 231.

5 Isaiah Berlin, *Against The Current*, ed. Henry Hardy (Oxford University Press, 1981), 48.

6 Charles Taylor, *Human Agency and Language, Philosophical Papers* vol. 1, especially chs. 1 and 4.

7 Taylor, 'The Concept of a Person', in *Human Agency and Language*, p. 97.

8 Roger D. Masters, *The Nature of Politics* (New Haven: Yale University Press, 1989), 21.

9 John M. Cooper, 'Political Animals and Civic Friendship', in Neeras Kapur Badhwar, ed., *Friendship: A Philosophical Reader* (Ithaca: Cornell University Press, 1993): 303–26, especially pp. 304–11.

10 Masters, *The Nature of Politics*, p. 150.

Richard Rorty, *Consequences of Pragmatism* (Minneapolis: University of Minnesota Press, 1982), xiii.

11 On these issues, see Bernard Yack, *The Problems of a Political Animal: Community, Justice and Conflict in Aristotelian Political Thought* (Berkeley: University of California Press, 1993), *passim*.

12 Masters, *The Nature of Politics*, pp. 16, 19.

13 Niebuhr, *Moral Man and Immoral Society*, p. 2.

14 Howard Williams, *International Relations in Political Theory* (Milton Keynes: Open University Press, 1992) provides an excellent account of international relations as a theme of political theory much of which involves description and analysis of the views of realists. However, since his anti-realism is rather evident, these views should be treated with some circumspection.

15 Tang Tsou, ' "Scientific Man vs. Power Politics" Revisited', in *A Tribute to Hans Morgenthau*, ed. Kenneth Thompson and Robert J. Myers (Washington, DC: The New Republic, 1977), 44.

16 John Burton, *World Society* (Cambridge University Press, 1972), 56.

17 Ibid., p. 55.

18 See Carl N. Degler, *In Search of Human Nature* (New York: Oxford University Press, 1991), especially ch. 11.

19 This is the opinion too of a distinguished biologist. See John A Moore, 'Science As a Way of Life', *American Zoology* 24 (1984): 478.

20 Richard D. Alexander, *Darwinism and Human Affairs* (London: Pitmann, 1980), 16.

21 Mary Midgley, *Beast and Man: The Roots of Human Nature* (London: Metheun, 1980), 132.

22 Donald L. McEachron and Darius Baer, 'A Review of Selected Socio-biological Principles: Application to Hominid Evolution', *Journal of Social and Biological Structures* 5 (1982): 125.

23 Ibid.

24 H. Kruuk, *The Spotted Hyena* (University of Chicago Press, 1972).

25 R. Fiennes, *The Order of Wolves* (New York: Bobbs-Merrill, 1976).

26 McEachron and Baer, 'A Review', p. 125.

27 Alexander, *Darwinism and Human Affairs*, p. 221.

28 Ibid., p. 222.

29 Martin Wight, *Power Politics* (Harmondsworth: Penguin, 1979), 132.

30 William H. Durham, 'Resource Competition and Human Aggression, Part I: A Review of Primitive War', *Quarterly Review of Biology* 51 (September 1976): 401.

31 Ibid., p. 411.

32 Napoleon Chagnon, 'Mate Competition, Favoring Close Kin and Village Fissioning Among the Yanomamo Indians', in *Evolutionary Biology and Human Behaviour*, ed. Chagnon and William Irons (North Scituate, MA: Duxbury Press, 1979), 89. See also Laura L. Betzig, *Despotism and Differential Reproduction* (New York: Aldine, 1986), *passim*.

33 Chagnon, 'Mate Competition', p. 92.
34 Ibid., p. 93.
35 Alexander Rosenberg, *Sociobiology and the Preemption of Social Science* (Oxford: Basil Blackwell, 1980), chs. 1–3.
36 Morgenthau held this view, I believe.
37 Quincy Wright, *The Study of International Relations* (New York: Appleton-Century-Crofts, 1955), 399.
38 Edward O. Wilson, *Sociobiology*, abridged edn (Cambridge, MA: The Belknap Press, 1980), 3. See also Wilson, *On Human Nature* (Cambridge, MA: Harvard University Press, 1978), ch. 7. Wilson has been criticised for this claim, somewhat unfairly, by Rosenberg, *Sociobiology and the Preemption of the Social Sciences*, 185ff.
39 Burton, *World Society*, p. 114.
40 Charles R. Beitz, *Political Theory and International Relations* (Princeton University Press, 1979), *passim*.
41 Ashley, 'Living on Border Lines: Man, Post-Structuralism, and War', *passim* and the other articles in James Der Derian and Michael J. Shapiro, *International/Intertextual Relations* (Lexington, MA: Lexington Books, 1989).
42 Richard D. Alexander 'Biology and Moral Paradox', *Journal of Social Biology Struct.* 5 (1982): 392.
43 Marshall Cohen, 'Moral Skepticism and International Relations', *Philosophy and Public Affairs* 13 (Fall 1984): 229–346.
44 Susan Wolf, 'Moral Saints', *Journal of Philosophy* 79 (August 1982): 421.
45 See, e.g., Steven Rose, Leon J. Kamin and R.C. Lewontin, *Not in our Genes* (Harmondsworth: Penguin, 1984) and Jay Gould, 'Sociobiology and the Theory of Natural Selection', in G. Barlow and J. Silverberg, eds., *Sociobiology: Beyond Nature/Nuture* (Boulder, CO: Westview, 1980), 257–69.
46 For the charge, see Gould, 'Sociobiology and the Theory of Natural Selection', *passim*.
47 Michael Carrithers, *Why Humans Have Cultures: Explaining Anthropology and Social Diversity* (Oxford University Press, 1992) admits that ethnography cannot meet the standards of naturalistic science at pp. 150–5 and argues, quite correctly, that it need not do so.
48 See, for example, John A. Vasquez, *The Power of Power Politics: A Critique* (London: Frances Pinter, 1983), especially ch. l.
49 One should perhaps say 'the early Wilson'. The 'later' Wilson is far more sophisticated and evidently less reductionist. See, for example, Edward O. Wilson and Charles Lumsden, *Genes, Mind and Culture* (Cambridge, MA: Harvard University Press, 1981).
50 Rosenberg, *Sociobiology and The Preemption of Social Science, passim*.
51 Glendon Schubert, 'Politics as a Life Science', in A. Somit, ed., *Biology and Politics: Recent Explorations* (The Hague: Moutan, 1976), 155–95.
52 Masters, *The Nature of Politics, passim*.
53 Roger D. Masters, 'Is Sociobiology Reactionary? The Political Implications

of Inclusive-Fitness Theory', *The Quarterly Review of Biology* 57 (September 1982): 275–92 and Masters, *The Nature of Politics*, pp. 160–86.

54   Roger D. Masters, 'Evolutionary Biology and Naturalism', *Interpretation* 17 (Fall 1989): 113.
55   Ibid., pp. 113–14.
56   Morgenthau, *Politics Among Nations*, p. 259.
57   Ibid.
58   Charles Taylor, 'The Concept of a Person', in *Human Agency and Language*, 2 vols., *Philosophical Papers* (Cambridge University Press, 1985), I, 97–114.
59   Ibid., p. 104.
60   On contextual *a priori* truths, see Hilary Putnam, *Meaning and the Moral Sciences* (London: Routledge & Kegan Paul, 1978), 137–8.
61   Charles Taylor, *Human Agency and Language*, *Philosophical Papers* (Cambridge University Press, 1985), I, ch. 4.
62   Roger Trigg, 'The Sociobiological View of Man', in S. C. Brown, ed., *Objectivity and Cultural Divergence*, Royal Institute of Philosophy Lecture Series 17 (Cambridge University Press, 1984): 93–110 at p. 106.
63   Masters, *The Nature of Politics*, p. 245.
64   See Leonard Krieger, *Ranke: The Meaning of History* (University of Chicago Press, 1977). See also Gunter A. Berg, *Leopold von Ranke als Akademischer Lehrer* (Gottingen: Vandenhoeck and Ruprecht, 1968), 180–218.
65   Richard Rorty, *Consequences of Pragmatism* (Minneapolis: University of Minnesota Press, 1982), xiii.

7 Evaluative political realism and historical realism

1   George Liska, 'The Vital Triad: International Relations Theory, History and Social Philosophy', *Social Research* 48 (1981): 700.
2   The trepidation has to do with the unusually large disagreement surrounding the term 'historical realism'. For example, Adrian Kuzminski claims, contrary to the view defended here, that historical realism is unreflective and 'anti-interpretive'. See his 'Defending Historical Realism', *History and Theory* 18 (1979): 316–49.
3   Kuzminski, 'Defending Historical Realism', p. 329.
4   Hubert Dreyfus, *Being-in-the-World: A Commentary on Heidegger's Being and Time, Division I* (Cambridge, MA: MIT Press, 1991), especially pp. 251–7.
5   Ibid., pp. 254–5.
6   Hans J. Morgenthau, 'Common Sense and Theories of International Relations', in John C. Farrell and Asa P. Smith, ed., *Theory and Reality in International Relations* (New York: Colombia University Press, 1967), 27.
7   Isaiah Berlin, *Vico and Herder: Two Studies In the History of Ideas* (London: Chatto and Windus, 1976), 107–8.
8   Ibid., pp. 22–3.
9   Sir Isaiah Berlin, *Concepts and Categories* (Oxford University Press, 1980), 137.
10   Ibid., p. 138.

11   Ibid., p. 139.
12   Thomas Nagel, *Mortal Questions* (Cambridge University Press, 1979), 165–80.
13   Ibid., p. 166.
14   Ibid., p. 174.
15   R.G. Collingwood, *The Idea of History* (Oxford: Clarendon Press, 1946), 213.
16   On this point, see Andrew P. Norman, 'Telling Like It Was: Historical Narratives on their own Terms', *History and Theory* 30 (1991): 119–35 at p. 120.
17   See William Dray, *On History and Philosophers of History* (Leiden: E. J. Brill, 1989), 92–110 at p. 102. The article which Dray analyses is Norman A. Graebner, 'The Mexican War: A Study in Causation', *Pacific Historical Review* 49 (1980): 405–26.
18   Dray, *On History and Philosophers of History*, p. 102.
19   Hans J. Morgenthau, *Politics Among Nations*, 5th edn (New York: Knopf, 1973); 5.
20   Karl W. Deutsch, *The Nerves of Government* (New York: The Free Press, 1966), 82–6.
21   William Dray, *Law and Explanation in History* (Oxford University Press, 1957), 122.
22   G.H. von Wright, *Explanation and Understanding* (Ithaca New York: Cornell University Press, 1971), 105. Von Wright's practical inference schema has been slightly reformulated.
23   Ibid., p. 27.
24   Ibid., p. 143.
25   Charles Taylor, *Sources of the Self* (Cambridge University Press, 1989), 72.
26   For Foucault's claim concerning the possibility of eliminating intentions, see 'Qu'est-ce qu'un auteur', *Bulletin de la societé française de la philosophie* 63 (1969). For Derrida's view, see 'Signature Event Context', in *Limited Inc* (Evanston, IL: Northwestern University Press, 1988). For the consequences of this for our understanding of texts, see Robert Scholes, *Protocols of Reading* (New Haven: Yale University Press, 1989), ch. 2.
27   Thomas Nagel, *The Limits of Objectivity*, The Tanner Lecture on Human Values. (Brasenose College, Oxford: Oxford University, 1979): 77–141.
28   See also Thomas Nagel, *The View From Nowhere* (New York: Oxford University Press, 1986) and *Equality and Partiality* (New York: Oxford University Press, 1991), especially ch. 2.
29   Nagel, *The Limits of Objectivity*, p. 83.
30   On this theme, see Nagel, *The View From Nowhere*, pp. 3–5.
31   Nagel, *The Limits of Objectivity*, p. 86.
32   Ibid.
33   Ibid., p. 88.
34   Ibid., p. 89.
35   Ibid., p. 90.
36   Ibid.

37 Ibid.
38 Ibid.
39 Ibid.
40 Colin McGinn, *The Subjective View* (Oxford: Clarendon Press, 1983), especially ch. 6.
41 Nagel, *Equality and Partiality*, p. 10.
42 See, for example, Bruce Baugh, 'Sartre, Aron et le relativisme historique', *Dialogue* 29 (1990): 557–73. See also H. Aram Veeser (ed.), *The New Historicism* (New York: Routledge, 1989).
43 Michael Foucault, *Power/Knowledge* (New York: Pantheon, 1980), 69.
44 Louis Mink, 'Narrative Form as a Cognitive Instrument', in Robert H. Canary and Henry Kozicki, eds., *The Writing of History* (Madison, WI: University of Wisconsin Press, 1978).
45 For the difficulties of doing this, see Donald Davidson, 'On the Very Idea of a Conceptual Scheme', in John Rajchman and Cornell West, eds., *Post-Analytic Philosophy* (New York: Columbia University Press, 1985): 129–43. The issue of conceptual relativism is discussed more fully in ch. 8 below.
46 Peter Winch, *The Idea of a Social Science* (London: Routledge & Kegan Paul, 1958).
47 W.B. Gallie, *Philosophy and Historical Understanding* (London: Chatto & Windus, 1964).
48 Michael Oakeshott, *On Human Conduct* (Oxford: Clarendon Press, 1975), 199.
49 Gallie, *Philosophical and Historical Understanding*, p. 38.
50 Henry Kissinger, *The White House Years* (London: Weidenfeld and Nicolson, 1979) and *Diplomacy* (New York: Touchstone Books, 1995).
51 Morton A. Kaplan, *System and Process in International Politics* (New York: Wiley, 1957), 44.
52 Ludwig Wittgenstein, *Philosophical Investigations*, G.E.M. Anscombe, trans., 3rd edn (Oxford, Blackwell, 1968), no. 201.
53 *Wittgenstein's Letters on the Foundations of Mathematics*, ed. Cora Diamond (Ithaca, New York: Cornell University Press, 1976), 202–4.

8 Evaluative political realism as moral realism

1 Vernon Van Dyke, *Political Science: A Philosophical Analysis* (Stanford: Stanford University Press, 1960), 192.
2 Sabina Lovibond, *Realism and Imagination in Ethics* (Minneapolis: University of Minnesota Press, 1983), 1.
3 Mark Timmons, 'Putnam's Moral Objectivism', *Erkenntnis* 34 (1991): 371–99.
4 David Hume, *A Treatise of Human Nature*, ed. L.A. Selby-Bigge (Oxford: Clarendon Press, 1946), bk. III, sect. I, Pt. 1. Hume's spelling has been modernised.
5 Max Weber, *The Methodology of the Social Sciences*, trans. and ed. Edward A. Shils and Henry A. Finch (Glencoe, IL: The Free Press, 1949), 11–12.

6 See D.C. Yalden-Thomson, 'Hume's View of "Is-Ought"', *Philosophy* 53 (1978): 89–93.
7 As recommended by Alasdair McIntyre, 'Hume on "Is" and "Ought"', in W.D. Hudson, ed., *The Is-Ought Question*, (New York: St Martin's Press, 1969), 36–50.
8 Quincy Wright, *The Study of International Relations* (New York: Appleton-Century-Crofts, 1955), 441.
9 Phillipa Foot, 'Moral Arguments', in *Virtues and Vices* (Oxford University Press, 1978), 102.
10 Bernard Williams, *Ethics and the Limits of Philosophy* (London: Fontana, 1985), 129.
11 Judith Jarvis Thomson, *The Realm of Rights* (Cambridge, MA: Harvard University Press, 1990), 16.
12 David Wiggins, *Truth, Invention and the Meaning of Life*, The Proceedings of the British Academy, vol. 62 (London, 1976): 331–78.
13 Ibid., p. 338.
14 Ibid., p. 357.
15 Hans P. Morgenthau, *Politics Among Nations*, 5th edn (New York: Knopf, 1973), 11.
16 Hans Morgenthau 'The Moral Dilemma of Political Action', in *Dilemmas of Politics* (University of Chicago Press, 1950), 246–7.
17 See, in particular, Albert Wohlstetter, 'The Delicate Balance of Terror', *Foreign Affairs* 37 (January 1959), 211–34.
18 Aristotle, *Nichomachean Ethics*, David Ross, trans. (New York: Oxford University Press, 1980), 1137 b 17.
19 Bernard Williams, *Moral Luck: Philosophical Papers, 1973–1980* (New York: Cambridge University Press, 1981), 72.
20 Isaiah Berlin, *Four Essays on Liberty* (Oxford University Press, 1969), li. From a different perspective, Bonnie Honig makes frequent theoretical use of the notion of remainder in her lucid and penetrating book *Political Theory and the Displacement of Politics* (Ithaca: Cornell University Press, 1993), *passim*.
21 Williams, *Moral Luck*, p. 72.
22 Adrienne Koch and William Peden (eds.), *The Life and Selected Writings of Thomas Jefferson* (New York: Modern Library, 1944), XXXVI; cf. 334–8 and 571–72.
23 Williams, *Moral Luck*, p. 75.
24 Winston S. Churchill, *The Second World War* 6 vols. *The Hinge of Fate*, IV (London: Cassell, 1950).
25 Churchill, *The Hinge of Fate*, p. 448.
26 Bernard Williams makes this point in 'Ethical Consistency', in *Problems of the Self* (Cambridge University Press, 1973), 166–86.
27 Phillipa Foot 'Moral Realism and Moral Dilemmas' *Journal of Philosophy* 80 (July 1983), 395–6.
28 Susan Wolf, 'Two Levels of Pluralism', *Ethics* 102 (1992): 785–98 at p. 788.

29   Ibid., p. 787.
30   Ibid., p. 788.
31   Ibid., p. 789.
32   Terry Nardin, 'The Problem of Relativism in International Ethics', *Millennium* 18 (1989), 150–1.
33   Wolf, 'Two Levels of Pluralism', p. 789.
34   Stuart Hampshire, *Morality and Conflict* (Oxford: Basil Blackwell, 1983) and Thomas Nagel, 'The Fragmentation of Value', in *Mortal Questions* (Cambridge University Press, 1989).
35   Wolf, 'Two Levels of Pluralism', p. 791.
36   Ibid., p. 792.
37   Ibid., p. 792.
38   Ibid., p. 793.
39   Ibid., p. 794.
40   Ibid., p. 795.
41   Ibid., p. 796.
42   Ibid.
43   James Wallace, *Moral Relevance and Moral Conflict* (Ithaca: Cornell University Press, 1986), 128–32.
44   William McNeill, *The Rise of the West* (The University of Chicago Press, 1963), 717n. Cited in Wallace, *Moral Relevance and Moral Conflict*, p. 128.
45   Wallace, *Moral Relevance and Moral Conflict*, p. 129.
46   Ibid.
47   Ibid.
48   Ibid., pp. 129–30.
49   Immanuel C. Y. Hsu, *The Rise of Modern China* (New York, Oxford University Press, 1970), 230.
50   Quincy Wright wrote many years ago that 'a profound sense of the relativity of all philosophies is necessary for peace. The world is composed of many states, many religions, many legal systems, many languages, many cultures. The claim of one to be absolute has been a major cause of wars and disorders. Most wars are fundamentally ideological wars, wars to make *my* vision of the perfect world prevail. There are many visions of the perfect world and they cannot all prevail in one world.' *The Study of International Relations* (New York: Appleton-Century-Crofts, 1955), 108.
51   Wolf, 'Two Levels of Pluralism', p. 796.
52   Ibid.
53   Williams, *Ethics and the Limits of Philosophy*, p. 158.
54   Martha C. Nussbaum and Amartya Sen, 'Internal Criticism and Indian Rationalist Tradition', in Michael Krausz, ed., *Relativism* (University of Notre Dame Press 1989), 299–325.
55   John McDowell, 'Virtue and Reason', in Stanley Clarke and Evan Simpson, eds., *Anti-Theory in Ethics and Moral Conservatism* (Albany: State University of New York Press, 1989), 88.

56 Wolf even goes so far as to say that her position 'acknowledges that culture may contribute to the determination of a person's moral requirements and prohibitions in a much more thoroughgoing way than absolutism appears to allow'. 'Two Levels of Pluralism', p. 796.

57 Raymond Aron, *Le développement de la société et la stratification sociale* (Paris: Plon, 1956), 10.

58 Morgenthau, *Politics among Nations*, p. 5.

59 Herbert Butterfield, writing in *The New York Times* of 3 January 1973 remarked that the US and the USSR 'may overlook the fact that it can make its own security complete only by destroying the security of the other altogether'.

60 Thomas Hobbes, *Leviathan*, ed. C.B. MacPherson (Harmondsworth: Penguin, 1968), 152.

61 *New York Review of Books*, 17 March 1988: 11–18 at p. 13.

62 Ludwig Wittgenstein, *Philosophical Investigations*, p. 185.

63 Ibid., p. 217.

64 *Nichomachean Ethics*, 1139b 11–13.

9 Conclusion

1 Sir Isaiah Berlin, *Concepts and Categories* (Oxford University Press, 1980), 110.

2 For one example of what amounts to an absolute demand, see Terry Nardin, 'The Problem of Relativism in International Ethics', *Millennium* 18 (1989): 149–61. For another, see Thomas L. Prangle, *The Ennobling of Democracy* (Baltimore: The Johns Hopkins University Press, 1992), 58.

3 Vaclav Havel, 'The End of the Modern Era', *New York Times*, 1 March 1992.

4 Ludwig Wittgenstein, *Philosophical Investigations*, para 352.

5 Ibid., para 393.

Select Bibliography

Alexander, Richard D. *Darwinism and Human Affairs*. London: Pitmann, 1980.

Alker, Hayward R. and Biersteker, Thomas J. 'The Dialectics of World Order: Notes for a Future Archaeologist of International *Savoir Faire*', *International Studies Quarterly* 28 (1984): 121–142.

Anderson, Perry. *In the Tracks of Historical Materialism*. London: Verso, 1983.

Aristotle. *Nicomachean Ethics*, David Ross (trans.). New York: Oxford University Press, 1980.

Arnold, N. Scott. *Marx's Radical Critique of Capitalist Society*. New York: Oxford University Press, 1990.

Aron, Raymond. *Le dévelopement de la societé et la stratification sociale*. Paris: Plon, 1956.

International Relations: Peace or War? New York: McGraw Hill, 1973.

Ashley, Richard K. 'Living on Border Lines: Man, Post-Structuralism, and War', in James Der Derian and Michael J. Shapiro eds., *International/Intertextual Relations*. Lexington, MA: Lexington Books, 1989.

'The Geopolitics of Geopolitical Space: Toward a Critical Social Theory of International Politics', *Alternatives*, 12 (1987): 403–34.

Banks, Michael. 'The Inter-Paradigm Debate', in Margot Light and A. J. R. Groom, eds., *International Relations: A Handbook of Current Theory*. Boulder, CO: Lynne Rienner, 1985.

'Where We Are Now', *Review of International Studies*, 11 (1985): 215–33.

Baugh, Bruce. 'Sartre, Aron et le relativisme historique', *Dialogue* 29 (1990): 557–73.

Beitz, Charles R. *Political Theory and International Relations*. Princeton University Press, 1979.

Berg, Gunter A. *Leopold von Ranke als Akademischer Lehrer*. Gottingen: Vandenhoeck and Ruprecht, 1968.

Berlin, Isaiah. *Vico and Herder: Two Studies In the History of Ideas*. London: Chatto and Windus, 1976.

Four Essays on Liberty. Oxford: Oxford University Press, 1969.

Concepts and Categories. Oxford: Oxford University Press, 1980.

Against the Current, Henry Hardy, ed. Oxford: Oxford University Press, 1981.

Booth, Ken. 'Security and Emancipation', *Review of International Studies*, 17 (1991): 313–26.

'Security in Anarchy: Utopian Realism in Theory and Practice', *International Affairs*, 67 (1991): 527–45.

Bull, Hedley. *The Anarchical Society: A Study of Order in World Politics*. London: Macmillan, 1977.

Burton, John. *World Society*. Cambridge University Press, 1972.

Butterfield, Herbert. *The Whig Interpretation of History*. London: Bell, 1931.

International Conflict in the Twentieth Century. London: Routledge, 1960.

Carrithers, Michael. *Why Humans Have Cultures: Explaining Anthropology and Social Diversity*. Oxford: Oxford University Press, 1992.

Cashman, Greg. *What Causes War? An Introduction to Theories of International Conflict*. New York: Lexington, 1993.

Churchill, Winston S. *The Second World War*, 6 vols., IV, *The Hinge of Fate*. London: Cassell, 1950.

Cohen, G. A. *Karl Marx's Theory of History: A Defence*. Oxford: Clarendon Press, 1978.

History, Labour, and Freedom. Oxford: Clarendon Press, 1988.

Cohen, Marshall. 'Moral Skepticism and International Relations', *Philosophy and Public Affairs*, 13 (Fall 1984): 229–346.

Collingwood, R. G. *The Idea of History*. Oxford: Clarendon Press, 1946.

Cooper, John M. 'Political Animals and Civic Friendship', in Neera Kapur Badhwar, ed., *Friendship: A Philosophical Reader*. Ithaca: Cornell University Press, 1993.

Cox, Robert W. 'Social Forces, States and World Orders: Beyond International Relations Theory', *Millennium* 10 (1981): 126–54.

Production, Power and World Order. New York, Columbia University Press, 1987.

Davidson, Donald. 'On the Very Idea of a Conceptual Scheme', in John Rajchman and Cornell West, eds., *Post-Analytic Philosophy*. New York: Columbia University Press, 1985.

Der Derian, James and Shapiro, Michael J., eds. *International/Intertextual Relations*. Lexington, MA: Lexington Books, 1989.

Descartes, René. *The Philosophical Works of Descartes*, E. S. Haldane and G. R. T. Ross, trans. New York: Cambridge, 1968.

Deutsch, Karl. *The Nerves of Government*. New York: Free Press, 1966.

Donelan, Michael. *Elements of International Political Theory*. Oxford: Clarendon Press, 1990.

Dray, William. *Law and Explanation in History*. Oxford University Press, 1957.

On History and Philosophers of History. Leiden: E. J. Brill, 1989.

Dreyfus, Hubert. *Being-in-the-World: A Commentary on Heidegger's Being and Time, Division I*. Cambridge, MA: MIT Press, 1991.

Elster, Jon. *Making Sense of Marx*. Cambridge University Press, 1985.

Ferguson, Yale H. and Mansbach, Richard W. *The Elusive Quest*. Columbia, SC: University of South Carolina Press, 1988.

Fine, Arthur. 'The Natural Ontological Attitude', in Jarret Leplin, ed., *Scientific Realism*. Berkeley: University of California Press, 1984.

The Shaky Game: Einstein, Realism and Quantum Theory. University of Chicago Press, 1986.

'Unnatural Attitudes: Realist and Instrumentalist Attachments to Science', *Mind* 95 (1986): 149–79.

Foot, Phillipa. 'Moral Arguments', in *Virtues and Vices*. Oxford University Press, 1978.

Foucault, Michel. *Power/Knowledge*, Colin Gordon, trans. and ed. New York: Pantheon, 1980.

Gallie, W. B. *Philosophy and Historical Understanding*. London: Chatto & Windus, 1964.

Gill, Stephen. 'Historical Materialism, Gramsci, and International Political Economy', in Craig N. Murphy and Roger Tooze, eds., *The New International Political Economy*. Boulder: Lynne Rienner, 1991.

Gillepsie, John. 'Why Mathematical Models?', in Dina Zinnes and John Gillepsie, eds., *Mathematical Models in International Relations*. New York: Praeger, 1976.

Gilpin, Robert. *War and Change in World Politics*. New York: Cambridge University Press, 1981.

'The Richness of the Tradition of Political Realism', in Robert O. Keohane, ed., *Neorealism and its Critics*. New York: Columbia University Press, 1986.

Gould, Jay. 'Sociobiology and the Theory of Natural Selection', in G. Barlow and J. Silverberg, eds., *Sociobiology: Beyond Nature/Nuture*. Boulder, Colorado: Westview, 1980.

Gray, John. 'Mill's and Other Liberalisms', in Knud Haakonssen, ed., *Traditions of Liberalism*. No place: Centre For Independent Studies, 1988.

Grieco, Joseph. *Cooperation Among Nations: Europe, America and Non-Tariff Barriers to Trade*. Ithaca: Cornell University Press, 1990.

Habermas, Jürgen. *Knowledge and Human Interests*, Jeremy J. Shapiro, trans. London: Heinemann, 1972.

Hampshire, Stuart. *Morality and Conflict*. Oxford: Basil Blackwell, 1983.

Harding, Sandra. *The Science Question in Feminism*. Ithaca: Cornell University, 1986.

Hartsock, Nancy. 'The Feminist Standpoint: Developing the Ground for a Specifically Feminist Historical Materialism', in Sandra Harding and Merrill Hintikka, eds., *Discovering Reality*. London: D. Reidl, 1983.

Havel, Vaclav. 'The End of the Modern Era', *New York Times*, 1 March 1992.

Heidegger, Martin. *Being and Time*, John Macquarrie and Edward Robinson, trans. New York: Harper & Row, 1962.

The Question Concerning Technology and Other Essays, William Lovitt, trans. New York: Harper & Row, 1977.

Hobbes, Thomas. *Leviathan*, C. B. MacPherson, ed. Harmondsworth: Penguin, 1968.

Hollis, Martin. *Models of Man: Philosophical Thoughts on Social Action*. Cambridge University Press, 1977.

Holsti, K. J. *The Dividing Discipline*. Boston: Allen & Unwin, 1985.

Honig, Bonnie. *Political Theory and the Displacement of Politics*. Ithaca: Cornell University Press, 1993.

Hume, David. *A Treatise of Human Nature*, L. A. Selby-Bigge, ed. Oxford: Clarendon Press, 1946.

James, Alan. *Sovereign Statehood: The Basis of International Society*. London: Allen & Unwin, 1986.

Jones, R. J. Barry. 'Concepts and Models of Change in International Relations', in Barry Buzan and R. J. Barry Jones, eds. *Change and the Study of International Relations*. London: Frances Pinter, 1981.

Kaplan, Morton A. *System and Process in International Politics*. New York: Wiley, 1957.

Keohane, Robert O. 'Reciprocity in International Relations', *International Organisation* 40 (1986): 1–27.

'International Institutions: Two Approaches', in *International Institutions and State Power: Essays in International Relations Theory*. Boulder, CO: Westview Press, 1989.

'Theory of World Politics', in Robert O. Keohane, ed., *Neorealism and Its Critics*. New York: Columbia University Press, 1986.

'Neoliberal Institutionalism', in *International Institutions and State Power: Essays in International Relations Theory*. Boulder, CO: Westview Press, 1989.

'International Relations Theory: Contributions of a Feminist Standpoint', *Millennium* 18 (1989): 245–54.

Kissinger, Henry. *The White House Years*, London: Weidenfeld and Nicolson, 1979.

Diplomacy, New York: Touchstone Books, 1995.

Koch, Adrienne and Peden, William, eds. *The Life and Selected Writings of Thomas Jefferson*. New York: Modern Library, 1944.

Krasner, Stephen. *Structural Conflict: The Third World Against Global Liberalism*. Berkeley: University of California Press, 1985.

'Toward Understanding in International Relations', *International Studies Quarterly* 29 (1985).

Krieger, Leonard. *Ranke: The Meaning of History*. University of Chicago Press, 1977.

Kripke, Saul. 'Identity and Necessity', in Stephen P. Schwartz, ed., *Naming, Necessity and Natural Kinds*. Ithaca: Cornell University Press, 1977.

Naming and Necessity. Oxford University Press, 1980.

Kuhn, Thomas. *The Structure of Scientific Revolutions*, 2nd edn. University of Chicago Press, 1970.

Laclau, Ernesto and Mouffe, Chantel. *Hegemony and Socialist Strategy: Towards a Democratic Politics*. London: Verso, 1985.

Lakatos, Imre. *The Methodology of Scientific Research Programs, Philosophical Papers*, John Worrall and Gregory Currie, eds. Cambridge University Press, 1978.

'Falsification and the Methodology of Scientific Research Programmes', in Imre Lakatos and Alan E. Musgrave, eds., *Criticism and the Growth of Scientific Knowledge*. Cambridge University Press, 1970.

Lapid, Yosef. 'The Third Debate: On the Prospects of International Theory in a Post-Positivist Era', *International Studies Quarterly* 35 (1989): 235–54.

'*Quo Vadis* International Relations? Further Reflections on the "Next Stage" of International Theory', *Millennium* 18 (1989): 77–88.

Linklater, Andrew. *Men and Citizens in the Theory of International Relations*. London: Macmillan, 1982.

'Realism, Marxism and Critical International Theory', *Review of International Studies* 12 (1986): 301–12.

Beyond Realism and Marxism. New York: St Martin's Press, 1989.

'Dialogue, Dialectic and Emancipation in International Relations at the End of the Post-War Age', *Millennium* 23 (1994): 119–31.

Loeb, Louis E. 'The Priority of Reason in Descartes', *The Philosophical Review* 99 (1990): 3–43.

Lovibond, Sabina. *Realism and Imagination in Ethics*. Minneapolis: University of Minnesota Press, 1983.

Lyotard, Jean-François. *The Postmodern Condition – A Report on Knowledge*. Manchester University Press, 1986.

The Differend. Manchester University Press, 1988.

The Postmodern Explained to Children: Correspondence 1982–1985. Sydney: Power, 1992.

Lyotard, Jean-François and Thébaud, Jean-Loup. *Just Gaming*, Wlad Godzich, trans. Minneapolis: University of Minnesota Press, 1985.

Macdonald, Graham and Pettit, Phillip. *Semantics and Social Sciences*. London: Routledge and Kegan Paul, 1981.

Marx, Karl. 'On the Jewish Question', *Collected Works*, Richard Dixon, et al., trans., 47 vols. London: Lawrence and Wishart, 1975, vol. III.

Marx, Karl. 'The Critique of Hegel's Philosophy of Right', in T. B. Bottomore, ed. *Early Writings*. London: McGraw Hill, 1963.

Masters, Roger D. *The Nature of Politics*. New Haven: Yale University Press, 1989.

Masters, Roger, D. 'Is Sociobiology Reactionary? The Political Implications of Inclusive-Fitness Theory', *The Quarterly Review of Biology* 57 (September 1982): 275–92.

McClelland, Charles A. *Theory and the International System*. New York: Macmillan, 1966.

McDowell, John. 'Virtue and Reason', in Stanley Clarke and Evan Simpson, eds., *Anti-Theory in Ethics and Moral Conservatism*. Albany: State University of New York Press, 1989.

McGinn, Colin. *The Subjective View*. Oxford: Clarendon Press, 1983.

McIntyre, Alasdair. 'Hume on "Is" and "Ought"', in W. D. Hudson, ed., *The Is-Ought Question*. New York: St. Martin's Press, 1969.

Midgley, Mary. *Beast and Man: The Roots of Human Nature*. London: Metheun, 1980.

Miller, J. D. B. 'Sovereignty as a Source of Vitality for the State', *Review of International Studies* 12 (1986): 79–89.

Mink, Louis. 'Narrative Form as a Cognitive Instrument', in Robert H. Canary and Henry Kozicki, eds., *The Writing of History*. Madison, WI: University of Wisconsin Press, 1978.

Modelski, George. *Principles of World Politics*. New York: Free Press, 1972.

Morgenthau, Hans J. 'The Moral Dilemma of Political Action', in *Dilemmas of Politics*. University of Chicago Press, 1950.

The Decline of Democratic Politics, in vol 1 of 3 vols, *Politics in the Twentieth Century*. University of Chicago Press, 1962.

Scientific Man vs. Power Politics. University of Chicago Press, 1962.

'Common Sense and Theories of International Relations', in John C. Farrell and Asa P. Smith, eds., *Theory and Reality in International Relations*. New York: Colombia University Press, 1967.

Politics Among Nations, 5th edn. New York: Knopf, 1973.

Nagel, Thomas. *The Limits of Objectivity*, The Tanner Lecture on Human Values. Brasenose College, Oxford: Oxford University, 1979: 77–141.

Mortal Questions. Cambridge University Press, 1979.

The View From Nowhere. New York: Oxford University Press, 1986.

Equality and Partiality. New York: Oxford University Press, 1991.

Nardin, Terry. 'The Problem of Relativism in International Ethics', *Millennium* 18 (1989): 149–61.

Neufield, Mark. 'Reflexivity and International Relations Theory', *Millennium* 22 (1993): 53–76.

Niebuhr, Reinhold. *Moral Man and Immoral Society*. New York: Charles Scribner's, 1932.

Norman, Andrew P. 'Telling it Like it Was: Historical Narratives on their own Terms', *History and Theory* 30 (1991): 119–35.

Northedge, R. S. *International Political System*. London: Faber and Faber, 1976.

Nozick, Robert. *Anarchy, State and Utopia*. Oxford: Basil Blackwell, 1974.

Nussbaum, Martha C. and Sen, Amartya. 'Internal Criticism and Indian Rationalist Tradition', in Michael Krausz, ed., *Relativism*. Notre Dame: University of Notre Dame Press 1989.

Oakeshott, Michael. *On Human Conduct*. Oxford: Clarendon, 1975.

Experience and Its Modes. Cambridge University Press, 1933.

Peterson, V. Spike. 'Transgressing Boundaries: Theories of Knowledge, Gender and International Relations', *Millennium* 21 (Summer 1992): 183–206.

Peterson, V. Spike, ed. *Gendered States: Feminist (Re)Visions of International Relations Theory*. Boulder: Lynne Rienner, 1992.

Pogge, Thomas. 'Rawls and Social Justice', *Canadian Journal of Philosophy* 18 (1988): 227–56.

Porter, Brian. 'Patterns of thought and practice: Martin Wight's international theory', in M. Donelan, ed. *The Reason of States*. London, George Allen & Unwin, 1978.

Puchala, Donald J. 'Woe To the Orphans of the Scientific Revolution', *Journal of International Affairs* 44 (1990): 59–80.

Putnam, Hilary. 'The Meaning of Meaning', in *Mind, Language and Reality*. Cambridge University Press, 1975.

Meaning and the Moral Sciences. London: Routledge & Kegan Paul, 1978.

Reason, Truth and History. Cambridge University Press, 1981.

Representation and Reality. Cambridge, MA: MIT Press, 1988.

Rorty, Richard. *Consequences of Pragmatism*. Minneapolis: University of Minnesota Press, 1982.

'Science as Solidarity' and 'Freud and Moral Reflection', in *Objectivity, Relativism, and Truth*, 2 vols, *Philosophical Papers*, I. Cambridge University Press, 1991.

Rose, Stephen, Kamin, Leon J. and Lewontin, R. C. *Not in our Genes*. Harmondsworth: Penguin, 1984

Rosenau, James N. ed. *Global Voices: Dialogues in International Relations*. Boulder, CO: Westview Press, 1993.

Rosenberg, Alexander. *Sociobiology and the Preemption of Social Science*. Oxford: Basil Blackwell, 1980.

Rosenberg, Justin. 'What's the Matter with Realism?', *Review of International Studies* 16 (1990): 285–303.

Russett, Bruce and Starr, Harvey. *World Politics: Menu For Choice*, 2nd edn. New York: W. H. Freeman, 1985.

Sandel, Michael. 'The Procedural Republic and the Unencumbered Self', *Political Theory*, 12 (1984): 81–96.

Schubert, Glendon. 'Politics as a Life Science', in A. Somit, ed. *Biology and Politics: Recent Explorations*. The Hague: Moutan, 1976.

Singer, J. David and Jones, Susan D. *Beyond Conjecture in International Politics*. Itasca, IL: Peacock, 1972.

Spegele, Roger. 'Richard Ashley's Discourse for International Relations', *Millennium* 21 (1992): 147–82.

Steinbrunner, John. *The Cybernetic Theory of Decision*. Princeton University Press, 1974.

Sylvester, Christine. 'Riding the Hyphens of Feminism, Peace, and Place in Four-(Or more) Part Cacophony', *Alternatives* 18 (1993): 109–18.

Feminist Theory and International Relations in a Postmodern Era. Cambridge University Press, 1994.

Taylor, Charles. 'Understanding and the Human Sciences', *Review of Metaphysics* 34 (1980): 30–7.

Human Agency and Language, 2 vols., I, *Philosophical Papers*. Cambridge University Press, 1985.

Sources of the Self. Cambridge University Press, 1989.

Thompson, Janna. *Justice and World Order: A Philosophical Inquiry*. London: Routledge, 1992.

Thompson, Kenneth W. 'Idealism and Realism: Beyond the Great Debate', *British Journal of International Studies* 3 (1977): 199–209.

Thomson, Judith Jarvis. *The Realm of Rights*. Cambridge, MA: Harvard University Press, 1990.

Trigg, Roger. 'The Sociobiological View of Man', in S. C. Brown, ed., *Objectivity and Cultural Divergence*, Royal Institute of Philosophy Lecture Series 17. Cambridge University Press, 1984: 93–110.

Tsou, Tang. ' "Scientific Man vs Power Politics" Revisited', in Kenneth Thompson and Robert J. Myers, eds. *A Tribute to Hans Morgenthau*. Washington, DC: The New Republic, 1977.

Van Dyke, Vernon. *Political Science: A Philosophical Analysis*. Stanford University Press, 1960.

Vasquez, John A. *The Power of Power Politics: A Critique*. London: Frances Pinter, 1983.

Veeser, H. Aram ed. *The New Historicism*. New York: Routledge, 1989.

von Wright, G. H. *Explanation and Understanding*. Ithaca: Cornell University Press, 1971.

Walker, R. B. J. 'Realism, Change, and International Relations Theory', *International Studies Quarterly* 31 (1987): 65–86.

    'The Prince and "The Pauper": Tradition, Modernity, and Practice in the Theory of International Relations', in James Der Derian and Michael J. Shapiro, eds. *International/Intertextual Relations*. Lexington, MA: Lexington, 1989.

    One World, Many Worlds: Struggles for a Just World Peace. Boulder, CO: Lynne Rienner, 1988.

    'The Territorial State and the "Theme of Gulliver" ', *International Journal* 39 (Summer 1984): 529–52.

Wallace, James. *Moral Relevance and Moral Conflict*. Ithaca: Cornell University Press, 1986.

Waltz, Kenneth. *Man, the State and War*. New York: Columbia University Press, 1959.

    Theory of International Politics. Reading, MA: Addison-Wesley, 1979.

    'Realist Thought and Neorealist Thought', in Robert Rothstein, ed., *The Evolution of Theory in International Relations*. Columbia, SC: University of South Carolina, 1991: 21–38.

Watson, Adam. 'Systems of States', *Review of International Studies* 16 (1990): 99–109.

Weber, Max. *The Methodology of the Social Sciences*, Edward A. Shils and Henry A. Finch, trans. and eds. Glencoe, IL: The Free Press, 1949.

Wettstein, Howard. 'Has Semantics Rested on a Mistake?', *Journal of Philosophy* 83 (April 1986): 185–209.

Whitehead, Alfred North. *Adventures of Ideas*. New York: Macmillan, 1954.

Wiggins, David. *Truth, Invention and the Meaning of Life*, The Proceedings of the British Academy 62. London (1976): 331–78.

    Sameness and Substance. Oxford: Basil Blackwell, 1980.

Bibliography

Wight, Martin. *Systems of States*, Hedley Bull, ed. Leicester University Press, 1977.

Power Politics. Harmondsworth: Penguin, 1979.

Williams, Bernard. 'Ethical Consistency', in *Problems of the Self*. Cambridge University Press, 1973.

Ethics and the Limits of Philosophy. London: Fontana Press, 1985.

Williams, Howard. *International Relations in Political Theory*. Milton Keynes: Open University Press, 1992.

Wilson, Edward O. *On Human Nature*. Cambridge, MA: Harvard University Press, 1978.

Sociobiology, abridged edn. Cambridge, MA: The Belknap Press, 1980.

Wilson, Edward O. and Lumsden, Charles. *Genes, Mind and Culture*. Cambridge, MA: Harvard University Press, 1981.

Winch, Peter. *The Idea of a Social Science*. London: Routledge & Kegan Paul, 1958.

Wittgenstein, Ludwig. *On Certainty*. Oxford: Basil Blackwell, 1971.

Philosophical Investigations, G. E. M. Anscombe, trans., 3rd edn. Oxford: Blackwell, 1968.

Wohlstetter, Albert. 'The Delicate Balance of Terror', *Foreign Affairs* 37 (January 1959): 211–34.

Wolf, Susan. 'Moral Saints', *Journal of Philosophy*, 79 (August 1982): 419–39.

'Two Levels of Pluralism', *Ethics* 102 (1992): 785–98.

Wolfers, Arnold. 'The Actors in International Politics', in William T. R. Fox, ed. *Theoretical Aspects of International Relations*. University of Notre Dame Press, 1959.

Wright, Quincy. *The Study of International Relations*. New York: Appleton-Century-Crofts, 1955.

Yack, Bernard. *The Problems of a Political Animal: Community, Justice and Conflict in Aristotelian Political Thought*. Berkeley: University of California Press, 1993.

Yalden-Thomson, D.C. 'Hume's View of "Is-Ought"', *Philosophy* 53 (1978): 89–93.

Young, Iris Marion. *Justice and the Politics of Difference*. Princeton University Press, 1990.

Zinnes, Dina A. 'Prerequisites in the Study of System Transformation', in Ole R. Holsti, Randolph M. Siverson and Alexander L. George, eds. *Change in the International System*. Boulder, CO: Westview Press, 1980.

Index

Index

psychological egoism 133
Puchala, Donald 43–4
Putnam, Hilary 16–17, 47, 114
Pyrrhonic sceptics 37–8, 49

quasi-realist ethics 19
Quine, W.V. 43, 90

radical historicism 37, 182
radical holism 121, 122
radical relativism 158
radical/Marxist approaches to
    international relations 5
Ranke, Leopold von 159
rational choice theory 15
    and concessional realism 89
    and moral dilemmas 205
    and positivism-empiricism 31, 33
rationalism
    and concessional realism 15
    in Cox 70
    and evaluative political realism 48
    and positivism-empiricism 7
rationality 50, 130, 238
realism
    commonsense xi, 14, 17, 83, 84–8, 90
    concessional (neorealism) 14–17, 83,
        84–5, 88–92, 240
    and human nature 127, 128, 129, 133–6,
        160–1
    and kin-selection theory 145–7
    metaphysical 16, 47
    natural ontological attitude (NOA) 91
    and the primacy of foreign policy 159
    revisionary 71–2, 79
    scientific xii, 69, 91
    and sovereignty 113
    state and state-system 125
    versus idealists xvi
    see also evaluative political realism;
        historical realism; political realism
realist paradigms 5
reason
    and critical international theory 10, 55,
        61
    and moral judgements 196
    and positivism-empiricism 24–5, 28, 31
    and practice 27
    theoretical and practical 167–8
reason-explanation, and historical realism
    234–5
reductionism
    historical 189
    and the historical state-system 121–2
    and human nature 156, 157–8, 232–3

regime theory 31
regular truth 199
relativism 161
    and historical realism 189
    and moral realism 212–24, 226–7, 238–40
restricted-historical sortals 110, 112
revisionary realism 71–2, 79
Rorty, Richard 47, 160–1
Rosecrance, Richard 30, 125
Rule of Basic Deterrence 202–3
rules/rule-following, and historical
    realism 181–9
Rummel, R.J. 30
Russett, Bruce 38–9, 40

Sartre, Jean-Paul 158
scepticism 244
    ethical/moral 38, 94
    historical 181, 189
    and moral dilemmas 210
    and moral realism 192
    and positivism-empiricism 22, 26, 44–9,
        83, 94, 100
    anti-sceptical strategies 41–4
science
    and ethics 191–2
    natural, and historical realism 163–4,
        167, 179, 185, 236
    and positivism-empiricism 31
    theory and practice 20
    see also philosophy of science
scientific empiricism
    and concessional realism 85, 88–92
    and factual supervenience 157
    and historical realism 166, 233–4
    and process-analytic systems theory
        106
    and scepticism 44–8
scientific knowledge, and historical
    knowledge 169
scientific method, and concessional
    realism 88
scientific naturalism, and concessional
    realism 89
scientific realism xiv, 69, 91
scientific theories 28, 43–4
scientism, and human nature 156
scientists, and international relations
    theory xvi
second-order studies xiii–xiv
secondary self 152
security, and state-systems 121
self-as-actor 32–6
self-interest 63, 133, 135
selflessness, rise of 63

CAMBRIDGE STUDIES IN INTERNATIONAL RELATIONS